Value investing

From Graham to Buffett and Beyond

BRUCE C. N. GREENWALD

JUDD KAHN   PAUL D. SONKIN

MICHAEL VAN BIEMA

John Wiley & Sons, Inc.

New York • Chichester • Weinheim • Brisbane • Singapore • Toronto

This book is printed on acid-free paper.∞

Published by John Wiley & Sons, Inc.
Published simultaneously in Canada.

The Wiley Finance series contains books written specifically for finance and investment professionals as well as sophisticated individual investors and their financial advisors. Book topics range from portfolio management to e-commerce, risk management, financial engineering, valuation, and financial instrument analysis, as well as much more. For a list of available titles, please visit our Web site at www.WileyFinance.com.

This publication is designed to provide accurate and authoritative information in regard to the subject matter covered. It is sold with the understanding that the publisher is not engaged in rendering professional services. If professional advice or other expert assistance is required, the services of a competent professional person should be sought.

Designations used by companies to distinguish their products are often claimed as trademarks. In all instances where John Wiley & Sons, Inc. is aware of a claim, the product names appear in initial capital or all capital letters. Readers, however, should contact the appropriate companies for more complete information regarding trademarks and registration.

Library of Congress Cataloging-in-Publication Data:
Value investing : from Graham to Buffett and beyond / Bruce C. N. Greenwald . . . [et al.].
    p. cm.
    Includes index.
    ISBN 0-471-38198-5 (cloth : alk. paper)
      1. Investment analysis. 2. Corporations—Valuation. 3. Investments.
    4. Graham, Benjamin, 1894–1976 5. Buffett, Warren. I. Greenwald, Bruce C. N., 1946–
    HG4529.V35 2001
    332.63′20242—dc21

                                   2001017635

Printed in the United States of America.

10 9 8 7 6 5 4 3

For Virginia Greenwald
who now only need find a ship
and Anne Rogin
who need not

Contents

PART III   VALUE INVESTING IN PRACTICE: PROFILES OF EIGHT VALUE INVESTORS

Preface

Benjamin Graham is commonly credited with establishing security analysis as a reasonably firm discipline within an investment world that had been dominated by speculation, insider information, and other practices at best unsound and at worst downright shady. The publication of *Security Analysis* with David Dodd in 1934 marks the start of a profession. Graham made his ideas and techniques more available to professionals and interested amateurs with *The Intelligent Investor*, which initially appeared in 1949. Each book has been revised several times. *Security Analysis* is available both in its initial, classic version and in a fifth edition that purists feel has little of Graham remaining. The New York Society of Security Analysts, an association Graham founded, contends that he "is to investing what Euclid is to geometry, and Darwin is to the study of evolution." Though this may carry the praise further than Graham himself would have allowed, his significance to investing is not in dispute.

Graham did more than put investing on a rational foundation. He also engraved on the minds of his students and devotees a strong preference for what would now be called *value investing*. To present the most succinct description, the value investor seeks to purchase a security at a bargain price, the proverbial dollar for 50 cents. There is considerably more to it than that, as this book attests. Still, despite all the changes in the investment world since the 1920s, Graham initiated an approach to investing that remains vital today. Our effort here is to build on his work and on that of his successors and to incorporate the advances in value investing that have appeared over the last three or four decades.

Starting in 1928, Graham began to teach a course on security analysis at Columbia University, his alma mater. The book he wrote with Dodd grew from that course. The course at Columbia lasted through several incarnations after Graham and Dodd and passed eventually into the hands of Roger Murray, an author of the fifth edition of *Security Analysis*. On Murray's retirement in 1978, the course and the tradition disappeared from the formal academic curriculum. Outside the university, the intellectual life of value investing remained robust in the world of practicing investors, thanks primarily to Warren Buffett, who had taken the original Graham and Dodd course in 1950 after having been exposed to *The Intelligent Investor*. He read the first edition of *Security Analysis* while on his honeymoon. Together with a number of other Graham students, Walter Schloss among them, Buffett established records of consistent investment success that attracted continuing attention to value investing.

Further generations of former students, including Mario Gabelli, who had taken the course with Roger Murray, continued to refine and extend the basic value approach. In 1992 Gabelli prevailed on Murray to offer a series of lectures on value investing to Gabelli's own analysts, who had found nothing like it in their formal MBA courses. As the newly appointed Heilbrunn Professor of Asset Management and Finance, I attended those lectures out of curiosity. Like generations of investors who preceded me, I was struck by the compelling logic of Graham's approach. As a consequence, in 1993 I dragooned Roger Murray into joining me in offering a revived and revised version of the value course. That course, which continues to attract large numbers of both MBA and professional-level students, is the point of departure for this book.

Meanwhile, in the 1950s and 1960s a new approach to investment analysis emerged from scholars who had been trained in economics or statistics. As a group they produced a body of work, sometimes called *modern investment theory*, that, if accurate, has several inescapable implications for investors:

- The market is efficient, and it is not possible to outdo its returns except by accident.
- Risk is measured by the contribution of individual securities to the volatility of returns of widely diversified portfolios, rather than the more common-sense understanding of risk as permanent loss of capital.

- The best strategy for investors is to buy a broad index of securities and adjust for the desired level of risk by combining investments in this index portfolio with greater or lesser amounts of a risk-free asset, such as cash.

There were always investment professionals who disagreed with this theory, especially as their livelihood depended on its being incorrect or at least difficult for their clients to swallow. But over the last 20 years, a number of academic studies began to challenge the efficiency hypothesis. In these studies, mechanical variants of value investing (e.g., low price to earnings, low price to book value) have bested the indexes, as have some variants of momentum investing (e.g., buy stocks that have gone up and sell them before they go down). The general outcome has been to tarnish if not destroy the efficient market orthodoxy and to reinforce the worth of Graham's approach.

Along with the purely statistical challenges to modern investment theory, a body of work labeled *behavioral finance* has built on psychological research to dispute the idea that investors act as dispassionate calculating machines. It turns out that like everyone else, investors respond to events in the world with certain powerful biases. New information is interpreted, not simply digested, and not all of that interpretation is rational. One powerful set of biases tends to give more significance to the most recent news, good or bad, than is actually warranted. The stocks of companies that report high rates of growth are driven to extremes, as are stocks of companies that disappoint. These findings about excessive reactions confirm a belief that value investors have held since Graham: Over the long run, performance of both companies and share prices generally reverts to a mean. The first edition of *Security Analysis* had as a frontispiece this quote from Horace's *Ars Poetica:* "Many shall be restored that now are fallen and many shall fall that now are in honor." If value investors have their own bias, Horace captured it. Again, modern academic research has moved the theory of financial market behavior in the direction of Graham and Dodd.

More surprisingly, Graham and Dodd's insights into the methods of valuing companies have also anticipated recent developments in the field. At the core of most investment approaches lies the practice of valuation, the techniques by which the real or intrinsic value of a company can be estimated. Most investors want to buy securities whose true worth is not reflected in the current market price of the shares. There is general agreement that the value of a company is the sum of the cash flows it will produce for investors over the life of the company, discounted back to the present. In many cases, however, this approach depends on estimating cash flows far into the future, well beyond the horizon of even the most prophetic analyst. Value investors since Graham have always preferred a bird in the hand—cash in the bank or some close equivalent—to the rosiest projection of future riches. Therefore, instead of relying on techniques that must make assumptions about events and conditions far into the future, value investors prefer to estimate the intrinsic value of a company by looking first at the assets and then at the current earnings power of a company. Only in exceptional cases are they willing to factor in the value of potential growth.

This skepticism regarding growth stems not from a prejudice against the future but from an understanding that in many instances growth is simply not worth very much at all. For most companies in a competitive market economy, all the value of the growth will be consumed to pay for the additional capital that is necessary to fund the growth. The growth that is profitable for investors is growth that produces returns that exceed the costs of this additional capital. As we discuss in detail in this book, the companies that produce these kinds of above-normal returns are those that operate protected by barriers to entry from competitors that would otherwise enter these profitable markets and drive down the excess profits. Growth has value only within a protected franchise. It is the rare company that can expand beyond its franchise and still retain its profitability. When value investors do try to put a value on growth, they therefore pay most attention to the strategic position of a company and attempt to assess how sustainable any current franchise is. Here suspicion rules; the burden of proof is always on those who argue that the franchise will swell and still thrive. This broad vision, now commonplace among the most sophisticated investors, that an assessment of the strategic position of a company is central to any useful valuation, is inherent in the Graham and Dodd approach.

A further advantage of the value investor's approach—first the assets, then the current earnings power, and finally and rarely the value of the potential growth—is that it gives the most authority to the elements of valuation that are most credible. Asset values depend on tangible aspects of a company's situation today. Earnings power valuations assess the value of today's earnings. It is much easier to establish with confidence the current market price of a piece of land or the current profitability of a division than it is to predict the size of a market, one company's share of that market, its profit margins, and its cost of capital 20 years, or even five, into the future. Ultimately the future does matter, but it is important to separate what we reliably know today from less secure conjectures about tomorrow. This is one of the strengths of the Graham and Dodd approach. Also, this discrete process allows investors to spot discrepancies between the asset value of a company and its current earnings power value. When this is a sign that the company suffers from poor management, some value investors have become activists to encourage management to take corrective action, sell the company, or just simply leave.

Graham loved his "net-nets," the stocks he could buy for substantially less than the current assets of the company minus all its liabilities. Who wouldn't? But in the contemporary investment world, net-nets are, with only the rarest exception, a distant memory. Modern value investors have had to develop new approaches to discovering and valuing assets that allow them to move beyond cash, accounts receivables, and inventory while still making their investment decisions on the basis of the value of the assets today, rather than earnings, cash flow, or whatever in the future.

In the last years of the last century, it looked as if value investors were an endangered species. The "New Economy," based on digital technologies and biotechnologies in all their manifestations, was thought to cultivate companies with prospects for unlimited growth in sales and even more growth in income. By now it is clear that at least some of these premises were mistaken. There is no need to review the history of those miraculous initial public offerings (IPOs) that came public at $20, spiked to $120, and then drifted or thudded back to earth, on the basis of earnings that no one had seen but were promised four or five years hence. The most fervid proponents of the New Economy hypothesis argued that some of the fundamental truths of economics had been repealed, such as the theory that competitors would be drawn to profitable industries and ultimately force profit margins down into a normal range.

This intellectual environment, when coupled with stock markets that for three or four years only went up, and up substantially, was not friendly to value investors. Even those whose long-term performance records were the stuff of legend fell behind those who either understood the New Economy or, more likely, were able to anticipate how other investors would respond to its prospects. At the end of the decade (and century and millennium), the debate between those who saw the current market level as tulip mania revisited and those who saw it as a stepping stone to 36,000 on the Dow was still raging. It has diminished, at least for the moment, as the year 2000 reminded investors that everything that rises may not rise forever. Like most value investors, we do not put much credence in predictions about the market—our own included. But we strongly believe that the laws of economics have not been repealed, and that in a market economy, competition will, in the absence of readily identifiable barriers to entry, eventually keep profits in check. In this sort of world, which has characterized most of recorded economic history, a book that offers an updated version of the Graham and Dodd approach is hardly out of place.

This book is intended for anyone interested in investing, from the casual weekend reader of *Barron's* or something similar to the seasoned professional bearing the sobering responsibility of managing other people's money. We have assumed nothing on the part of our readers except a willingness to follow an argument and to examine some financial tables and charts. There are redundancies within this book; we excuse them on the grounds that it is easier to skip repetitions than to search back for the first time an unfamiliar concept was introduced. Though much here will be familiar to experienced money managers and academics, we believe that there are enough new ideas and novel applications of established ones to satisfy almost everyone.

BRUCE GREENWALD

New York, NY
2001

PART I

AN INTRODUCTION TO VALUE INVESTING

Chapter 1

Value Investing
Definitions, Distinctions, Results, Risks, and Principles

What Value Investing Is

Value investing in the manner initially defined by Benjamin Graham and David Dodd rests on three key characteristics of financial markets:

1. The prices of financial securities are subject to significant and capricious movements. Mr. Market, Graham's famous personification of the impersonal forces that determine the price of securities at any moment, shows up every day to buy or sell any financial asset. He is a strange fellow, subject to all sorts of unpredictable mood swings that affect the price at which he is willing to do business.

2. Despite these gyrations in the market prices of financial assets, many of them do have underlying or fundamental economic values that are relatively stable and that can be measured with reasonable accuracy by a diligent and disciplined investor. In other words, the intrinsic value of the security is one thing; the current price at which it is trading is something else. Though value and price may, on any given day, be identical, they often diverge.

3. A strategy of buying securities only when their market prices are significantly below the calculated intrinsic value will produce superior returns in the long run. Graham referred to this gap between

3

value and price as 'the margin of safety'; ideally, the gap should amount to about one-half, and not be less than one-third, of the fundamental value. He wanted to buy a dollar for 50 cents; the eventual gain would be large and, more important, secure.

Starting with these three assumptions, the central process of value investing is disarmingly simple. A value investor estimates the fundamental value of a financial security and compares that value to the current price Mr. Market is offering for it. If price is lower than value by a sufficient margin of safety, the value investor buys the security. We can think of this formula as the master recipe of Graham and Dodd value investing. Where their legitimate descendants differ from one another—where each may add his or her unique flavor—is in the precise way they handle some of the steps involved in the process:

- Selecting securities for valuation
- Estimating their fundamental values
- Calculating the appropriate margin of safety required for each security
- Deciding how much of each security to buy, which encompasses the construction of a portfolio and a choice about the amount of diversification the investor desires
- Deciding when to sell securities

These are not trivial decisions. To search for securities selling below their intrinsic value is one thing; to find them is quite another. It is because the descendants have devised alternative methods that value investing has remained a vital discipline through all market conditions in the more than six decades since Graham and Dodd first published *Security Analysis*. Profiles of some of the more prominent descendants constitute the second half of this book.

What Value Investing Isn't

No rational investor admits to searching for securities selling for more than their underlying value. Everyone is looking to buy low and sell high.[1] What is it that differentiates real value investors, who are actually quite rare, from all the others who trade in the securities markets?

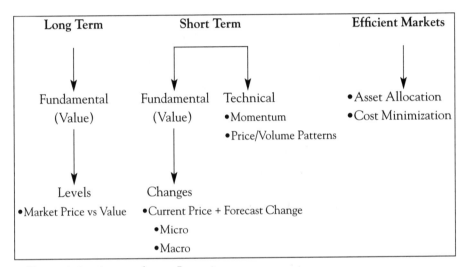

Figure 1.1 **Approaches to Investing**

One large class of investors who obviously do not qualify are "technical" analysts, or technicians (see Figure 1.1). Technicians avoid fundamental analysis of any kind. They pay no attention to a company's balance sheet or income statement, its line of business, the nature of its product markets, or anything else that might concern a fundamental investor of any stripe. They care nothing for its economic value. Instead, they focus on

[1] We are going to confine our discussion throughout this book to the 'long' position side of investing and ignore those investors who 'short' (sell without owning) securities that they think are priced at more than their fundamental value. At certain points in his career, Graham used short sales to hedge other positions he had taken, and there may be bona fide value investors today who make active use of shorting securities. In the main, however, value investing is identified with uncovering fundamental value and buying it at bargain price.

trading data, that is, the price movements and volume figures for any security. They believe that the history of these movements, reflecting the supply and demand for that security over time, traces patterns that they can analyze to infer future price movement. They construct charts to represent this information, and they scrutinize them for signs that will predict how prices will move next and thus allow them to make a profitable trade. For example, momentum investors extrapolate the current price trend and buy securities whose prices are rising in the expectation that they will continue to go up. Sometimes they compare the day's price for the security to a trend line made up of the average prices of the last 30, 90, 150, or some other number of days. Crossing that trend line, up or down, can indicate a change in direction. Surely they intend to buy low and sell high, but *low* and *high* here refer to the previous and future prices of the security, unconnected to its fundamental value. For technical investors, Mr. Market is the only game in town. It is also a game that lends itself to trading—buying and selling over a very short term. Very few traders ignore technical information.

Even when we turn back to people who legitimately see themselves as fundamental investors, concerned with the real economics of the companies whose securities they buy, Graham and Dodd value investors are a distinct minority.

We can divide the class of fundamental investors into those who focus on macroeconomic issues and those who concentrate on the microeconomics of specific securities. *Macrofundamentalists* are concerned with broad economic factors that affect the universe of securities as a whole, or at least in large groups: inflation rates, interest rates, exchange rates, unemployment rates, and the rates of economic growth at the national or even international level. They closely monitor the actions of policy makers, like the Federal Reserve Board, and aggregate investor and consumer sentiment. They use their information to forecast broad economic trends, and they then use the forecasts to decide which groups of securities (or even individual issues) are likely to be most affected by the changes they predict. Their approach is often referred to as *top down*, starting with the overall economy and working down to specific companies and securities. Like every other investor, they intend to buy low and sell high, using what they hope are their superior predictions to move before the market as a whole recognizes what is happening. They do not, as a rule, do direct calculations of the value of individual securities or particular classes of securities, though such calculations could be consistent with a macrofundamentalist approach. Although there are some famous and successful macrovalue investors, most value investors in the Graham and Dodd tradition are microfundamentalists.

Even within the society of microfundamentalists—those who analyze the economic fundamentals of companies and look at securities one by one—value investors in the Graham and Dodd tradition are still a minority. A more common approach to microfundamentalist investing takes the current price of a stock or other security as the point of departure. These investors study the history of this security, noting how the price has moved in response to changes in those economic factors that are thought to influence it: earnings, industry conditions, new product introductions, improvements in production technology, management shake-ups, growth in demand, shifts in financial leverage, new plant and equipment investments, acquisitions of other companies and divestitures of lines of business, and so on. There is more than enough to examine. They then try to anticipate how the critical variables on this list are likely to change, relying in large measure on company and industry sources as well as on their more general knowledge.

Most forecasts focus on company earnings. Security prices incorporate the market's collective prediction about future earnings. If these investors find that their estimates of future earnings and other important variables exceed the market's expectations, then they purchase the securities. They assume that when new information about earnings and the other matters is released, their predictions will be validated, and the market will drive up the price of the securities. They have bought low, based on superior knowledge of the future, and they intend to sell high.

Though this approach shares with value investing a concentration on economic fundamentals and specific securities, there are major differences. First, it focuses on prior and anticipated *changes* in prices, not on the *level* of prices relative to underlying values. One could apply this analysis equally well to a stock trading at 10, 20, or 50 times the forecast earnings.

A value investor would not regard these situations as equivalent. Second, this approach does not incorporate an identifiable margin of safety to safeguard the investment from the capricious behavior of Mr. Market, who, after all, has been known to sink the price of shares in response to good news. So while Graham and Dodd value investing is most frequently a microfundamentalist approach, not all, or even most, microfundamentalists are value investors.

Each of these alternatives to value investing can lead to a successful investment record, provided it is carefully and diligently pursued. Statistical studies increasingly suggest that security prices and volumes do trace consistent and recognizable patterns (there are positive serial correlations in the short run and reversion to the mean over the longer term). There are successful technical investors. Macroeconomic variables can be forecast with some accuracy and will affect securities markets in systematic and identifiable ways. There are successful macrofundamentalist investors. Analysts who energetically pursue information from company and industry sources, ferreting out trends ahead of the pack, should in theory—and sometimes do in practice—obtain above-average investment returns.

Nevertheless, it is important to remember that security trading is a zero-sum game. For every buyer there is a seller, and the future will prove one of them to have made a mistake. Indeed, when we take effort and expense into account, approximately 70 percent of active professional investors have done worse than they would have by adhering to a passive and low-cost strategy of simply buying a share of the market as a whole—a representative sample of all available securities. We can acknowledge the effectiveness of passive management without having to subscribe to the idea that the price Mr. Market offers for a security is the best estimate of its fundamental value.

Does Value Investing Work?

The case for value investing as a superior approach is both theoretical and factual. We develop the theory in our detailed discussion of the procedures of modern value investing. We contend that these methods embody a surer practical use of economics and statistics than do the most popular alternatives. But investing is like other contact sports: The best proof of the theory is in the results. The historical record confirms that value investing strategies have worked; over extended periods, they have produced better returns than have both the leading alternatives and the market as a whole.

Three distinct sources provide evidence of this superiority. The first comes from a battery of mechanical selection tests. They work like this:

1. Take all the stocks in some large universe, say the New York Stock Exchange or all the stocks in the Compustat database.
2. Sort them into groups (deciles, quintiles, quartiles) using some measure of value, like market price to book price or market price to earnings; the value portfolios are those with low price-to-book or low price-to-earnings ratios.
3. Record the prices at the start date, usually the first trading day of the year.
4. Hold these portfolios for a fixed period of time, generally one year.
5. Record the prices at the end of the year.
6. Add the dividends paid to the change in prices to get the total return on holding each portfolio for that one year period.
7. Compare the total returns of each portfolio.

Many studies have been conducted employing different versions of this approach. The results demonstrate almost invariably that the value portfolios produce better than average returns (*average* here meaning returns on the entire market) in almost all periods and all kinds of markets. Low market-to-book portfolios have outperformed the market by 3 to 5 percent a year or more, since the 1920s, and low price-to-earnings portfolios have had similar success. By contrast, portfolios constructed of highly priced stocks, measured by high market-to-book and high price-to-earnings ratios, have done poorly. Some studies refer to these as glamour portfolios. They are highly priced mainly because the companies have experienced rapid sales and earnings growth in the recent past. Unfortunately, all that success and expectations of more have already been incorporated into the stock price by the time the portfolios are constructed.

These mechanical selections of stocks do produce portfolios that look very much like those that a diligent value investor, analyzing stocks one by one, would construct, especially as value investing was practiced in its early period. But value investing is not the same thing as a mechanical approach—a computer program—that selects stocks on the basis of a statistical measure indicating which ones are cheap. Calculations of intrinsic value are usually more intricate and require more detailed knowledge of company and industry economics than can be disclosed by simple financial ratios. Nevertheless, the striking historical success of these value portfolios produced by mechanical selection should remind us of the high standards that an active value investing strategy must meet. Seventy percent of active professional money managers underperform the market; imagine how few exceed market performance by 3 to 5 percent annually over many decades.

It is reassuring, therefore, that some large investment management institutions that have adopted systematic value strategies in the Graham and Dodd spirit, such as Oppenheimer and Company and Tweedy, Browne, have records comparable to the mechanical value portfolios and superior to the market as a whole.[2] The performance of these institutions is the second source of support for the argument that value investing produces superior returns. Unlike the mechanical studies, which are backtests of selection rules applied to historical data, these institutions have generated real returns for real clients. Value investing works in the world as well as in the lab.

The final piece of evidence is those money managers whom Warren Buffett called the 'superinvestors of Graham and Doddsville.' To a remarkable extent, value investors in the Graham and Dodd tradition have dominated the select ranks of those money managers who have markedly outperformed the market over an extended period of time.[3]

---

[2] From 1975 through 2000, the S&P 500 had a total return of 16.1 percent per year, well above its average since inception. For the same period, the Oppenheimer Capital Large-Cap Value Composite returned 17.4 percent per year; Tweedy, Browne and Company's Common Stock Portfolio gained 20.4 percent per year.

[3] We provide long-term results for some of the value investors we profile in the second half of this book. Their returns have continued to excel in the years since Buffett wrote his essay, even during the greatest bull market in history.

Is Extra Return the Reward for Extra Risk?

It is certainly possible that the higher returns achieved by value investing from each of these three sources—mechanically selected portfolios, value-oriented institutions, and individual Graham and Dodd investors—occur only because these portfolios are riskier than the market as a whole. If that were so, then their superior returns would be nothing more than an appropriate reward for bearing this increased risk. Academic financial experts have been emphatic in arguing not only that higher return is the reward for higher risk, but also that there is no way to beat the market's average return other than by assuming additional risk.

The problem with this argument is that when standard academic measures of risk—either annual return variability or beta as defined by modern finance theory—have been calculated for our value portfolios, they have generally been lower than the same risk measures applied to the market as a whole. In addition, value portfolios have proven to be less risky than the market as a whole when tested by other measures of risk, such as how much a stock drops in reaction to bad news about the company, the extent of price declines during bear markets, or simply the level of maximum loss experienced. These measures are closer to our common-sense understanding of risk and are more appropriate for value investors, who regard price fluctuations as opportunities to buy or sell, not as accurate estimates of the intrinsic worth of the security.

For our mechanically selected value portfolios, which have been subjected to the most thorough statistical scrutiny, their average one-year returns have been higher; their average three-year holding period returns have been higher; their average five-year holding period returns have been higher; they have provided superior returns during recessions; and they have outperformed glamour portfolios during the worst months for the stock market as a whole. The value approach, even in its mechanical application, is no fair-weather friend.

As another alternative approach to risk, we can refer to Warren Buffett's account of how he came to buy a large chunk of the shares of the Washington Post Company. The date was late 1973. It was a miserable time for the economy, the stock market, and the national temperament, and, naturally, a great moment for value investors. The market capitalization of the Washington Post Company had dropped to $80 million. At that moment, the whole company could have been sold to any of 10 buyers for at least $400 million. Clearly, Mr. Market was in a dreadful mood. Now, Buffett asked, had the market value of the stock declined again, from $80 million down to $40 million, would that have made a purchase of the shares more risky? According to modern investment theory, the answer is yes, because it would have increased the volatility of the prices. According to Buffett, the answer is not at all, because it would have increased an already ample margin of safety and lowered whatever risk—he thinks there was none to begin with—existed in the purchase. As a calculation of risk, the margin of safety has nothing in common with the volatility of a security's price. In order to use it, you have to acknowledge the existence of an intrinsic value and feel confident about your ability to estimate it.

Finding Value

The physical universe is probably expanding, but perhaps not any faster than the universe of securities and other investment vehicles, such as derivatives and mutual funds. To keep from losing their way in the vastness of investment space, value investors have relied on a three-phase process to direct their work:

1. A search strategy to locate potentially rich areas in which value investments may be located;
2. An approach to valuation that is powerful and flexible enough to recognize value in different guises, while still protecting the investor from succumbing to euphoria and other delusions;
3. A strategy for constructing an investment portfolio that reduces risk and serves as a check on individual security selection.

We will discuss each of these steps in the chapters that follow.

Value investing is an intellectual discipline, but it may be that the qualities essential for success are less mental than temperamental. First, a value investor has to be aware of the limits of his or her competence. You have to know what you know and be able to distinguish genuine understanding from mere general competence. Most value investors are specialists in either particular industries or certain special circumstances, such as bankruptcy workouts. Not every stock that looks like a bargain is worth more than its price. You must be able to tell the difference between the underpriced and the merely cheap. Even the most broad-gauged investor does better operating within his or her circle of competence.

Second, value investing demands patience. You have to wait for Mr. Market to offer you a bargain. Fortunately, you are not compelled to act until that bargain is available. In Warren Buffett's useful analogy, investing is like batting without called strikes. You can take as many pitches as you want until you spot the one you like. Then you swing, and if you have done the analysis intelligently, your chances of success are high. What big league hitter wouldn't love to play under these rules? Patience is also necessary after the securities are bought. Even if you are correct about the intrinsic value, it generally takes time for the rest of the market to come around. After all, you bought it because it was out of favor. The market's estimate of its worth does not change overnight. A value investor needs to be able to sit still.

Sitting still need not mean doing nothing. What does a value investor do when he or she cannot find securities to buy that meet the dual criteria of falling within his or her circle of competence and being priced low enough to permit an adequate margin of safety? At one point in his career, Warren Buffett sent the money he had been managing back to the limited partners on the grounds that the market was so highly priced that he could find no place to invest it. (He did convince William Ruane to establish a mutual fund to accommodate those who wanted to stay invested.) But most money managers are reluctant to part with funds under their control. Value investors have traditionally parked the funds temporarily in money market instruments or other secure investments. That has been the default strategy. There are other default alternatives. An institutional equity manager, for example, whose performance is judged by comparing it to that of a benchmark portfolio like the Standard & Poor's 500, ought to select that benchmark as his or her default and only purchase stocks individually when they meet all the value criteria he or she has established. We will talk more about this issue when we discuss portfolio construction and diversification.

The Rest of the Book

Chapter 2 describes appropriate search strategies for value investors. Just as geologists hunting for oil, gold, or some other precious resource have created models that indicate what type of terrain is most likely to reward their drilling, value investors have methods for identifying areas of potentially rich investment opportunities. We explain why certain types of securities are more likely to be undervalued than the market as a whole, and how these securities can be identified.

Chapter 3 discusses valuation proper. We examine the standard approach to valuation—discounted cash flow analysis—and identify the serious flaws inherent in the application of this method. We then offer some alternatives originally presented by Graham and Dodd. The first is to put a value on the assets of a company by starting with its financial statements and then adjusting certain assets to reflect their true economic value, which is the cost of reproducing them at current prices. The most obvious candidate for a desirable security is a stock that is selling below the reproduction cost of its current assets—cash, receivables, inventory—after all liabilities have been paid. These are Benjamin Graham's famous net-net stocks, and although it was easier to find them during the Depression than it is today, such opportunities can occasionally be located.

A second way to calculate the company's intrinsic value is to examine its stream of earnings over a period of years and to estimate how much the company should earn on average over the course of a business cycle. This figure should correspond to a market-level return on the intrinsic (reproduction) value of the assets. When the earnings repeatedly exceed this norm, the company may have earnings power that supports an intrinsic value higher than its adjusted net worth. These situations are not common, but they are much less rare than Graham's net-nets. Finally, but only for those rare companies that possess a sustainable competitive advantage, the profitable growth of the firm needs to be incorporated into the valuation.

Chapter 4 provides a more detailed discussion and a real-world example of how a company should be valued on the basis of the reproduction costs of its assets. Chapter 5 presents a method for analyzing the earnings power value. For a company to generate earnings in excess of an average return on its adjusted net worth on a sustainable basis, it must have a franchise, which is a special and defensible competitive advantage. We explain the economics behind these competitive advantages, show how to recognize a franchise, and demonstrate how to value the securities in cases where a franchise exists. Chapter 6 applies this analysis to the recent history of a company with a franchise.

Chapter 7 deals with the least reliable ingredient of valuation: the value of growth. Wall Street loves growth, and companies love to grow; this is a match made in heaven. Managers gain recognition and power; they have more positions to fill and can promote generously; budgets expand; corporate jets abound. Growth means a move up in class. The problem is that most growth is not profitable in the crucial sense that there must be money left over after the additional capital required for growth has been compensated. The only profitable growth is growth within the franchise. This is hard to accomplish, and value investing as a discipline tries to inoculate the investor against paying for growth outside the franchise or for franchise growth that may never materialize. For value investors who are determined to buy growth—and who are willing to pay for it—this chapter describes approaches that put growth investing within a value framework and thus help guard against the siren call of profits increasing without end. The framework is the history of Intel as a company and as a potential investment.

Chapter 8 demonstrates how value investors construct portfolios to reduce risk over and above what is provided by the margin of safety for individual securities. There are times when Mr. Market is so euphoric that he puts a high price on everything he owns. Value investors have to be able to just say no and wait until Mr. Market comes to his senses—or better, until he turns so sour and negative that he will part with anything at a bargain price. At the same time, each value investor needs a default position for funds that have not found a value home. The default stance depends on the standards against which the investor is measured and on other circumstances that vary with the situation. We present some alternative default strategies.

In Part III we explore the distinctive approaches of eight value investors. Some of them are household names; others are known only to value investing aficionados. For most of them, we offer one or two live cases to show specifically how they put their methods to work. We believe that value investing is a genuine academic discipline, and that it is closely tied to economic and financial theory. But it is also a way to invest real money, and as such, the arguments are tested by results in the market.

Chapter 2

Searching for Value
Fish Where the Fish Are

The investment world offers so many choices that any serious investor needs to carve out a limited part of that world before beginning his or her analysis. We are going to make the task simpler by ignoring whole regions of the investment universe: government and federal agency debt issues, state and municipal bonds, bank savings accounts and certificates of deposit, currencies, commodities, collectibles, direct investments (ownership of the entire enterprise), derivatives, mutual funds of every imaginable stripe, and just about everything that is not a stock or corporate bond. Even here, our focus is going to be on selecting equity investments, although there are certainly times in which value investors buy bonds, convertibles, and other kinds of securities. Our approach to valuation is a method for evaluating businesses; it has nothing to say about foreign exchange, commodities, or most of the other investment vehicles mentioned. Corporate securities may be only a small part of the investment universe, but there are more than enough of them to keep an investor occupied with trying to discover intrinsic value selling at a discount. And, for the patient investor, there is enough value to be found to make the search rewarding.

The Industrial Approach to Uncovering Value

In Chapter 1 we mentioned a legion of studies that employ a mechanical approach to stock selection for testing various investment styles. This research uses one or several variables to rank the universe of stocks at a start time, to divide these ranked lists into equally sized groups, and to compare the investment returns of these groups (now considered portfolios) over one year or more. As a group, these works demonstrate convincingly that portfolios of stocks ranked high on value outperformed the market as a whole and trounced portfolios ranked high on glamour. But it is not enough to report the findings; we also need to understand why value has bested glamour so that we can confidently adapt the mechanical approach to our own tastes.

Let's look at the variables along which the stocks are sorted and placed into various ranks. They come in three varieties. First are the fundamental variables. These refer only to a company's performance, not the relationship between that performance and its share price. Studies have sorted stocks using the following fundamental variables:

- Return on equity or on total capital
- Growth in earnings per share, for both one year and multiple years
- Growth in sales
- Growth in assets
- Profit margins

Companies with high marks on these variables are the successful firms, the businesses whose shares everyone wants to own. The only problem is that when portfolios are created using these variables, it is the lowly companies, those with low return on equity or narrow profit margins, whose stocks have produced higher returns for investors. In Michelle Clayman's telling phrase, "in search of disaster" has been a better investment guide than "in search of excellence."

A second type of variable looks only at price changes in the stock, without reference to any fundamental data. We are now in the world of technical investing, which focuses on momentum. The measure most frequently used is relative strength, which is simply the price performance of the stock relative to all other stocks in the pool. Choosing a portfolio of last year's best performing stocks is a bet that winners will continue to excel, and the bet has paid off. From 1952 through 1994, the top 50 stocks selected on the basis of relative strength bested the market as a whole by an average of 3.7 percent a year (O'Shaughnessy, 1994, p. 193). This is confirmation of all those slogans that advise, "Don't fight the tape"; "The trend is your friend"; and "Sell your losers and let your winners run."

But momentum plays out fairly quickly. When stocks are selected on the basis of price change over three prior years, rather than last year alone, the results are different: The worse do better. The high flyers fall back to earth; the downtrodden arise. We witness that phenomenon found so frequently in nature and culture: reversion to the mean. The children of tall parents do not, on average, exceed their parents in height; if they did, centers in the NBA would not command the salaries they do. And if prior winners in the stock market continued to outperform over sustained periods, their market capitalizations would rise to the sky, leaving behind any fundamental value that might support the share price. There are manias in the history of investment; they also collapse.

Finally, the most commonly employed variables are those that do relate the price of the shares to some fundamental company information: share price to earnings, share price to cash flow, share price to book value, share price to sales, or share price to dividends. In all of these cases, the value stocks—those with low share prices relative to each of these other variables—outperform the glamour stocks. These ratios offer slightly different snapshots of the same underlying picture: how much investors are willing to pay for the future success of the company, whether measured by earnings, cash flow, sales, net assets, or dividends. The less investors want to pay, the better the prospects of the shares, if not of the company itself.

There is one other factor about a company that has had a major effect on the rate of return that investors would earn from owning its shares: market capitalization. This variable does not fit neatly into any of the three classes of variables we have identified—purely fundamental, purely price history, or the ratio of market price to some fundamental variable like sales or earnings. We can think of the market capitalization as the number of shares outstanding times the current share price, which itself is the book value per share times the price-to-book ratio; we could just as easily use sales or earnings ratios. (We have to add outstanding debt to each of these.) But the point about market capitalization is that it is an important explanatory factor independent of the value-oriented ratios. That is, the stocks of small companies, measured by market capitalization, have outperformed the shares of large companies even when the price-to-book ratios are similar (see Fama articles). Size matters, and smaller has been better most of the time. But not always; there have been periods, such as the current one, when large capitalization stocks have outperformed the small fry. But over the 60-odd years for which we have a detailed history of company fundamentals and share prices, betting on smaller companies has paid off.

The Anomaly of Value

Superior investment returns from value stocks over time constitute an anomaly. Once investors know that cheap stocks outperform expensive stocks, they should bid up the price of the cheap stocks and eliminate the superior performance. That the differential has persisted is what makes it an anomaly. There have been two distinct responses to the evidence that cheap stocks provide superior performance. One seeks to explain it, the other to explain it away. We will start with the latter. Essentially a defense of the efficient market hypothesis, the argument is that the superior performance occurs only because the value portfolios bear more risk than do expensive portfolios or the market as a whole. Because the theory holds that additional risk should indeed produce extra returns, the anomaly dissolves once risk is taken into account; superior performance is explained away. As we indicated in the previous chapter, however, the data reveal that value stocks outperform and that they are less risky, so the argument of extra return for extra risk doesn't work.

The second response tries to explain why the value anomaly might persist in the face of intelligent and energetic investors who are trying to outperform the market averages. The answer, in a word, is biases. Investors, both as individuals and institutions, are in the grip of systematic biases that induce them to pay too much for winners (potential growth companies with great stories and bright futures) and too little for losers (companies that are boring, poor performing, unknown, and unloved). These biases shape the investment returns. The glamorous companies may indeed do well, but the price of their shares already anticipates stunning performance. The unexciting companies may indeed just plod along, but the price of their shares anticipates that they will perpetually stumble and foul up. All they need to do is to get back to normal, and they will surprise investors.

What accounts for the strength of these biases? To answer this question, we need to understand how investment decisions are made, and by whom. Even though most investment dollars are in the hands of institutions, institutions do not make investment decisions; individuals working for institutions do. These people have their own interests and agendas, some of which may not be in line with the interests of the institution for which they work. They also have their own psychologies, over which they may have little control. On the other hand, institutions normally have investment policies that are mandated by authority and that are intended to constrain the decisions of current investment managers. Therefore, it makes sense to think of three different entities whose biases affect investment decisions: (1) institutions, (2) institutional managers pursuing their own needs and interests within the institutional setting, and (3) individuals investing for themselves (or as agents for others) whose outlook is influenced by psychological dispositions.

For institutions, investment biases are generally a consequence of either policy or size. We'll start with policy. Many institutional investment funds are prevented—by charter, by stated investment policy, or by legislative intervention—from owning certain kinds of stock. Shares of companies that engage in businesses deemed socially irresponsible, whether for environmental, health, or regime related reasons, are not allowed to be bought. If many funds adopt policies that compel them to avoid the same companies, the normal demand for these shares may be substantially reduced. Unless there are enough funds with socially irresponsible investment mandates (i.e., buy only stocks of tobacco companies or manufactures of defective infant car seats), shares of the "dirty companies" may be permanently undervalued, as measured by current earnings or growth prospects. It will take a change in investment policy, a change in corporate social behavior, or a reorganization of the business to eliminate this bias and allow the shares to be revalued upward. As long as the prohibition is stable, the stocks may remain permanently depressed.

The issue of size bias is more important and more interesting. Many funds cannot invest in small companies, either because their mandates do not allow it or, more frequently, because they have too much money to manage and small companies just can't absorb enough of it to make it worthwhile. If a diversified investment company (most mutual funds) with $5 billion to invest wants to own stock in 100 companies, it needs to buy on average $50 million in each. Because the fund does not want and is not allowed to own more than 10 percent of any company's stock, that limits the universe of investment choices to firms with market capitalization of $500 million. The specific sizes of funds, market capitalizations of suitable firms, and percentages of ownership will vary, but the impact of company size persists. Many funds simply cannot buy shares in small companies. The consequence is that the shares in small companies are cheaper, all other things being equal, than shares in large companies. Among the "all other things" that need to be held constant, growth prospects are the most important. Small companies typically have the opportunity to grow faster than large ones, which already control major segments of the market in industries that are likely to be well developed.

The only thing that small companies need do to enter the set of investments acceptable for large funds is to grow. There are plenty of other investors out there to raise the value of the company's shares as its revenues and earnings increase. At some point, last year's tiny company, with a market capitalization of $50 million, becomes next year's small firm, with a capitalization of $150 million. In a few years more, it reaches $500 million. As it matures, it becomes an eligible purchase for more funds; its shares are priced at less of a discount. It ceases to be an opportunity and emerges as a success. But this cycle is one of perpetual renewal, and new tiny firms spring up to take its place in the shade. The shares of companies too small for big funds are always available on sale.

A standard measure of the small capitalization discount compares the price to earnings (P/E) ratio for companies in the Standard & Poor's 500 to the P/E multiple of a small cap index (e.g., Salomon Smith Barney Emerging Growth Index). This ratio varies over time, but generally the small cap P/Es are higher, befitting their more realistic prospects for growth. In 1983, just after the start of the longest bull market in U.S. history, the small cap

P/E ratio reached a pinnacle of more than 2.3 times the P/E of the S&P 500. That marked the end of small cap superior performance. By the end of 1998, the ratio had fallen along a very jagged course to around 1 to 1. As we might suspect, large company stocks had outperformed small company shares for a sustained period. The ups and downs in the relative valuations of small and large cap stocks does not negate the argument that small capitalization stocks have historically been undervalued, and as a consequence have performed better than large capitalization stocks. Because they are not acceptable to a large part of the investor universe, they tend to be a bargain until they grow bigger.

A striking example of the size bias as it affects stock performance concerns the record of corporate spin-offs. Sometimes a company rids itself of a division or other unwanted unit of business by issuing stock in this new corporation and distributing it to existing shareholders. The shares in this spin-off company now trade on their own. In most cases, the new firm is small, especially when compared with the giant from which it has just been separated. Funds that owned stock in Giant now find themselves holding shares in New Midget enterprise, with a market capitalization of $50 million. They may know little about the new business, but of one thing they are certain: it isn't big enough for them to spend much time learning about it because it is too small for them to buy. So they sell—dump—the shares on the market and pocket the money. Spin-offs are a wonderful opportunity for investors who are not constrained by questions of corporate size. Because many of the shares are sold for reasons unrelated to the company's prospects, there are bound to be gems tossed away by the large funds for whom a small company stock, though perhaps a jewel, is still a nuisance. Spin-offs intensify the small company bias. The normal small company has its shares ignored by the large funds; the spin-off has them prejudicially sold off. This is only an extreme illustration of the institutional bias against the shares of small companies that has made them, over time, a fertile field for value investors.

When we examine the actual people making investment decisions within the institutions, we find a different source of bias. Most money managers are employees, hired to produce results by following prescribed investment policies. Though original thinking that leads to extraordinary success may be rewarded, the safest path is to look pretty much like everyone else who is investing with the same mandate. The old corporate adage of data processing managers, that nobody was ever fired for buying computers from IBM, applies as well to money managers. Nobody loses a job for average performance or for holding the same securities as the rest of the group. If you take a chance and buy stock in a company that nobody else wants, the payoffs are skewed. Should the company recover and the stock rise, the praise is real but short-lived. If the company does poorly and the stock falls, everyone remembers that you chose that "dog." Investment managers running large pools of money are often described as following a herd mentality. And why not, since there is safety in numbers? The situation becomes most extreme toward the end of a reporting period, when managers window-dress their portfolios, dumping the stocks that have fallen in price and loading up on the past year's (or quarter's) successes. This pruning has the effect of driving up the price of currently successful stocks and depressing even further stocks that are already downtrodden. The end of the year has historically been a good month to pick up the value stocks that window-dressing managers have tossed out in order to avoid listing them in the year-end report.

These comments about investment managers are gross generalizations. There are successful and renowned investors who have pushed against prevailing sentiment, buying the apparent dogs and steering away from stocks anointed by Wall Street. But we think they are clearly a minority (the fact that the public knows the names of some famous contrarian investors may be a sign of their rarity), and our effort here is to explain why enduring biases create opportunities that should not exist were money managers guided solely by reason and evidence. That explanation does not require all money managers to move as a pack and to sanitize their portfolios before they publish reports. All it takes is for a preponderance of them to work that way, and the field has been tilted enough to permit significant mispricing of some stocks that are currently performing poorly.

The last source of investor bias is human psychology. As we know from literature, from science, and only too well from experience, people are not dependably rational. They—we—do not carefully weigh evidence; we repeatedly stumble into logical pratfalls; we confuse cause with effect; we generalize on the basis of a few exceptional cases; we remember selectively. What makes these defects interesting and material for investors is that the errors we make are not strewn about randomly as ungainly blots on the smooth canvas of human reason. They cluster in certain locations, which makes them statistically predictable and therefore useful.

There is a considerable body of scholarship on the question of flawed intuitive inference. It has been imported from cognitive psychology into economics, where it is known as behavioral finance. For our purpose here, which is to explain why anomalies in stock performance can endure in a world of smart, motivated, and diligent investment managers seeking to profit by eliminating them, we can concentrate on a few of the most telling findings.

1. People remember the recent past better than the distant past, and they informally generalize from a few cases that are memorable rather than incorporate the full body of data into their analysis. As a consequence, people assume that companies that have performed well over the prior year or two are good bets for the future and expect that companies that have disappointed will continue to perform poorly. We predict by *extrapolation*. A more thorough examination of the correlation of past performance with future return would reveal just the opposite: over a two- or three-year period, yesterday's laggards become tomorrow's leaders, and vice versa. Wall Street lore is filled with wisdom that reminds us that no acorn grows to the sky, but that doesn't stop professionals and amateurs from overweighting recent history, both good and bad, in estimating the future. Reversion to the mean is not a concept we embrace naturally.

2. We dislike risk and hate losing money. There's nothing wrong with that, except that we confuse past fiascoes with future disappointments. Stocks that have declined in price are tainted, even though the lower price at which we can buy them covers a multitude of old sins. So we let our analysis be colored by an emotional taint that hinders our efforts at producing an unbiased picture of a company's prospects and a security's value. We love winners more than we

should, and we avoid losers so that we don't notice when situations improve and yesterday's failure is tomorrow's comeback of the year.

If we put all of these biases together, we can see why a particular approach to investing—buying value stocks even when value is established mechanically—should provide abnormal returns over a long period, well after evidence about its exceptional performance has been widely publicized. Thus, in a world where there are colossal rewards for uncovering discrepancies between the current price of a stock and its true, intrinsic, or ultimate worth, some discrepancies persist. These discrepancies outline the fields in which a search for fundamental value is more likely to be rewarded.

Other Hunting Grounds

In addition to the disappointing, dispiriting, downtrodden, and thus discarded, there are other places to look for hidden value. First, there are securities that are obscure. They tend to be the stock of smaller companies, untouchable by large investment funds and therefore lacking in coverage by security analysts who want to get paid for their work. Companies spun off from larger firms fit into this category, and they have the extra attraction that they may be actively discarded by the large funds that don't want to be bothered. Finally, boring companies make for boring stocks and lower levels of interest. The company that has been doing the same thing for years, growing slowly and profiting modestly, is not going to spend its funds courting attention from analysts. A change in the fortunes of this kind of firm is more likely to go unnoticed than if the firm were doing something with a lot more flash.

Undesirability has other signs. Companies in bankruptcy or suffering from severe financial distress are clearly undesirable, except to the knowledgeable investor who sees the real value of the assets and the business that may emerge after reorganization. Companies in industries that are suffering from overcapacity, a sudden increase in imports, general decline, or the threat of legislative or regulatory punishment, may also be undesirable.

Lawsuits, both current and potential, may make companies undesirable. And there is nothing more depressing than protracted underperformance. We are not referring here to the stock whose price drops by 50 percent in a week, or even a day, but to one that has substantially lagged the market for two or three years. These indicators of undesirability identify potential areas of opportunity; as investors flee from bad news or poor performance, they discard stock at prices that may exaggerate the company's distress. Not always, of course. Sometimes things are worse than even the gloomiest analyst imagines, and the current low price of the stock is actually too high. But overreaction is frequent enough that the informed and diligent investor may find bargains in the trash(ed).

Finally, there are securities that are mispriced because of institutional constraints or mandates and other temporary aberrations. When the Resolution Trust Company disposed of assets it had acquired in taking over failed savings and loan companies, its aim was to get itself out of business and get these assets back onto the tax rolls. Investors who had the expertise and made the effort to value these assets, whether real estate, junk bonds, or the savings institutions themselves, were able to purchase them at sale prices. Though opportunities such as these are not everyday events, they happen with enough frequency to keep value investors attentive to the next opportunity. There are also companies with divisions performing so poorly that the record of the whole company suffers. If the stock price reflects the earnings (often losses) of the whole company, then the only thing management needs to do to turn things around and boost the share price is to kill the division. Most of these situations do not escape notice from the sharp eyes of Wall Street analysts, but there are always a few with situations novel or complicated enough to avoid detection. They await the value investor with the knowledge and time to disaggregate the company's results and spot the earnings potential. They require as well some catalyst to encourage the company's executives to rid themselves of the albatross and let the true value emerge. It doesn't always work out that way.

We want to emphasize that all of this work is a starting point. The purpose of the search effort is to reduce the investment universe to a manageable size so that we can begin valuation analysis in depth. We can use computerized screens of company or stock databases. We can look at the financial press for notice of spin-offs, other restructurings, or new bankruptcy filings. We can read trade publications to see which industries are distressed and where there is potential for consolidation and other value-enhancing changes. We are examining possibilities for our portfolio, and those that pass these screens or eyeball searches have made our short list. But this is only the first step. The actual work of valuation begins after the candidates have been selected.

PART II

THREE SOURCES
OF VALUE

Chapter 3

Valuation in Principle, Valuation in Practice

Adherents to value investing as an investment discipline believe that financial securities, like all other assets, have an *intrinsic value* that can be determined by careful analysis. Opportunities for profitable investment emerge when the current market price of the securities deviates significantly from this intrinsic value. The essential task of the successful value investor is to determine intrinsic value with enough accuracy to take advantage of the market's mispricing. There are methods in abundance for estimating an asset's true value, but some work better than others. This chapter argues that the methods pioneered by Graham and Dodd possess significant practical advantages over the commonly used alternatives. Therefore, the historical success of the value approach has not been an accident.

The Present Value of Current and Future Cash Flows

There is wide agreement in theory that the intrinsic value of any investment asset—whether an office building, a gold mine, a company selling groceries at the corner or groceries over the Internet, a government bond, or a share of General Motors stock—is determined by the present value of the distributable cash flows that the asset supplies to its owner. Present value is properly calculated as the sum of present and future cash flows, both outlays and receipts, with each dollar of future cash flow appropriately discounted to take into account the time value of money (see Appendix to this chapter). Graham and Dodd disciples accept the concept and the calculation of present value, as do all other fundamental investors. The techniques are taught at every undergraduate and graduate school of business. Investment bankers and corporate financial officers use them. Governments depend on them to evaluate the returns from potential capital projects and other investments. Calculators are programmed to produce present value figures, and electronic spreadsheets have financial functions that will do the work. Present value analysis is inescapable. But what is true in theory need not provide an appropriate model for finding intrinsic value in actual practice. (Perhaps we should say that the practical value of present value analysis should be discounted.)

The standard way of calculating present values, and hence intrinsic value, is to begin by estimating the relevant cash flows for the current and future years out to a reasonable date, perhaps 10 years in the future. Then one selects (estimates) a rate for the cost of capital that is appropriate to the riskiness of the asset in question. With these two figures it is possible to calculate the present value of each annual cash flow; summing them gives us the present value of all the cash flows for the years in question.

The customary practice for dealing with the cash flows in the distant future is to come up with what is called a terminal value. The terminal value is invariably calculated by assuming that beyond year 10 (or whatever year is the last for which we have done annual cash flow calculations) cash flow grows perpetually at a constant proportional rate. Under this assumption, the value of those cash flows, looking forward from the end of year 10, will be the projected cash flow for year 11 times a multiple. This multiple is equal to 1 divided by the difference between the cost of capital and the perpetual growth rate. (For example, if we project a cost of capital of 10 percent and a growth rate of 5 percent a year, then the multiple is 1/[10% − 5%] = 20.) Since we won't see this terminal value until we look forward from the end of year 10, we need to discount the terminal value back to the present. We add that to the present value of our first 10 years of cash flows to get an intrinsic value for the current and all future cash flows.

We should be struck here by a glaring inconsistency between the precision of the algebra and the gross uncertainties infecting the variables that drive the model. We estimate rates of growth for 10 years and then another growth rate from the end of year 10 to forever. This is a heroic, not to say foolhardy, exercise. Suppose that in two or three years, the company faces more competition, technological challenges, a spike in its costs of materials that it cannot pass on to customers, or any of a host of reasonable possibilities that will curtail, and may even eliminate, the growth of its cash flow. Imagine how accurate our estimates are likely to be for even a stable company like General Motors, much less for dynamic firms like Microsoft or Cisco Systems. We also assume that our company will have access to long-term financing at a predictable cost of capital on an ongoing basis. Yet who knows today what lenders will demand in five years, or how much potential share purchasers will require to buy new stock? Profit margins and required investment levels, which are the foundations for cash flow estimates, are equally hard to project accurately into the far distant future.

Worse still, valuations vary significantly if the underlying assumptions are off by only small amounts. Consider the terminal value and the cash flow multiple. If future perpetual growth is 4 percent and the future cost of capital is 8 percent, then the terminal value multiple is 25(1/[8% − 4%] = 25). If our estimate is wrong by only 1 percent in either direction for the cost of capital, the growth rate, or both, the terminal value multiple can vary from a high of 50 (7 percent cost of capital minus 5 percent growth rate) to a low of 16 (9 percent cost of capital less 3 percent growth rate). This is a range greater than three-to-one. In many—probably most—valuations, the terminal value is the largest component of the total present value.

Investors are certainly aware of these difficulties, and there are ways of attempting to deal with them. One method is to simplify the valuation process by relying on multiple-based value calculations. Here one chooses a measure of cash flow, such as net income, operating income (EBIT), or operating income plus depreciation and amortization (EBITDA), and multiplies that by an appropriate factor, like the price to earnings (P/E) ratio, the EBIT multiple, or the EBITDA multiple, taken from market valuations of other, supposedly comparable, companies. The problems with this approach are legion: the secondary origins of the valuation, dependent on someone else's uncertain projections for other companies; the noncomparability of the companies chosen to provide the multiple factor; and the failure to use much current, short-term information on the company's competitive position, its margins, its cyclical sensitivity, and other available data. However, the key shortcoming of this approach is that multiple-based valuations are nothing more than present value calculations with some simplifying assumptions tacked on. In effect, they are terminal value calculations as of today. They do not avoid the problems with present value calculations; they merely sweep them under the rug.

Another widely employed approach to dealing with the uncertainties of present value is to perform an exhaustive number of sensitivity analyses. Here the analyst varies the company's projected operating parameters that determine the future cash flows—growth rates in sales, profit margins, investments required per dollar of sales, the cost of capital—and then looks at the corresponding variations in the company's valuation. The purpose is to capture the full range of valuation possibilities. The problem here is that the range is usually quite large. Because the underlying parameters are linked together in complicated ways, it is not clear which of the many possible valuations is the likely one. Sensitivity analysis has the virtue of making explicit the unreliability of present value estimates, but pointing out the problem is not the same as solving it.

In fact, the unreliability problem is intrinsic to the practice of present value analysis as a means of determining intrinsic value. As commonly applied, that approach suffers from two fundamental defects. First, present value is the sum of individual cash flows from now into the distant future. It may be possible to make correct projections for the next few years; as the time lengthens, the projections invariably become less accurate. In present value calculations, however, all these terms are simply added together. As every engineer knows, adding inaccurate to accurate information produces inaccurate information. An improved approach to valuation would attempt to protect reliable information from being corrupted; the present value method does not.

Second, the present value approach in practice relies on information—parametric values for operating variables—that is often simply not knowable, especially in the far distant future. Even the best informed analyst covering the auto industry will be unable to say with certainty whether Ford's return on sales will be 10 or 12 percent in the years after 2010. Yet there are predictions that the professional analyst should be able to make about those far future years: whether the auto industry is likely to be economically viable, whether Ford will continue to operate at whatever competitive advantage (or disadvantage) it may enjoy today relative to its major rivals (GM, Toyota, DaimlerChrysler, etc.), and whether Ford will develop any new competitive advantage in the future. These are broad strategic judgments, and thoughtful analysts are better at making them than at predicting operating margins or costs of capital. Yet the present value approach cannot be readily adapted to incorporate the implications of these judgments for a valuation of the company.

The Graham and Dodd approach to valuation avoids both of these problems. It segregates information affecting valuation by reliability class, so that good information is not contaminated by poor information. It also directly uses the valuation implications of broad strategic judgments.

A Three-Element Approach to Valuation: Assets, Earnings Power, and Profitable Growth

The skepticism with which Graham and Dodd investors regard present value calculations of future cash flows might be nothing more than a worldly cynicism toward all systematic efforts at valuation if these investors did not offer an alternative approach that avoids the pitfalls of present value. Fortunately for them, and for us, they have developed another valuation method. It is based on a thorough grasp of the economic situation in which a company finds itself. It puts more emphasis on information about the firm that is solid and certain, and it values the company's future prospects with more realism and less optimism than is customary on Wall Street. It refuses to pay anything for even the rosiest prediction that has no current or historical foundation. Charlie Munger of Berkshire Hathaway said that if he were giving a test calling for an analyst to value a new dot-com internet company, he would fail anyone who answered the question. To quote Wittgenstein, "Whereof one cannot speak, thereof one must be silent."

Of what then can we speak? Let's go back and look at Ford Motor Company. It would be rash to predict its cash flow in 2010, but there are some things we can state with confidence.

Element 1: The Value of the Assets

First, we can speak about the present condition of the company. Following Graham and Dodd, we are going to start with an asset value for the firm. We begin with the balance sheet and examine the value of the company's assets at the end of the most recent operating period, as determined by the company's accountants. We know that these accounting values are going to be more accurate for some assets than for others. Thus, as we work down the balance sheet, we accept or adjust the stated numbers as experience and analysis dictate. We do the same for the liabilities side of the balance sheet. At the end, we subtract liabilities from assets to obtain the current net asset value. There is no need for us to forecast the future. The assets and liabilities exist today. Many of them are tangible (or quasi-tangible, like money in the bank account as confirmed by the bank), and these can be valued directly with great precision.

Starting at the top of the balance sheet has another advantage. As we work down the asset list from cash at the top, whose value is unambiguous, to various intangible assets like goodwill, whose value is often highly problematic, we are made naturally aware of the decreasing reliability of the stated values. Graham himself preferred to rely totally on current assets that could be realized within a year and whose accounting values did not vary far from the actual cash that could be obtained by selling them. From these current assets he subtracted all the firm's liabilities to arrive at his famous net-net working capital figure for the value of the company.

Another aspect of asset valuation of which we may speak concerns the principle we employ to assign a value to each asset type. For our Ford example, the choice depends on a strategic judgment regarding the future of the automobile industry in which the company operates. If the industry is not economically viable, if it is in the process of terminal decline, then the assets must be valued at what they are likely to yield in liquidation. The more specialized the assets are for use in the automobile industry, the greater is the discrepancy between what the balance sheet says and the actual cash they will bring in a sale. Cash and accounts receivable will be fully valued, more or less, while plants, equipment, and even some units in the inventory will be valued at scrap. Any goodwill or other intangibles the company lists on its balance sheet, representing what it paid for customer relationships or product designs bought when it acquired other companies, will be worth nothing.

On the other hand, if the automobile industry is not going away, then these assets should be valued at *reproduction* costs, meaning the amount Ford or a competitor would have to pay to replace them today, at the currently most efficient way of producing them. They are still used in an economically viable industry, and as they wear out, they will be reproduced at some cost. Again, the reproduction costs of cash, accounts receivable, and inventory are relatively easy to calculate and are close to accounting book value. The farther down the list, the harder it is to make an accurate estimate of the value. But there are appraisers who make a living by valuing plant and equipment, so we are still dealing with a more solid item than the earnings growth rate 10 years into the future.

Another judgment we may be qualified to make—especially if we are at all expert in the automobile industry—is a strategic judgment about where Ford will fit within the industry. We may say something like "Ford is unlikely to enjoy significant competitive advantages or suffer from significant competitive disadvantages, relative to other global auto companies, of which we are not already aware." Given the mature, highly competitive nature of the industry, this prediction is no surprise. But the implications of this strategic situation—no competitive advantage or disadvantage for the firm—are important. In these cases, the reproduction cost of the assets is going to be the most appropriate measure—the intrinsic value—of the company's worth.

Competitive advantages enjoyed by incumbent firms in any industry are equivalent to barriers to entry against potential competitors. In fact, the two terms are simply different ways of identifying an identical situation. If there are no barriers, we have a level economic playing field. All the firms, both those already in the business and new entrants who might like to take part, have equal access to production technologies, resources, and customers. There is nothing to prevent either existing competitors from trying to expand or new players from joining in.

Imagine that we find a company, First-In, operating on a level playing field. The reproduction costs of its assets (including intangibles not necessarily listed on the balance sheet) are $1 billion. Its market value is $2 billion. What happens? Existing competitors and new entrants will calculate that by spending $1 billion to reproduce the assets, they can create an enterprise with a market value of $2 billion. Why should they have a different economic experience from First-In, since there is nothing it can do that they can't do as well? So we see First-In confronted by newcomers, expanding competitors, or both. A load of new capacity starts to come on line. As the level of customer demand hasn't changed much, there is now more competition for the same business. Either prices fall or, for differentiated products, each producer sells fewer units. In both cases, profits decline, and market value drops with them.

Capacity continues to expand, and profits and market value continue to sink. The game is over when the market value of First-In has been driven down to the $1 billion reproduction costs of its assets. Competitors suffer the same fate; everybody sinks. Certainly this process doesn't happen as smoothly or automatically as we have described, but things do ultimately turn out this way. The incentives to get into the business and take advantage of the market's excessively generous valuation are too powerful, until the market takes back its free money.

This basic process also works in the opposite direction. If the market value of First-in falls substantially below the $1 billion asset reproduction cost, then existing producers will stop replacing their assets. Capacity will decline until either prices rise or sales increase to generate enough profit so that the market raises the value of First-In back to $1 billion. Asset value in strategic terms corresponds, therefore, to the free-entry (no competitive advantage, level playing field) value of the firm—a circumstance that probably characterizes a substantial share of all industries and markets.[1] For these firms, the intrinsic value is the asset value.

---

[1] "Free-entry" is not the same as "commodity product." We will make the distinction clear in Chapter 5 when we discuss franchise values. There is often free-entry into industries with differentiated products, but the same asset valuations hold. We did not indicate whether First-In produces a commodity or a differentiated product; without a sustainable competitive advantage, it makes no difference.

Thus, for Ford, calculating the reproduction value of the assets in the spirit of Graham and Dodd enables us to say a number of important things with reasonable confidence. Unless mismanagement of the company impairs their worth—a situation not unheard of—the Ford Motor Company is worth at least this identifiable asset value. But without barriers to entry or competitive advantages, it is worth no more.

Element 2: Earnings Power Value

The second most reliable measure of a firm's intrinsic value is the second calculation made by Graham and Dodd, namely, the value of its current earnings, properly adjusted. This value can be estimated with more certainty than future earnings or cash flows, and it is more relevant to today's values than are earnings in the past. To transform current earnings into an intrinsic value for the firm requires us to make assumptions both about the relationship between present and future earnings and about the cost of capital. Because we need to rely on these assumptions, intrinsic value estimates based on earnings are inherently less reliable than estimates based on assets.

The traditional Graham and Dodd earnings assumptions are (1) that current earnings, properly adjusted, correspond to sustainable levels of distributable cash flow; and (2) that this earnings level remains constant for the indefinite future. Using these assumptions, the equation for the earnings power value (EPV) of a company is EPV = Adjusted Earnings $\times$ $1/R$, where R is the current cost of capital. Because the cash flow is assumed to be constant, the growth rate G is zero. The adjustments to earnings, which we discuss in greater detail in Chapter 5, include

1. Rectifying accounting misrepresentations, such as frequent "one-time" charges that are supposedly unconnected to normal operations; the adjustment consists of finding the average ratio that these charges bear to reported earnings before adjustments, annually, and reducing the current year's reported earnings before adjustment proportionally.
2. Resolving discrepancies between depreciation and amortization, as

reported by the accountants, and the actual amount of reinvestment the company needs to make in order to restore a firm's assets at the end of the year to their level at the start of the year; the adjustment adds or subtracts this difference.

3. Taking into account the current position in the business cycle and other transient effects; the adjustment reduces earnings reported at the peak of the cycle and raises them if the firm is currently in a cyclical trough.

4. Considering other modifications we discuss in Chapter 5.

The goal is to arrive at an accurate estimate of the current distributable cash flow of the company by starting with earnings data and refining them. To repeat, we assume that this level of cash flow can be sustained and that it is not growing. Although the resulting earnings power value is somewhat less reliable than the pure asset-based valuation, it is considerably more certain than a full-blown present value calculation that assumes a rate of growth and a cost of capital many years in the future. And while the equation for EPV looks like other multiple-based valuations we just criticized, it has the advantage of being based entirely on currently available information and is uncontaminated by more uncertain conjectures about the future.

Also, there is an important and close connection between the EPV of a firm and its strategic situation, and the line of connection runs through the reproduction cost of the assets. When we consider economically viable industries, there are three possible situations. In the first, the firm's EPV may fall substantially below the reproduction value of its assets. In this case, management is not using the assets to produce the level of earnings that it should. The cure is to make changes in what management is doing. In the second, the EPV and the asset value are more or less equal. This is the situation we would expect to see in industries where there are no competitive advantages. If a careful analysis of the structure of costs and customer demand supports this conclusion (we discuss this type of competitive advantage in Chapter 5), then the asset valuation and EPV reinforce one another, and our confidence in both is increased.

We have ignored here the value of the future growth of earnings. But we are justified in paying no attention to it because in evaluating companies operating on a level playing field, with no competitive advantages or barriers to entry, growth has no value. The return these companies earn on the capital invested in them just equals the cost of acquiring that capital, and there is nothing left over for the previous investors. Thus, the EPV that equals the asset value defines the intrinsic value of the company, regardless of its growth rate in the future.

In the third situation, if the EPV, properly calculated, is significantly higher than the reproduction costs of the assets, then we are looking at an industry setting in which there must be strong barriers to entry. Firms within the barriers will earn more on their assets than will firms exposed to the humbling experience of seeing new entrants join the party with no handicap for arriving late. For the EPV to hold up, the barriers to entry must be sustainable at the current level for the indefinite future.

The difference between the EPV and the asset value is the value of the *franchise* enjoyed by the company in question. Competitive advantages enjoyed by incumbent firms constitute barriers to entry that protect the incumbents from profit-eroding competition. These advantages and barriers are responsible for the firm's franchise. In fact, the three terms all describe the same basic phenomenon. The defining character of a franchise is that it enables a firm to earn more than it needs to pay for the investments that fund its assets. The EPV is greater than the asset value; the difference between the two, as we said, is the value of the franchise. Therefore, the intrinsic value of a firm is either the reproduction costs of the assets, which should equal the EPV, or those assets plus the competitive advantages of the firm that underlie its franchise.

The initial judgment that has to be made in this connection is whether the firm currently has a competitive advantage, and, if so, how strong and sustainable it is. This is a judgment that we can sensibly make. For Ford, we forecast that no competitive advantage was likely to emerge over the next two or three decades. We might be proven wrong, but given the history of competition in the motorcar world, that is the way to bet. The opposite would be true for Coca-Cola. It has had 100 years of higher-than-normal profitability. It makes sense to believe that its competitive advantage will persist, neither more nor less powerful, into the foreseeable future.

Element 3: The Value of Growth

When does growth contribute to intrinsic value? We have isolated the growth issue for two reasons. First, this third and last element of value is the most difficult to estimate, especially if we are trying to project it for a long period into the future. Uncertainty regarding future growth is usually the main reason why value estimations based on present value calculations are so prone to error. By isolating this element, we can keep it from infecting the more reliable information incorporated into the asset and earnings power valuations.

Second, under many commonly encountered strategic situations, growth in sales and even growth in earnings add nothing to a firm's intrinsic value. This statement seems to contradict an article of faith about a company's sales and profits—growth is good. However, as we explained earlier, growth on a level economic playing field creates no value. It will be useful to review why. Growth in sales that finds its way to the bottom line (net income) would seem to imply that there is more money available to investors. But growth generally has to be supported by additional assets: more receivables, more inventory, more plant and equipment. These extra assets that are not offset by higher spontaneous liabilities[2] have to be funded by extra investment, whether from retained earnings, new borrowings, or sales of additional shares. That cuts into the amount of cash that can be distributed and thereby reduces the value of the firm. For firms that are not protected by barriers to entry and thus do not enjoy sustainable competitive advantages over their rivals, the new investment produces returns that are just enough to offset the costs of the new investment. The net gain is zero.

Recall the example of the firm operating on a level playing field. With

---

[2] *Spontaneous liabilities* is our term for those liabilities the company incurs in the course of its business: accounts payable, wages payable, accrued expenses, accrued taxes, and occasionally a few other items. They are not the result of formal contracts, and they generally don't require that the company pay for their use with interest or a share of the profits. When business expands, so do accounts receivable and accounts payable. To the extent that the growth of accounts payable offsets the growth of accounts receivable, no additional capital is required.

free entry, a $1 billion investment should produce $1 billion in added value. For the firm that raises an additional $1 billion to expand operations, its cost of capital eats up all the additional earnings that the new investment produces. Its intrinsic value has grown not at all. For firms operating at a competitive disadvantage (i.e., those outside the barriers to entry but still insisting on staying in the game), additional growth will actually destroy value. We shall discuss this phenomenon in more detail in Chapter 5. The only growth that creates value is growth in markets where the firm enjoys a competitive advantage.

Situations in which growth has value arise when the firm's EPV substantially and sustainably exceeds its asset value. In the language we used earlier, only franchise value creates growth value. Thus, judging the existence and sustainability of a company's franchise/competitive advantages/barriers to entry is central to assessing the value of future growth. Again, there is a direct connection between strategic industry conditions and the sources of a firm's intrinsic value. The magnitude of this last element of value is not easy to calculate when it is positive. The growth-related uncertainties of valuation cannot be eliminated completely. However, we know that in many—if not most—situations, the value is zero (no franchise) or even less (competitive disadvantages). By paying careful attention to the strategic underpinnings of a franchise, we may actually obtain superior estimates of the value of growth (as we discuss in Chapter 7). Nevertheless, growth is the most uncertain source of value and is, therefore, the element of value for which the Graham and Dodd–oriented investor is least willing to pay full price.

Integrating the Elements and Strategic Valuation within the Graham and Dodd Framework

The elements of the Graham and Dodd approach to valuation are summarized in Figure 3.1 for a firm with a powerful franchise. The first slice represents the asset value. Under conditions of free entry and no competitive advantage, this is all the value there is.

The second slice, which is the difference between the asset value and

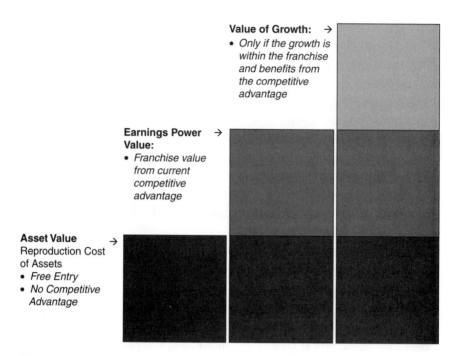

Value of Growth: →
- *Only if the growth is within the franchise and benefits from the competitive advantage*

Earnings Power Value: →
- *Franchise value from current competitive advantage*

Asset Value →
Reproduction Cost of Assets
- *Free Entry*
- *No Competitive Advantage*

Figure 3.1   Three Slices of Value

EPV, represents the franchise value of the firm. Superior management may be considered here as a variety of franchise value, though it is probably less durable than a competitive advantage in its pure form. Estimates about the value of this slice are less reliable than estimates of asset value.

The third and last slice is the difference between the EPV and the full value of growth within the franchise. Of all the estimates, this one is the most difficult to make and therefore the least reliable. A value investor may in fact conclude that the intrinsic value of the firm lies somewhere within this slice, and then compare that (after a suitable reduction to provide for a margin of safety) to the market price to see if a purchase makes sense. But our investor will understand how much detailed knowledge of the industry and good judgment this decision requires. He or she will have a far better idea of what he or she is paying for than will someone relying on a net present value calculation, even one that includes every conceivable sensitivity analysis.

Each of the elements of valuation—assets, earnings power, and growth—is useful in its own right, but the best insights into a firm's value come from comparisons among them, especially the direct comparison between the asset value and the EPV. Consider the case in which the asset value of a company—the reproduction costs of the assets—is greater than its EPV, properly calculated. There are only two conditions in which we are likely to find these results. In the first, the firm's management is doing a poor job by failing to earn as much on the assets as it should. In the second, the industry is operating with more than normal excess capacity. Either it has expanded too rapidly ahead of an anticipated increase in demand or it has not shrunk quickly enough to adjust to a permanent decline.

Careful investigation can determine which of these conditions, poor management or excess capacity, is responsible. If it is poor management, then potential value may be unlocked by a catalyst, such as a takeover or even the threat of one, that will either bring in new faces or concentrate the attention of the incumbents. If the problem is overcapacity, the firm's value will increase no faster than the rate at which the excess capacity is absorbed by new demand or eliminated as assets decay and are not replaced. In both situations, the true value investor will ignore the higher asset value and use the lower earnings power figure as his or her measure of the firm's intrinsic value. He or she will also look to purchase shares when the market prices them far enough below this intrinsic value to provide a sufficient margin of safety. Discrepancies between asset value and EPV suggest both an opportunity and a caution. If the gap can be closed because of better management, then the intrinsic value of the firm will increase, which should be quickly reflected in its market price because the earnings will grow (i.e., return to normal). On the other hand, the fact that the assets are not producing the earnings they should may indicate that the firm is operating at a competitive disadvantage. If the firm raises additional capital to invest for growth, that investment will tend to destroy rather than add to value.

When separate valuations of the assets and of the earnings power produce figures that are approximately the same, we have confirmation of the accuracy of the intrinsic value estimate. The agreement between the two approaches suggests that the quality of the management is average and that the firm enjoys no competitive advantages over its rivals. These conditions may be directly verified. Do newcomers regularly enter the industry to take advantage of overvaluation or poor management, or are conditions more stable? Does current management produce average returns on invested capital, or are they consistently better or worse? Value investors will purchase shares when there is a margin of safety between this intrinsic value and the market price, and they will assign no value to any future growth.

Finally, if the EPV is substantially greater than the asset value, that difference is due to either superior management or the fact that the firm benefits from significant competitive advantages. In any reasonably large group of competing firms, a few will be blessed with exceptional management. Their virtue is already reflected in the higher earnings power. It can only decline with any fall off in the quality of management in the future. Therefore, a realistic value investor will make a negative adjustment to EPV, realizing that management is not going to get better and that it may certainly deteriorate. In the short run, this superior management may squeeze some value out of growth, provided that growth is in areas where it has expertise. But a value investor is not likely to pay for the full EPV of this firm in the hope that future profitable growth will provide the margin of safety, unless he or she is convinced that this superior management is young, healthy, loyal, and deep.

The more common condition that explains an EPV that is greater than the asset value is when a firm enjoys substantial competitive advantages over potential rivals, thanks to barriers to entry, and thus can earn more on its assets than is possible in a more competitive environment. We have called this extra earnings power the *franchise value* of the firm. The critical question here is the franchise's strength and sustainability. We will discuss franchise value and how its durability can be assessed in Chapter 5.

The value of the franchise lies not only in its current earnings power but also in the possibilities for profitable growth. The only kind of growth that adds to the firm's intrinsic value is *growth within the franchise*—growth that, because of the competitive advantages of the firm, can earn more than the cost of the capital necessary to support it. If the value investor identifies a firm with a franchise and good prospects for growing the franchise, then he or she might pay for the full EPV of the firm, in the expectation that the margin of safety will be created by the difficult-to-measure but clearly genuine value of growth.

We have described a situation in which one approach to valuation—net present value calculations—is theoretically correct and precise and can be applied equally well to any asset that produces a flow of income or cash to its owner. Unfortunately, this approach has two defects: (1) it lumps together estimates based on good information with those based on very uncertain assumptions, tainting the lot; and (2) it relies on making accurate estimates of events that are a long way in the future. The other approach to valuation puts more emphasis on current information and on fundamental competitive conditions. It depends on specific knowledge about particular industries and assets, and it places less faith in projections of rosy futures unless substantiated by current hard data. This is the discipline of value investing in the Graham and Dodd tradition. During periods of investor euphoria, value investing will appear stingy and pessimistic in its estimates of intrinsic value. Its requirements that value be found in assets and earnings power will seem antediluvian when radically new technologies or other innovations are promising a boundless future for cutting-edge companies whose first profitable quarter is always a few quarters away. Value investors understand that there are some games at which they are not adept, and the only sensible course is to decline to play. A canon they rely on is, "Use knowledge to reduce uncertainty." This canon has served them well, and it would be foolish to jettison it and buy into tenuous projections of future wealth, no matter how seductive they might be.

Appendix

The Present Value of Future Cash Flows

The process by which money to be received at various dates in the future can be equated with money in hand today is called *discounting*. The term *discount* refers to the fact that we prefer to have a dollar in hand today rather than the promise—even the iron-clad guarantee—of a dollar at some time in the future. The bank will pay us *interest* if we give them the dollar, as will other collectors of funds. In one year's time, at 8 percent simple interest, the bank will return $1.08. At 8 percent simple interest, $1.08 in one year is the equivalent of $1.00 today; put differently, $1.00 is the *present value* of $1.08 one year hence, *discounted* at 8 percent. The algebra is rudimentary: $1.00 × (1 + .08) = $1.08; $1.08 × [1/(1 + .08)] = $1.00. The expression [1/(1 + .08)] is the discount factor. We can think of the discount rate as the equivalent of the interest rate in reverse, the rate at which the future money is reduced to determine its present value. As with the interest rate, part of the discount is to compensate the investor for inflation, and the rest is for risk and the willingness to part with the money.

At 8 percent interest, compounded annually, in two years a dollar deposited today will be worth $1.00 × (1 + .08) × (1 + .08), or $1.164. Conversely, a dollar guaranteed to us two years in the future, at a discount rate of 8 percent, has a present value of $1.00 × 1/(1.08) × 1/(1.08), or $.857. The present value of the future cash flow is reduced more the longer we have to wait for it. The expression that captures this relationship is the *time value of money*. Combined with the right algebra, the concept allows us to transform a whole series of future values into their value today. The two variables we need are time, which is almost always stated in years, and the other expression that we have called both interest and the discount rate. Both terms refer to the rate at which people will voluntarily commit funds to acquire the asset in question. Other phrases for this concept that are more or less equivalent are *rate of return* (which is how much the investor demands) and *cost of capital* (which is how much the user of the funds has to pay for them). The general equation for the present value (PV) of a dollar received in the future is $PV = \$1 \times (1/1 + R)^T$, where R is the cost of capital (or rate of return) per year, expressed as a percentage, and T is the number of years until payment, with the current time as 0.

Let's see how this works out with a bond. We buy a 10-year government bond with a face value of $1,000, which for simplicity's sake pays us $80 at the end of each year. At the end of year 10, it also repays the principle amount. What is the present value of the bond, given this stream of payments? If our rate of return is 8 percent, then the present value exactly equals the face value of $1,000. Here are the calculations:

$$\text{Discount Factor} = (1/1 + R)^T; R = 8\%$$

Year	Payment ($)	Discount Factor	Present Value ($)
1	80.00	0.93	74.07
2	80.00	0.86	68.59
3	80.00	0.79	63.51
4	80.00	0.74	58.80
5	80.00	0.68	54.45
6	80.00	0.63	50.41
7	80.00	0.58	46.68
8	80.00	0.54	43.22
9	80.00	0.50	40.02
10	1,080.00	0.46	500.25
			1,000.00

Everything looks perfect because the bond's stipulated interest payments, at 8 percent, are identical to the rate of return we require or can earn on an equivalent investment elsewhere. But suppose that after the bond is issued, interest rates on this kind of investment increase to 9 percent. That becomes our required rate of return; we don't want to take less than everyone else. What happens to the present value of the bond? The only change is that R now equals 9 percent, but as a consequence, the present value of the bond drops by $64.

$$\text{Discount Factor} = (1/1 + R)^T; R = 9\%$$

Year	Payment ($)	Discount Factor	Present Value ($)
1	80.00	0.92	73.39
2	80.00	0.84	67.33
3	80.00	0.77	61.77
4	80.00	0.71	56.67
5	80.00	0.65	51.99
6	80.00	0.60	47.70
7	80.00	0.55	43.76
8	80.00	0.50	40.15
9	80.00	0.46	36.83
10	1,080.00	0.42	456.20
			935.82

The only difference between the term *present value* and the almost identical expression *net present value* is that the latter includes the initial flow, which is usually the money laid out in year zero. In the first example, we pay $1,000 for the bond, which is a negative flow unreduced by a discount factor because it happens today. The net present value of the cash flows would be zero, which only means that we receive back the present value of our current outlay. If interest rates go to 9 percent and we still insist on paying $1,000 for the note with the $80 coupon, then the net present value of the investment turns out to be negative, since we only receive back funds with a present value of $935.82. One of the cardinal rules of investing is not to make investments that have a net present value of less than zero.

Chapter 4

Valuing the Assets
From Book Value to Reproduction Costs

The first step in a Graham and Dodd valuation is to calculate the asset value of the company. For many traditional value investors, this has been essentially the only step. But even within this restricted approach, the investor has to make judgments about the reliability of the information and the strategic situation of both firms and industry in order to make accurate calculations of the value of the assets.

The strategic judgments concern the future economic viability of the industry (or industries) in which the firm operates. If the industry is in serious decline, then the asset values of the company should be estimated based on what they will bring in *liquidation*. Since there will be no market for capital goods tailored to specific requirements of the industry, they will basically be sold for scrap. On the other hand, if the industry is stable or growing, then the assets in use will need to be reproduced as they wear out. These assets should be valued at their *reproduction cost*.

The reliability issue is largely a question of how far down the balance sheet the investor chooses to go. At one extreme, Benjamin Graham considered only current assets (cash, accounts receivable, inventory, etc.) in his valuation. These can be determined within a narrow margin of error using either a liquidation or reproduction cost basis. With the virtual disappearance of Graham's net-net stocks (market price less than current assets minus liabilities), contemporary value investors have moved down the balance sheet to include in their valuations plant, property, and equipment and even intangibles such as product portfolios, customer relationships, brand images, and trained employees. The error band here is certainly wider, and valuing these assets, especially the intangibles, has required both skill and imagination. Obviously, this effort is worthwhile only for firms operating in viable industries; intangibles are worthless if the industry disappears.

Assets for Sale: Values in Liquidation

The first question we need to ask about the value of a company's assets is whether the industry of which the firm is a part is economically sustainable. If the industry has no future, then neither does the firm, at least in its present form. In that case, the income will shrink and drag down the value of those assets that cannot be transferred, particularly specialized equipment and intangibles such as organizational capital and customer relationships. If the industry is thriving, even a failing firm may sell transferable assets for decent prices to more successful companies in the industry.

When the company's own profitability has plummeted, when it faces financial duress in the form of one or another of the chapters of the bankruptcy code, and when the industry looks feeble, then the firm may be worth no more than the liquidation value of the assets. Table 4.1 presents the balance sheet for a fictional company that appears to be either on the rocks or floundering a few yards away.

Between 1997 and 1998, the company's retained earnings fell by almost $4,000, putting its net worth below zero. Perhaps this was a temporary setback and the firm will be able to convince its lenders to extend it more money to meet its interest obligations. We can't tell from this fragment of information, and we really don't care. All we want to be able to do is estimate the value of the assets if the firm is to be liquidated (see Table 4.2).

For cash and marketable securities, there should be no discount from the amount stated on the company's books, provided that the securities are short-term or have been marked to the market. Accounts receivable will probably not be recovered in full, but since it is trade debt and there are

Table 4.1 Balance Sheet of In the Red, Inc.

In the Red, Inc.	1998	1997
Assets		
Current assets		
Cash	150	145
Marketable securities	25	70
Accounts receivable	1,667	1,525
Inventories	2,329	2,250
Total current assets	4,170	3,990
Property, plant, and equipment (net)	7,500	7,750
Goodwill	2,250	2,400
Deferred taxes	150	155
Total assets	14,070	14,295
Liabilities and equity		
Current liabilities		
Notes payable	2,200	0
Accounts payable	1,417	850
Accrued expenses	1,250	725
Current portion of long-term debt	520	500
Total current liabilities	5,387	2,075
Long-term debt	9,500	9,250
Deferred taxes	125	150
Preferred stock	350	350
Paid-in capital	850	850
Retained earnings	(2,016)	1,770
Total liabilities and equity	14,070	14,295

Table 4.2 Assets and Liquidation Value of Fictional Firm

Assets	1998	Percentage Realized	Value
Current assets			
Cash	150	100	150
Marketable securities	25	100	25
Accounts receivable	1,667	85	1,417
Inventories	2,329	50	1,164
Total current assets	4,170		2,756
Property, plant, and equipment (net)	7,500	45	3,375
Goodwill	2,250	0	0
Deferred taxes	150	0	0
Total assets	14,070		6,131

plenty of specialists who know how to collect it, we estimate that we can realize 85 percent of the stated amount. What the inventory will bring depends on what it is. For a manufacturing firm, the more commodity-like the inventory, the less the discount necessary to sell it. It is those tie-dyed T-shirts that have to be marked down, not the cotton yarn. If, on the other hand, the inventory consists of cartons of last year's unsalable toys, then it may be necessary to pay someone to cart it away. We estimate in this case that we can realize 50 percent on the inventory; if the inventory is highly specialized, then the valuation would have to be substantially lower. In those situations in which the value of the inventory is critical to the overall valuation, an expert appraiser can be called in to determine a value that is more precise than our back-of-the-envelope estimate.

The same holds true for property, plant, and equipment. Detailed knowledge of the real estate and the equipment is necessary to come up with an accurate estimate. Certain broad principles apply. Generic assets such as office buildings will be worth far more, relative to their book value, than will specialized structures such as chemical plants. We have put down 45 percent as another quick and dirty valuation; if this entry is critical, we can hire another expert to do the appraisal. We ascribe no value to the goodwill; it merely represents the excess over fair market value that the firm paid in making those acquisitions that may have gotten it in trouble.[1] Deferred tax assets, the refunds the company can expect over time from the IRS, are offset against deferred taxes owed. Putting all these figures together, we come up with a value of $2,756 for current assets and $3,375 for property, plant, and equipment, for a total of slightly more than $6,000.

Who might want to invest in this company's securities? Certainly not

---

[1] In theory, the accounting entry for goodwill represents the cost of acquiring intangible assets like product, customers, and market positions that are "real" but are not represented on the balance sheet of the company being acquired. The natural way to proceed in putting a value on goodwill is to identify the tangible measures—product lines, numbers of customers, trained workers, or the accessible population—underlying the accounting entry and to value each of them separately. But for a company in a nonviable industry, these highly specialized assets are not likely to have any significant value. Thus, our bottom line for goodwill is zero.

a traditional equity purchaser, no matter how value-oriented. But there is room for gain here, provided one is a specialist in buying up distressed debt. Though it looks fairly certain that if the company is liquidated there will not be enough money left to pay anything to owners of either common or preferred shares, there probably will be funds for the owners of the debt. Accounts payable and accrued expenses amount to only $2,660, even if they receive dollar for dollar. Everything else can flow to the holders of the debt. Debt on the books comes to $12,220, but given the condition of the company, the bonds would certainly have been available for substantially less. If the discount is steep enough, and there is enough value in the property, plant, and equipment, this might be a lucrative opportunity for an expert in distressed debt securities and liquidation values.

Assets for a Going Concern: How Much to Get into the Business?

Many of the values in liquidation are based, if not on fire-sale prices, then on far from the best use to which the asset might be devoted. Our principal purpose in valuing a firm based on its assets is to discover if the economic value of the assets is accurately reflected in the price at which the firm's securities are being bought and sold. Opportunities lie in the gap between value and price. We have already made the case that for a firm in a viable industry, the economic value of the assets is their reproduction costs—that is, what it would take a would-be competitor to get into this business. How do we make these estimates?

We will start with another fictitious firm, this one involved in developing and manufacturing some highly engineered and specialized connectors used in computers, communications, and other electronic equipment. Table 4.3 presents the asset information from the company's published financial report.

What adjustments do we need to make here to get at reproduction costs? Cash is cash and nothing is required. For marketable securities, we have to find the current market prices. This may be difficult if the securities are not liquid, but generally this category is used only for securities that

Table 4.3   Adjustments to Assets for Fictional Firm

Assets	Book Value	Adjustments to Arrive at Reproduction Costs
Current assets		
Cash	2,250	None
Marketable securities	6,750	None
Accounts receivable (net)	31,250	Add bad debt allowances; adjust for collections
Inventories	25,000	Add last in, first out reserve, if any; adjust for turnover
Prepaid expenses	5,900	None
Deferred taxes	4,250	Discount to present value
Total current assets	75,400	
Property, plant, and equipment (net)	54,000	Original cost plus adjustment
Goodwill	26,250	Relate to product portfolio and research and development
Total Assets	159,900	

are actively traded. The serious work starts with accounts receivable; from here on, the book value should be adjusted up or down to get a more realistic reproduction cost. A firm's accounts receivable, as reported in the financial statement, probably contain some allowance built in for bills that will never be collected. A new firm starting out is even more likely to get stuck by customers who for some reason or another do not pay their bills, so the cost of reproducing an existing firm's accounts receivables is probably more than the book amount. Many financial statements will specify how much has been deducted to arrive at this net figure. That amount can be added back, or an average of similar firms can be used.

Valuing the inventory is more complicated. The stated number may be too high or too low by a substantial amount. Our attention should be drawn to an inventory that has been piling up if it equals 150 days worth of the cost of goods sold in the current year, whereas previously it had averaged only 100 days, then the additional 50 days may represent items that will never sell or will sell only at closeout prices. In this instance we would be justified in reducing the reproduction cost downward. By contrast, if the company uses a last in, first out (LIFO) method for keeping track of inventory costs, and if the prices of the items it sells have been rising, then the reproduction cost of the inventory is higher than the published figures indicate. This difference is the LIFO reserve, the amount by which the current cost of any item exceeds the old, recorded cost. The new entrant can't build this year's inventory at last year's prices and therefore will have to pay more to reproduce it.

Prepaid expenses, like rent or insurance, are what they are: small and realistic. They generally require no adjustment. Deferred taxes, as an asset, are future deductions or refunds the company will get from the government. Since we are interested in the value of the assets today, we ought to get the timing of the reductions or payments and calculate their present value. In our example, deferred taxes are listed as a current asset; this firm expects to cash them in within the year. But they might just as easily have been noncurrent, in which case the present value analysis has more significance.

The adjustments we end up making to the book value of current assets in most cases are not going to be large enough to matter. After all, the assets are current because we expect them to be turned into cash within a year, so there has been little time for great disparities between recorded costs and reproduction costs to build up. The situation changes when we examine noncurrent, or fixed assets. The land that cost $1,000 an acre in 1965—purchased because it was cheap, plentiful, and close enough to an adequate labor market, even though a little remote from a decent restaurant—may now sit 200 yards from the intersection of two interstate highways and be choice property in the eyes of trucking and other companies for whom transportation is primary. Our company owns 1,000 acres; last month, property similarly situated sold for $7,500 an acre. Either the land is worth that much to our company because of the easier access it provides, or else we sell it and move elsewhere, pocketing the difference. In either case, the gap between the book value and either the costs of reproducing it or the net gains from an outright sale is large enough to catch our eye.

Property, plant, and equipment, generally stated as net of accumulated depreciation, are the largest noncurrent assets for most companies. Though listed together on one line in the balance sheet, they are distinct from one another in the manner and degree to which their reproduction cost may deviate from book value. *Property* as land does not depreciate. Depending on one of the three cardinal rules of real estate (i.e., location), the land may be worth a lot more than is indicated on the books, as in our example. The company may have to sell the property or change the use to which it puts the land in order to realize this added value. It may still cost the new entrant extra funds to acquire similar property, but perhaps not so much as the market value of this particular parcel. In any case an adjustment to the book value is called for.[2]

Plant can refer to a legion of different investments. It may mean structures, like the factory, the office building, the string of motels that run from Bangor to Bakersfield, or the oil refinery. It may also mean that fiber-optic cable our company has just installed to link together every large city in the country and several outside it. The disparity between book value and reproduction cost of a company's plant is potentially enormous for two reasons. First, the depreciation rules by which the company reduces the value of its plant may bear only the slightest resemblance to what is actually happening to the economic value of the asset. Buildings may be depreciated over a 30-year period, down to zero, when in fact their market value and the cost of reproducing them is going up. The same is true for parts of the telecommunications infrastructure that has become so central to our economy; the cable may last for decades, but our company has written it down to nothing. Second, inflation can warp the values just as radically. The depreciation we charge ourselves to replace this year's use of the economic value of the asset is based on its historical cost, which is now as relevant as the price of wheat in Minneapolis in 1925. We may be overstating our income by understating the real expense. Our potential competitors, on the other hand, have to pay for the asset in today's dollars; their costs should reflect this increase.

Equipment may be the easiest to value at reproduction costs. It is de-

[2] If the market value of the land exceeds the reproduction cost, the situation is analogous to a firm that has more cash than it needs to run the business. There is a surplus here that the new entrant will not have to reproduce, but the additional cash or the higher market price of the land certainly adds to the asset value of this particular company.

preciated over its useful life, and if it lasts somewhat longer, we are ahead of the game. In fields where electronic controllers and other recent innovations are making today's equipment significantly more productive, the new entrant may have an advantage over the incumbent in starting with state-of-the-art tools. The book value of the incumbent may inflate the true costs of reproduction; no one would reproduce the equipment in place. The adjustments made to equipment require a case-by-case analysis, which in turn depends on specific knowledge of the firm and the industry. The adjustment made to the equipment account, like that for plant, may be up or down, but it is not so likely to be massive.

A goodwill entry within a company's long-term assets generally means one thing, and that isn't a reputation for probity, charity, or public-spirited behavior that the company has accumulated over the years. A company adds goodwill to its assets when it purchases another firm and pays more than the fair market value of the company's assets net of all liabilities. The difference between the two is tossed into the goodwill account, where it will be reduced over a long period of time by an annual amortization charge against earnings. This deduction lowers the company's income; because it does not require an outlay of cash, it is one of the adjustments that needs to be made to get from income to cash flow. Our question here is not annual cash flow but the reproduction cost of goodwill to the new entrant. Can we ignore it entirely because it is so intangible, or do we have to analyze it carefully to see whether it represents an economic value?

Analysis wins out, as always. Imagine that your business wants to buy the entire Coca-Cola Company, every share, every vat of syrup, every copyrighted jingle, every red logo. In the 1990s, shares of Coca-Cola (KO) traded between 6 and 26 times book value. If you are rich enough to get your hands on the whole thing, the single largest entry on the asset side of your new balance sheet is almost certainly going to be goodwill. Is it economically worthless? Obviously not. Any potential competitor will have to pay dearly for the value of the brand, consumer loyalty, distribution networks, and all the other things that make Coca-Cola one of the two or three best franchises in the world. Most of the company's value is goodwill; how else can it make so much money selling tinted sugar water?

But there are cases in which the economic value of goodwill is suspect.

A company may simply pay too much to acquire another firm, because of either perceived competitive threats or grandiose plans that don't work out; or it just makes a mistake. There is a goodwill entry for the extra money needed to buy the other firm, but it does not represent any economic value. A new entrant does not need to reproduce anything here in order to compete. This goodwill represents a prior blunder, and we are justified in ignoring it entirely in coming up with our asset-based valuation. So, to the question, "Is goodwill worth anything?" the answer is that it all depends on the source of the goodwill, and for that we need information and industry knowledge.

Goodwill appears because of a corporate takeover or other transaction that requires an accounting entry to keep the balance sheet in balance. The same business practices that made the acquired firm worth more than the fair market value of its tangible assets (e.g., investments in research and development, advertising, and promotion to create a brand identity, or money spent each year on developing loyal customers) will also have a value even if the company is not taken over. The would-be competitor will have to spend heavily on research, advertising, or customer relations in order to reproduce what we can call *hidden assets*, which don't appear on the balance sheet. In trying to determine the intrinsic value of the firm, we need a way to estimate the real worth of these hidden assets.

The main purpose of R&D expenses is to invent, design, and produce products or services for sale. Many firms will have no R&D expenses; others will spend modest amounts that don't merit their own entry in the income statement but may be specified in the notes; and some companies will list R&D as an entry separate from cost of goods sold or selling, general, and administrative expenses. As a general rule, the higher the technology, the more the R&D, although there are exceptions. Table 4.4 presents the R&D spending of some leading corporations as a percent of sales.

How many years worth of R&D spending would the new entrant have to invest to reproduce the value that these firms have already created? That depends on how long a product keeps generating sales for the company. Boeing's R&D total looks meager compared to most of the other companies. But suppose we find that the average lifespan of an aircraft frame design in its product portfolio is 15 years. To match Boeing's range of prod-

Table 4.4   R&D Spending of Major U.S. Firms

Firm	1997 (%)	1998 (%)
Boeing	4.2	3.4
Cisco Systems	18.7	19.1
Coca-Cola	1.7	1.5
Eli Lilly	16.2	18.8
General Electric	1.7	1.5
IBM	5.5	5.5
Merck	7.1	10.7
Microsoft	16.9	17.3
Pfizer	15.4	16.8

Source: Compustat data tapes.

ucts, we would have to spend 15 years worth of R&D, somewhere between 50 and 60 percent of current annual sales. The drug companies present an even more forbidding hurdle. Even if the life cycle of a profitable drug is only five years—and we know that patent protection lasts longer than that, although its clock starts to tick before the drug is commercially available—we would need to spend at least one year's worth of revenue to replicate any company's pharmacopoeia.

Developing customer relationships also costs money—money that never appears as an asset. Although this information may be difficult for outsiders to obtain, a well-run company knows how long it takes to woo a new customer before an initial sale is made. We can regard the money spent on sales before the order is signed as an investment in future business relationships, some of which will never materialize. A new competitor does not start with an order book full of business or a list of devoted customers; it has to build or buy established customer relationships. The amount it needs to spend depends on the sales cycle: how many months of selling, general, and administrative expenses the company has to pay out before it starts to take orders and make sales. It also needs time to develop the internal systems that allow it to function. These systems, which include information technology, human resource policies, and other unglamorous but essential procedures, are vital to its functioning. No company—certainly no public company—springs like Athena, fully armed from the brow of Zeus. So we need to add some multiple of the selling, general, and administrative line, in most cases between one and three year's worth, to the reproduction cost of the assets.

There are other potentially valuable assets that may not be fully recognized on the company's financial statements. The company may hold licenses from government agencies that permit it to operate in certain areas, such as the right to broadcast radio and television signals, to sell alcoholic beverages from a particular address, or to run a gambling casino. It may hold a real franchise that is difficult or impossible to reproduce; owners of professional sports teams need franchises to play in the league, and bottlers of Coca-Cola need franchises to turn concentrate into soda. There may be limitations on the rights of the holders of some of these licenses and franchises to dispose of them to third parties, but even the most restricted of them are assets that new entrants will have to reproduce in order to compete. And some certainly can be sold, generally with approval from the license or franchise grantor.

The surest method for assigning a value to the license or franchise is to see what similar rights have sold for in the private market, that is, to a knowledgeable buyer who is paying for the whole business. There are ways to compare situations that initially look dissimilar. There is almost always a "per" number: price per subscriber, per regional population, per caseload, per stadium seat. Recent sales in the private market provide a benchmark for valuing the license or franchise of the company under analysis.

The same approach can be used in valuing a subsidiary business within the corporation. Private market purchases of similar businesses provide a basis for determining the worth of the subsidiary. Instead of using the price paid per subscriber or other operating figure, the standard practice is to use a multiple of cash flow, like EBITDA. Say, for example, that a property and casualty insurance company has bought or built a subsidiary that provides online information to insurance adjusters on the price and availability of replacement auto parts. This information is available to all insurance firms, who pay for it by a combination of subscription fees and usage charges. Although it serves the insurance industry, the subsidiary is really a different business. Its success has nothing to do with careful underwriting or skillful investing. It is an information services provider, and it has the added appeal of living on the Web, at times the neighborhood of choice. In arriving at a value for the whole insurance company, it makes sense to break out the earnings and assets of the information subsidiary and to look at the price at which comparable information services companies have sold in the private market. Perhaps the insurance company will take advantage of the higher price to earnings multiples afforded to Web-based businesses and sell this subsidiary, or spin it off and retain some of the shares. Whatever it decides to do, its value is enhanced by the ownership of this other business, which deserves a separate valuation.

The assets are one side of the balance sheet, the liabilities the other. The oldest principle in accounting is that assets have to equal liabilities plus equity. The arithmetic reason is simply that equity is what is left after liabilities are subtracted from assets, so the balance sheet balances by definition. But the financial reason is that liabilities and equity are the sources of funds that support the assets, which are the uses to which those funds are put. If our task is to determine the value of a company based on the reproduction costs of its assets, we really want to know how much money an investor or business person would have to lay out to acquire or replicate those assets. To arrive at an answer, we have to examine the liabilities side of the balance sheet to see what we would need to spend.

For this purpose and many others, it is useful to think of liabilities as falling into three categories. First are those liabilities that arise intrinsically from the normal conduct of the business: accounts payable to suppliers, accrued vacation and other wage costs due to employees, accrued taxes due to governments, and other accrued expenses. Most of these are current liabilities, due within a year. They represent credit extended to the company for which the company pays no interest. Within reason—unreason here being that suppliers are so annoyed at late payments that they refuse to ship new orders—the larger these spontaneous liabilities are, the less investment the company needs to fund its assets. We can simply subtract the book value of these liabilities from the reproduction value of total assets to arrive at the reproduction value of net assets. This is what a new entrant would have to pay to duplicate what this firm has.

The second class of liabilities consists of those obligations that arise from past circumstances that are not pertinent to a new entrant. For example, deferred tax liabilities or liabilities incurred because of adverse legal judgments (e.g., our company broke the law and owes fines or settlement payments) are probably not relevant for the newcomer. The tax law may have changed, or this firm's experience may effectively deter the new people from making the same mistakes. Liabilities like these do not reduce the investment a potential entrant will have to make, but because they are genuine obligations that will have to be paid, they do need to be subtracted from the asset value to see what this firm is worth to investors.

The third class of liabilities is the outstanding formal debt of the company. The appropriate treatment of the debt is a matter of choice. When we start with the reproduction cost of the assets and then subtract the first two categories of liabilities (spontaneous and what we have called circumstantial), we are left with the asset value of the whole enterprise to which investors have claims. This value will be divided between those who hold the debt and those who own the equity. If we are shareholders or are looking to make an equity investment, we need to subtract the value of the debt from this figure. We use the market value of the debt, if available; if not, the book value is generally an adequate alternative. Because, the value of the debt is solid except in situations of financial distress, any errors made in measuring the enterprise value will directly affect the value of the equity. In a highly leveraged firm, where debt accounts for a large share of the asset value of the enterprise, a slight error in estimating the asset value will have a major impact on the value of the equity. For example, let's say we estimate the asset value of a company, after deducting spontaneous liabilities, at $100 million, and it has $80 million in debt. That leaves the value of the equity at $20 million. But if we are off by 10 percent, and the true value is $90 million, the value of the equity shrinks to $10 million, a 50 percent decline. Our margin of safety may be eliminated and then some. Because leverage can be the foe of the margin of safety, many value investors shy away from companies that have high levels of debt.

The other way to treat the debt is to consider it alongside the equity as part of the investment in the company. Using what is called the enterprise value approach, we add the market value of the debt to the market value of the equity and then subtract cash. This is the enterprise value. We compare that to the asset value less spontaneous and circumstantial liabilities.

Table 4.5   Various Asset Value Approaches

Approach	Graham and Dodd	Book Value	Reproduction Costs
Opportunities	None	Limited	More extensive
Value in practice	Yes	Yes	Yes
Industry knowledge required	None	None	Substantial
Stability/reliability	High	Low	Intermediate
Value of goodwill	0	Book	Reproduction costs
Value of debt	Book (low debt)	Book	Market

If we can buy the whole company for less than this asset value figure and still have our margin of safety, we may have discovered a good investment opportunity.

Reproduction costs are one of three methods used to establish an asset-based valuation of a company (see Table 4.5). Another is the traditional Graham and Dodd net-net approach, in which all the liabilities are subtracted from current assets to arrive at a conservative—even bulletproof—figure that is hard to beat and even more difficult to find. The third approach is simply to use the value as stated on the company's books. Even though we have pointed out how much the intrinsic value may deviate from this book figure, in practice the investment strategy of buying shares selling in the market for a significant discount to book value has proved difficult to improve upon. Finding the reproduction cost of a firm's assets and liabilities takes more work, more knowledge, and more everything than relying on book value or net-net figures. You have to do it well to make it pay off.

Assets under a Rock: Complex Structures and Concealed Values

It may pay to strain the eyes and devote hours in the examination of a company's financial accounts, searching for some formally legitimate figure that understates intrinsic worth. We can shorten the odds if we concentrate on firms with complex structures, multiple businesses, subsidiaries off on their own, and other features that confuse security analysts, and perhaps the company's management as well. Firms such as these present financial statements that may be full of places where undervalued assets can get lost, overlooked by the investment community and the chief executive—or, if not overlooked by the insiders, then secreted out of sight until they have the chance to get their own hands on the value. Whatever the proximate cause, simple companies produce financial statements with no place to hide. Complicated organizations, by contrast, have financial statements full of dark corners and secret passageways, terrifying to the novice but potentially rich in treasure for the seasoned explorer.

We can find a sufficiently complex situation in the annual report for 1998 of the Hudson General Corporation. A glance at the company's income statement (see Table 4.6) over three years suggests that something out of the ordinary has transpired. Revenues have declined by more than 96 percent, while net income has only been cut in half. We are not looking at the same animal in 1998 that we saw in 1996.

In fact, as the discussion tells us, in 1996 the company created a separate limited liability company (LLC), Hudson LLC, to run its major line of business, providing maintenance and other services to airlines at major airports. Hudson LLC (HLCC) sold 26 percent of itself to a branch of Lufthansa Airlines for almost $24 million; it gave Lufthansa the option to buy up to 49 percent at a price linked to profitability within the aviation business. Hudson General reports its 74 percent ownership of HLLC under the equity method of accounting, in which only its share of the LLC's earnings shows up on its income statement. The remaining revenue is largely

Table 4.6 **Hudson General Income Statement**

	1996	1997	1998
Revenue	157,100	5,064	5,783
Operating income	19,436	(3,755)	(2,724)
Equity in earnings of Hudson General LLC	855	11,955	9,426
Equity in loss of Kohala joint venture	(3,021)	(11,292)	(2,822)
Interest income	379	3,985	4,156
Earnings before taxes	17,649	866	8,036
Provision for taxes	7,183	391	2,780
Net earnings	10,466	475	5,256

Note: Amounts are in thousands of dollars.

from overhead that it charges HLLC. The other business is a land investment in Hawaii that, at least for the three years we can witness here, is not faring very well. With this background, we are in a position to take a closer look at the assets of Hudson General.

Table 4.7 presents the balance sheet of the company as of June 30, 1998, with the equity accounts omitted. We have included the costs of reproducing these assets. The only changes to book value are the minor effect of discounting future tax liabilities and the major effect of having to come up with a value for the two operating businesses in which the company is a partner. We will put that to the side for the moment and also ignore any benefit the company may gain from not having to pay those taxes until some time in the future. Without adjustment, and ignoring the two partnership interests, the assets are worth $46 million and the liabilities are $5 million, leaving the net worth at $41 million.

Table 4.7 **Reproduction Cost of Hudson General Assets**

	Book Value 1998	Reproduction
Assets		
Cash	19,001	19,001
Marketable securities	19,002	19,002
Receivables	563	563
Advances to HLLC	2,057	2,057
Prepaid expenses	56	56
Total current assets	40,679	40,679
Plant, property, and equipment (net)	2,389	2,389
Investment in HLLC	22,306	?
Investment in Kohala joint venture (net)	4,962	?
Notes receivable from HLLC	3,130	3,130
Total assets	73,466	46,198
Liabilities		
Accounts payable	200	200
Other current liabilities	2,628	2,628
Total current liabilities	2,828	2,828
Deferred income taxes	2,197	Present Value ≈ 2,000
Total liabilities	5,025	≈ 5,000
Net worth		≈ 41,000

Note: Amounts are in thousands of dollars.

What is the intrinsic value of Hudson General's interest in HLLC and the Hawaiian land investment? It carries its 74 percent stake in HLLC at $22 million, which would put the book value of all of HLLC at $30 million. But we already have two reliable pieces of information that make us think that this number is ridiculously low. First, Lufthansa paid $23 million for 26 percent two years ago, and now it is going to spend an additional $30 million for another 23 percent. At those prices, HLLC must be worth at least $130 million, and probably more. Hudson General has a controlling interest, for which there is a premium paid in the private market for control. Second, HLLC has measurable earnings. In 1998 its earnings after tax were $12.7 million, down from $16 million the year before. The company has no debt, and its earnings stream is secured by long-term contracts with airlines and airports. If the stock market were to pay 10 times for those earnings, then the LLC is worth $130 million, proportionally the identical price that Lufthansa is laying out. Those contracts are a hidden asset that don't show up on the balance sheet. They are, from another perspective, the specific competitive advantage that allows HLLC to earn more than it would on a level playing field.

Let us say that HLLC has an intrinsic value of $130 million. How much goes to Hudson General? After Lufthansa buys its next slice, Hudson General will be left with 51 percent. It will also have the $30 million that Lufthansa hands over. So, as of the date of the statement, we can conservatively value Hudson General's share of HLLC at

$130 × 51%   = $66.5 million
Cash received from Lufthansa = $30.0 million
Total $96.5 million

even before we include any extra premium for control.

The Hawaiian joint venture is another matter. How does a company specializing in aviation services end up a partner in a land development in the middle of the Pacific? Perhaps the executives who made the investment traveled a lot. Whatever the origins of the enterprise, it hasn't worked out well. Hawaiian real estate in general sank in price during the 1990s. Hudson's share of the venture's loss—primarily a massive write-down of the assets in 1997, coupled with annual operating losses—was $3 million in 1996, $11 million in 1997, and slightly less than $3 million in 1998. (How do you make a small fortune in the islands?) At the time of this financial statement, Hudson owns 50 percent of slightly more than 1,800 acres. How much are they worth? If they were desirable, then there would have been no need for the write-offs. Hudson records their value on the books at $4.9 million, which comes to $5,500 per acre. Is that too high? We can be conservative and eliminate the asset entirely, or we can hire a land appraiser in Hawaii to take a look and send us a report. Given the scope of the rest of the assets, it probably won't make much difference. For the moment, we will set the value to zero and merely mention it as potentially worth something.

We are ready to adjust our asset valuation of Hudson General to take into account the intrinsic value of HLLC (see Table 4.8). The new figure

Table 4.8   Reproduction Cost of Hudson General Assets, Round 2

	Book Value 1998	Reproduction
Assets		
Total current assets	40,679	40,679
Plant, property, and equipment (net)	2,389	2,389
Investment in HLLC	22,306	130,000 × 51% = 66,300
Plus cash from sale to Lufthansa		30,000
Investment in Kohala joint venture (net)	4,962	(even if we get nothing) 0
Notes receivable from HLLC	3,130	3,130
Total assets	73,466	142,498
Liabilities		
Accounts payable	200	200
Other current liabilities	2,628	2,628
Total current liabilities	2,828	2,828
Deferred income taxes	2,197	(a modest reduction 2,000 for present value)
Total liabilities	5,025	5,842
Net worth	68,441	
Adjusted net worth		137,670

Note: Amounts are in thousands of dollars.

is almost twice the book value, even with the 910 acres in Hawaii entirely written off. The stock market also underestimates the intrinsic value of Hudson General. At a share price high of $50 in 1998, the entire market capitalization of the company came to $88 million. That left a prize of more than $50 million available for the enterprising investor who could find a way to encourage the management to close the gap between the market price and the intrinsic value.

Management did not need much prompting. In November 1998 it offered to purchase the company for $100 million. Fortunately for the shareholders, the managers' move just initiated the bidding. By February 1999, when Globeground, the Lufthansa unit that by then owned 49 percent of HLLC, put in its winning bid of $133 million, there had been a sweetened offer from management at $106 million and several bids from other companies in the aviation services industry. All this attention kept management from enriching itself at the expense of outside shareholders, though who knows what door prizes they were able to cart away? Did Globeground pay top dollar? From our analysis, we know that they got both the Hawaiian acreage and control of HLLC for nothing. Since they were the logical purchasers from a strategic sense, it is probably unreasonable to expect anyone to have bid more.

One moral of this story is that an asset valuation based on reproduction costs provides an accurate estimate of what the company might be worth, as demonstrated by the arrival of a willing buyer to purchase it for roughly that amount. But—and this is a second moral—it generally requires more than analysis to levitate depressed asset values off the floor, namely, some catalyst to upset the status quo and propel a change. In this instance, it was the opportunism of existing management, which sought to walk away with the company by paying only a pittance more than the current share price. Had management not been greedy, Hudson General might be independent today, its stock selling at substantially less than the Lufthansa takeover provided its shareholders.

Chapter 5

Earnings Power Value
Assets Plus Franchise

Toasted Earnings

Consider a hypothetical company—we will call it Top Toaster because toasters are what it makes—that has been particularly successful. For the last five years it has earned around $10 million each year. To keep things simple, we will state that there is no substantial difference between reported net income and the amount of earnings it can distribute to shareholders. Investors in the company are willing to accept a 10 percent annual return on their investment. Applying the earnings power value (EPV) equation we developed in Chapter 3, the EPV of the toaster company is earnings × 1/cost of capital, or $10 million/10% = $100 million. Assume next that the company's asset value is $40 million. This figure includes all the tangible assets (cash; accounts receivable; inventory; and plant, property, and equipment—each adjusted to reflect any differences between the figures on the company's books and the money a competitor would need to spend to reproduce them) and the intangibles as well, including consumer recognition and reputation, product design, production know-how, worker training, and distribution channel development, whose reproduction also requires expense. There is a $60 million discrepancy here between the asset value and the EPV. And if the stock market should value the company at $150 million, then the gap above the asset value would be wider still.

Unfortunately for Top Toaster, the EPV of $100 million and the market value of $150 million will be a green flag to potential competitors.

Some bright entrepreneur—perhaps someone already in the small appliance business or an executive at another toaster company with access to investment capital and experience with retail outlets—will recognize that he or she can produce this income stream worth $100 million for an investment of only $40 million. Or, to put it differently, he or she can earn $10 million a year on a $40 million investment, a 25 percent return that almost qualifies as exorbitant.

The entrepreneur enters the toaster business by opening a new plant, expanding the capacity of an existing one, or finding a contractor to produce the toasters. He or she finds or buys an acceptable design, develops attractive packaging, and hires experienced sales agents to hawk the stuff. Assume for the moment that toasters are a *commodity product*, meaning that they are more or less interchangeable with one another and are selected entirely on the basis of price. Increased competition means more toasters on the market, and more toasters means lower toaster prices. As toaster prices fall, the profits of all toaster companies fall in tandem with one another. As the earnings of Top Toaster start to shrink, so does its earning power. After the first competitive wave hits, suppose that earnings were to decline to $8 million.

Unfortunately, the waves continue to break. Earnings of $8 million, with a desired return of 10 percent, value the company at $80 million. The assets cost $40 million to replicate. That leaves a $40 million gap, sufficient inducement for a second entrepreneur to start churning out toasters. In fact, only after the gap disappears and the EPV falls to $40 million will new entrants—or incumbents expanding their production—stop their invasion of Top Toaster's lush financial territory. The process ends, in other words, when there are so many indistinguishable toasters on the market that prices and profits have fallen to the level at which none of the suppliers earns more than the cost of capital that investors demand on their money.

The problem of declining profits in the face of increased price competition has challenged thousands of companies that cannot distinguish their goods or services from those of other players. It is a truth universally acknowledged that all sensible people abhor commodity businesses. The standard advice for avoiding this fate is to *differentiate* your product or service from all the others. For Top Toaster, that means spending money on advertising, adding product features, or changing the design. All of these may work to insulate Top Toaster from the immediate pressure to cut its price. But the competitors are still there, aiming for a share of Top Toaster's attractive market. Nothing prevents them from introducing competing designs, adding their own features, and matching Top Toaster's spending on advertising. Inevitably they take away some of Top Toaster's business; even if its prices do not decline, it sells fewer units. Unit volume shrinks, but fixed costs like product development, package design, and advertising do not decrease proportionately; in the face of active competition, they may actually rise. Top Toaster finds itself staggered by two blows: It is selling fewer units, and because the fixed costs are spread over fewer toasters, its profit margin on each one has also declined. Thus earnings take another hit. Differentiating the toaster is at best a short-term response. The company cannot separate itself from the competition. Earnings drop again, now to $6 million.

Unfortunately, this isn't the end of the story. As long as the company's EPV, now $60 million, exceeds the $40 million it costs to get into the game, new entrepreneurs will keep showing up, or old competitors will continue expanding. Toaster production will keep increasing until the profit opportunity motivating it disappears—until, that is, the $40 million of assets produces an income stream of $4 million (provided that investors still will take a 10 percent return on their capital). At that point, the EPV and the reproduction cost of the assets are equal to one another, and there is no easy money to be made by entering or expanding in the toaster business.

It doesn't matter whether the toaster is a commodity and sells only on price or it is a differentiated product and sells on features. Ultimately, new entrants will appear until the EPV comes to equal the asset value. This equality is not an accident; it is a fundamental economic connection, and it results from the corrosive influence of competition on prices and profit margins. The process of competition displays itself in this instance by the ability of other firms to enter or expand in quest of a profit opportunity. Although it is tough on the Top Toasters of the world, and on their investors, it is a blessing for consumers, meaning all those who were financing the difference between the EPV and the asset value with the price they paid for toasters.

Automobiles: Value in the Nameplate?

Top Toaster and its competitors are figments of our imagination, but the process through which the value of the firm in the long run is going to equal the value of the assets, in the absence of barriers that interfere with entry, is real enough. And this process works even in situations where companies and products benefit from strong brand images. An example from recent history should confirm the theory.

In the entire world there are few brand names as widely recognized as Mercedes-Benz. It is universally associated with a superior product that is high in quality and prestige. The cars themselves are immediately distinguishable from other automobiles by the Mercedes-Benz star, which serves as both a hood ornament and an icon for the corporate commitment to excellence. By all rules of product differentiation, Mercedes-Benz ought to enjoy a strongly protected market position and, as a consequence, high profitability. Yet for the years 1995 to 1997, before the company acquired Chrysler, Daimler's pretax return on the identifiable assets in its automotive business averaged 7.2 percent. If there is a franchise here, it does not show up in the returns being generated; they are at or below any reasonable cost of capital for the automobile industry.[1]

We can also analyze this situation from a value perspective. Suppose that the cost of capital to Daimler-Benz is 10 percent. In 1997 the automotive division earned DM3.5 billion, pretax. Based on these figures, its EPV would be DM35 billion, again pretax. The reproduction value of its assets is at least equal to these amounts. The book value of capital was approximately DM30 billion at the end of 1997. This excludes the cost of reproducing the engineering knowledge, images, dealer network, and or-

[1]The investment bank Goldman Sachs, in its fairness opinion regarding the merger of Daimler with Chrysler, estimated the cost of capital for comparable companies at between 10 and 12 percent. See DaimlerChrysler AG, Initial Tender Offer Statement, Form SC 14D1, September 24, 1998.

ganizational experience of the corporation. At a minimum, that would amount to an additional DM10 billion, representing three years of R&D. A new entrant would gain precious little above this asset value of DM40 billion by entering Mercedes-Benz's market.

The history of the automobile industry explains why Mercedes does not have a profitable franchise. In the late 1960s, the luxury car market in general and Daimler in particular enjoyed abnormally high profits. Seeking to benefit from this situation, other European luxury car makers, such as BMW, Jaguar, Rover, Citroen, and Peugeot, all expanded aggressively. In the 1980s, the Japanese car makers—first Acura (Honda), then Lexus (Toyota), and finally Infiniti (Nissan)—all entered the market. The results turned out exactly as theory predicts; more competition meant a substantial erosion of profit margins. They shrunk for Mercedes in Europe and for Lincoln and Cadillac in the United States. Globalization of the luxury car market proved to be profitability's foe. Both in theory and in practice, product differentiation and a strong brand are not the same as a profitable franchise.

The Nature of a Franchise

The critical element in both the Top Toaster fable and Mercedes-Benz history is the process of entry and the ability of entrants to compete on equal terms with the established firms. As long as newcomers can develop and distribute new products on an equal footing with incumbents (e.g., they have an equal ability to differentiate), all products effectively are commodities. Companies that have above-average earnings for sustained periods of time profit from the inability of competitors, both actual and potential, to do what they do, and such companies are generally awarded high valuations in the market. None of this means that brands have no value. A strong brand is an asset like any other; its value is equal to its reproduction cost. However, if the value of a brand is equal to what it costs to create the brand, then branding by itself is not the source of value.

Value is only created when the incumbent has abilities that new entrants cannot match. When a potential entrant sees Top Toaster earning

$10 million per year on assets of $40 million, it must recognize that it will not be able to do as well. In the language of modern management theory, Top Toaster must enjoy a *competitive advantage* over would-be rivals. The newcomer will stay out of the market if it sees that it cannot compete on equal terms. Top Toaster's competitive advantage acts as a barrier to entry and puts a brake on the profit-eroding process that occurs when entrants are able to compete on potentially equal terms. Another way to say the same thing is that the continued existence of Top Toaster's profitable franchise depends on the existence of the competitive advantages it enjoys; these act as barriers to entry and deter competitors. These three concepts—franchises, barriers to entry, and incumbent competitive advantages—amount to the same thing. They are the major sources, in a modern market economy, of any value that exceeds the cost of reproducing a firm's assets.

Contrary to popular management discourse, there are only a few types of competitive advantages, and examples of sustained competitive advantages in the business world are uncommon. The simplest form is the advantage created by the government when it grants a license to one or several firms to engage in some kind of business, leaving everyone else excluded. Cable franchises, broadcast television stations, telephone companies, and electric utilities all enjoyed exclusive local franchises. Potential competitors were deterred by law. As technology has changed, so have the regulatory and licensing regimes under which these firms operated, and some formerly protected businesses have had to learn to compete. But it is unlikely that all forms of exclusive, governmentally generated franchises will disappear.

Other types of competitive advantages follow from the basic profit equation of any business: Revenues minus costs equals profits. One key term in the equation is costs. Potential competitors to Top Toaster or Mercedes-Benz might be deterred because they are unable to meet the (low) costs of these firms. The only way such cost advantages are sustainable is if the incumbents possess production techniques or products that the entrants cannot match. For example, patents, whether on the products themselves or on the process of producing them, create one kind of cost-based competitive advantage. Know-how, otherwise known as the downward-sloping learning curve, is another important advantage. Even as the entrant gains experience, it will always trail the incumbent in the necessary expertise required to make things efficiently. The test here is whether the required technology, including the human-based skill, is accessible to the entrant on the same terms as it is to the incumbent. Neither Top Toaster nor Mercedes-Benz has access to technology or other knowledge that is not equally available to potential competitors.

Another possible cost advantage is access to cheap resources such as labor and capital. This advantage is hardly ever found in practice. Most resources are mobile and plentifully available on a global basis, and there is nothing that inhibits entrants from acquiring them on the same terms as incumbents. Some firms with unionized labor or other constraints may be forced to operate with high resource costs, but the incumbent has to worry about its most efficient competitor, not its least.

There are situations in which incumbents are at a cost disadvantage. Where technology is changing rapidly, the newcomer may be able to leapfrog the incumbent and set up with the latest equipment at a lower cost. But this situation ultimately benefits no one. Today's entrant is tomorrow's incumbent, and as the technology continues to change, it relentlessly erodes any incumbent advantage.

The other key term in the profit equation is revenues, which stem from customer demand. For the incumbent to have a competitive advantage here, it must have a degree of access to customers that a potential entrant cannot match. But for this incumbent demand advantage to persist, customers must in some way be captive to those incumbents. In an open and competitive economy, there are only a limited number of ways in which customer behavior leads to captivity. Habit, usually associated with high purchase frequency, is probably the most powerful. For a soda company to compete with Coca-Cola, it must induce Coca-Cola drinkers to stop drinking their favorite beverage. This is no easy task. Consumer studies and historical experience suggest that Coke drinkers are fiercely attached to their Cokes. By comparison, the attachment to Budweiser, another leading beverage brand, is weaker. When diners go to Chinese, Japanese, or Mexican restaurants, they are not reluctant to ordering a beer from that country, but the chances that they will ask for a local cola are slim. Neither

Top Toaster nor Mercedes-Benz is likely to be a beneficiary of habit-based purchases.

For items that are not on the weekly shopping list, there are other processes through which customers are made captive to specific products or services. If the cost of searching for an alternative to the existing supplier is high, then new entrants have a difficult time attracting customers who are not actually dissatisfied with their current arrangements. Take the case of the residential insurance market. There are many dimensions to a policy in addition to its cost: coverage, deductibles, levels of service, exceptions, creditworthiness of the carrier, and several others. Unless they are strongly motivated, few home owners are going to take the trouble to search for a replacement. Their aversion to change is reinforced in this example by the painful results that may ensue from an inappropriate choice; it hurts to have the wrong insurance carrier or policy after the disaster strikes.

Given these difficulties and dangers, a new entrant into this market will find it challenging to induce customers who have had decent experiences with their existing carriers even to begin searching for a replacement. Practically the only way the entrant can make any inroads is by offering to write the insurance at premiums substantially lower than those the incumbents are charging. But as this is almost always a losing proposition, entry in situations like this stops before the high profit levels of the incumbents are completely eliminated. In the model we have proposed here, the high search cost limits the arrival of new entrants, and the gap between the asset values and the earnings power values of the incumbents does not disappear.

High switching costs are the third and probably most common source of customer captivity. If it costs money, time, and effort for a customer to switch from one supplier to another, incumbents have an advantage over entrants. For example, when a company changes software systems for payroll, benefits management, internal communications, funds transfer, or other important functions, the company has to spend not only on the software but also on extensive retraining of the staff. That is bad enough; even worse, the error rate on the new installation still goes up. It is no wonder that there is a powerful bias toward keeping the current system. And if this is true for functions like payroll, it is 10 times truer for the aptly named "mission critical" or even "enterprise critical" systems that manage order entry, purchasing, production, inventory, shipping, billing, and accounts receivable. The corporate graveyard is filled with firms that bet the business on introducing a new, improved, integrated, and full-featured system, and lost.

The term *switching costs* applies to situations like this, of which software is the most obvious but hardly the sole example. They are the final major source of customer captivity and a powerful source of competitive advantage for companies like Microsoft and, in a previous computer era, IBM. An entrant going after this business will not be playing on a level field. Because most users are already familiar with Microsoft systems, any successful entrant must overcome the costs to those customers of switching to an unfamiliar alternative. Additionally, as computer users increasingly communicate with each other, any single user incurs additional costs of switching to a new software supplier unless all others do so at the same time. It doesn't pay to have the best communication program in the world if there is no one else connected to it. Less dramatically, there is a cost to switching any time the new supplier has to master the particulars of the customer, client, or patient. This applies to new lawyers, banks, service companies such as mechanics who are familiar with the existing systems, health insurance plans, and drugs for a doctor who must learn the risks and potentials of the new medication.

We contended earlier that although the term *barriers to entry* was frequently used by investment analysts, generally to justify the high price of a particular security, in the world where businesses fiercely compete with one another, real barriers come in very few forms. The clearest cut are governmental privileges, such as licenses, patents, copyrights, or other protections that keep potential competitors at a safe distance. The other barriers we have described stem from either cost (supply) or customer (demand) advantages. Now we turn to what is probably the most significant and sustainable source of competitive advantages, and it does not fit neatly into either category but results from the conjunction of the two.

On the cost side are *economies of scale*, the situation in which the more units a company makes, the cheaper its average cost per unit. Substantial economies of scale exist for products in which the fixed costs are high relative to the variable costs for each unit, and these unit variable costs remain stable as the output of units rises. The more units produced, the less burden each has to shoulder to pay its share of fixed costs. In our age, the archetypal example is shrink-wrapped software. It costs a fortune to organize the operation, design the program, write the code, debug it, and get it tested by hundreds of users. It costs virtually nothing to publish one more box of diskettes or CD-ROMs, and even less to distribute the program via Internet downloads. Clearly, under these conditions a competitor who can acquire a majority share of the market will enjoy lower unit costs than other firms in the business.

By itself, being a large firm in an economies of scale situation does not constitute an incumbent competitive advantage. Consider the case in which 10 firms compete on basically equal terms in the same market. In the absence of customer (demand) advantages, they will divide the market more or less equally. With similar levels of output, the companies will experience similar average costs per unit, economies of scale notwithstanding. If the scales of operation are roughly the same, any potential economies of scale advantages are eliminated. In order for economies of scale to be worth something and have implications for the valuation of a particular company, they must be combined with customer (demand) advantages that provide the company with a predominant share of the market in question. By themselves, economies of scale aren't sufficient to produce meaningful competitive advantages.

These demand advantages can be small and still matter. Suppose an incumbent company whose cost structure is characterized by economies of scale has won a disproportionate share of the market. If it can retain its existing customers at a price, product quality, and marketing budget that just match those of potential entrants—which is a very weak form of captivity—then it will hang on to its outsized market share even if it operates on an otherwise level playing field. Even with only this minor demand advantage, economies of scale in the cost structure will translate that superior market share into lower costs, higher margins, and higher profitability. This incumbent should also be able to attract a disproportionate share of newcomers into the market, who may be captive only to the extent of se-

lecting the more familiar incumbent among otherwise equivalent competitors.

The priorities of management and the basic business strategy should be
designed to take advantage of the particular situation in which the firm
finds itself. For example, a company protected by government barriers to
entry should concentrate both on raising prices as high as is reasonable and
on operating efficiently. To the extent possible—that is, within the limits
of the law—funds and managerial effort should be spent to strengthen the
original governmental limits on competition.

A similar imperative applies when captive customers are the source of
competitive advantages. Firms with captive customers should work to enhance their ties in the following ways:

- By raising switching costs through adding features and services to
  the original offering, which has been a Microsoft strategy;
- By reinforcing habits through increasing frequency of purchases due
  to obsolescence or with leasing plans for automobiles;
- By raising search costs through extending and complicating the offered range of services and enhancing existing customer satisfaction.[2]

At the same time, companies benefiting from these competitive advantages should exploit them with aggressive pricing strategies and raise
prices whenever they can. Those that do not capitalize on their protected
positions may be concealing substantial value in unused pricing power.
The same holds for firms with patent protection or process (cost) advantages; the strategy is to reinforce the advantages while making full use of
pricing opportunities.

But for the firm whose competitive advantage is rooted in economies
of scale, the first priority is to protect the market share on which this advantage rests. It has to match and even anticipate the introduction of new

[2] Entrants, of course, should do just the opposite: minimize search and switching
cost. Credit card companies offer switchers preapproved credit balances and rewards
on any credit balances that are transferred.

product features and advertising campaigns. It must meet or beat competitors' prices. All this is essential because once its market share starts to erode, the underlying cost advantages shrinks with it. Companies with economies of scale advantages earn superior returns by having lower average costs—not by being able to charge more. For them to reinforce their advantage, they need to focus on offering consumer benefits whose costs are largely independent of the number of units sold. These include new products and features, image advertising, and levels of service support that depend on a geographically dense, fixed cost infrastructure.

A second factor that differentiates competitive advantages based on economies of scale is reproducibility. Cost advantages based on superior production systems survive only as long as the underlying technology. Rapid change in technology will often mean that, in the absence of economies of scale, cost structure advantages are very short-lived. On the other hand, even if the technologies are long lasting, patents do expire, learning curves flatten, and the associated competitive advantages still disappear. Sustainable cost advantages are confined to an intermediate range of technological environments—change not too fast and not too slow— and even they have limited lives. As an example, Cisco in the late 1990s and RCA in the 1920s enjoyed significant technological superiority over their competitors. But just as RCA's lead eroded, so we predict will Cisco's. In the long run, manufactured items all look like toasters. Competition is the rule, not the exception.

Something similar happens to companies with captive customers. These customers will disappear over time; some will die, and others will change tastes and buying habits as they mature. Children are captive customers with strong habitual preferences, but they don't remain children forever. A company marketing to youngsters has to capture each generation of children anew.

Consumer franchises that are sustainable over decades must have a competitive advantage in recruiting new customers as well as in retaining existing ones. The only competitive advantages that meet this challenge are those based on the conjunction of economies of scale and demand preferences. This combination can provide an important degree of franchise longevity, even in the face of changing technology.

Consider the competition between Intel and Advanced Micro Devices (AMD) to produce the next generation of microprocessors for desktop computers. Because Intel has established access to customers through long-standing relationships with computer manufacturers, supplemented by the "Intel Inside" campaign, it can expect that a successful next-generation chip will capture roughly 90 percent of the processor chip market. Even if AMD beats Intel to the market, its successful chip will, at least initially, grab a much smaller share. If Intel responds quickly and effectively, it will relegate the AMD chip to a minor—say 10 percent—market share. Thus, AMD's spending on R&D, ignoring for the moment any difficulties it may have in financing that spending, will be paid for by future sales that are small compared to those of Intel. Assuming that R&D spending rises proportionately with sales, Intel will be able to spend much more than will AMD on next-generation technology. In fact, as we show in Chapter 7, Intel only spends five times as much; the difference is still potent. Provided the company doesn't get distracted or otherwise fail to perform, Intel's economies of scale help transform a temporary into a durable—if not eternal—competitive advantage.

A company enjoying large economies of scale will be able to spend more on advertising and service, charge less than its smaller competitors, and still remain profitable. Because these three attractions apply to both new and old customers, companies benefiting from economies of scale are better able to retain current customers and recruit new ones. These advantages help extend the life of the franchise. The strategy that companies with franchises based on economies of scale advantages should follow is to attack the competition and win new customers, rather than exploit their positions for maximum current profit. Microsoft is the obvious example here. Somewhat less conspicuously, Wal-Mart pursues this course with everyday low prices, as does Intel when it reduces prices whenever me-too chips appear.

Finally, we must not confuse mere size—no matter how enormous—with competitive advantages based on economies of scale. These arise only when a firm enjoys a disproportionate share of the relevant market. *Relevant* here means the market that determines the level of fixed spending. For retailers like Wal-Mart or any of its competitors, distribution systems and advertising program costs are fixed by geographic region. A high market share within this area leads to regional economies of scale; the advertising blankets the region, and the distribution system serves it. If Wal-Mart's revenues and fixed costs were spread evenly across many regions, its economies of scale advantages would shrink or disappear. The identical situation applies to health maintenance organizations (HMOs). The HMO that has a 60 percent share of households in the New York metropolitan area will be able to benefit from economies of scale to a much greater extent than would considerably larger HMOs with 30 percent shares of the Chicago, Miami, Dallas, San Diego, and Seattle markets.

For manufacturers, development costs are usually fixed by product line, making market share within the product line what counts for economies of scale. General Electric is a giant company, but it only benefits from economies of scale where it dominates the market for a particular product line. Competitive advantages grounded on regional and product-line economies of scale are the ones we are most likely to encounter in practice. Only rarely do firms achieve national or global advantages, and these hardly ever spread across a range of product lines. To cite the most obvious example, IBM could not extend its dominance in mainframe computers into the desk-top era, even though it established the standards for the microcomputer. That advantage went to Microsoft, which itself has not been successful in dominating markets beyond operating systems and standard office applications. Those markets, as we know, have been enormous.

To sum up the arguments of this chapter, one striking advance in modern value investing has been recognition of the value of the franchise. This development is rightfully identified with Warren Buffett, who loves the Coca-Colas and Gillettes of this world because of the intense customer loyalty that they have built up over the years. Our operational definition of franchise value is the amount by which the EPV of the firm exceeds the reproduction cost of the assets, provided that both have been accurately estimated.

A franchise only exists where a firm benefits from barriers to entry that keep out potential competitors or insure that if they choose to enter, they will operate at a competitive disadvantage relative to the incumbents. The competitive advantages that the incumbents enjoy need to be identifiable and structural. Good management is certainly an advantage, but there is nothing built in to the competitive situation to guarantee that one company's superiority on the talent count will endure over time. Structural competitive advantages come in only a few forms: exclusive governmental licenses, consumer (demand) preferences, a cost (supply) position based on long-lived patents or other durable superiorities, and the combination of economies of scale thanks to a leading share in the relevant market with consumer preference.

The symbols by which securities are identified in the public markets do not include labels that allow investors to differentiate companies with genuine franchises from those without. No visitor to the corporate headquarters needs to climb over barriers to entry, should they exist, in order to meet with company executives. And of the many advantages a firm proclaims for its flagship products, durable competitive advantages are generally not among them. Spotting franchises is a difficult skill—one that takes time and work to master. Also, it is not easily extensible. Value investors like to operate within their own circles of competence, where the knowledge they have accumulated about newspapers, insurance companies, cable stocks, natural resource companies, or other types of investments can be applied in a new but still familiar situation. When Benjamin Graham went scouring financial statements looking for his net-nets, it did not concern him that he may have known little about the industry in which he found his targets. All he was concerned with were asset values and a margin of safety sufficiently large to protect him from too frequent losses. But in the world where market prices already exceed asset values, and the margin of safety by that measure is negative, a contemporary value investor had better be able to identify and understand the sources of a company's franchise and the nature of its competitive advantages. Otherwise he or she is just another punter, taking a flier rather than making an investment.

Appendix

The Value of Brands—Less than Meets the Eye?

Brands are identifiable product images that exist in the minds of consumers and affect their behavior in ways beneficial to the company that owns the brand. That brands are an important element in the value of any company is an idea broadly accepted by investors and marketing professors. It is also alleged that strong brands represent an important source of competitive advantage. Although these two positions appear more or less interchangeable, in fact these two aspects of brand based behavior are not at all the same thing. Understanding the differences between them is critical for a proper assessment of the implications that brands may have for the value of the company.

The terms *brand* and *brand equity* apply to a broad range of consumer phenomena. At its simplest, a brand may represent part of the value that a product brings to a consumer. Prestige brands have this characteristic; firms like Louis Vuitton–Möet Hennessey are managed to cash in on this appeal. Mercedes-Benz is perhaps the world's premier brand in this regard. Consumers on every continent seem willing to pay a substantial premium over what basic comfortable transportation would cost them for the status of being Mercedes-Benz owners. Yet Daimler-Benz had not been able to translate this "brand-mediated" desirability into a franchise value, meaning a high return on its invested capital. The history of the luxury car market suggests that this kind of brand-mediated pricing power does not create a significant barrier to entry that would protect Daimler from the ravages of competition. Even a marque as illustrious as Mercedes-Benz is not a major competitive advantage in this regard.

Why not? Despite the many years that Daimler has spent investing in the brand, there is nothing to keep competing car companies from following its lead. As long as they have equal access to the means of creating a premium image—advertising, endorsements, public relations, high product quality, innovative technology, luxurious dealerships, extraordinary after-sales services, and high prices—at costs that are essentially equivalent to those of Daimler, they will enter this profitable market. The Mercedes-

Benz brand does not maintain itself; it needs to be replenished with fresh advertising and image-burnishing expenses. The new competitors will drive up these costs for Daimler, making it more costly, and consequently less profitable, for Daimler to maintain the brand.

The brand may be an essential element of the perceived value of the product. But by itself the brand does not construct barriers to entry, establish competitive advantages, or create a franchise. The aspects of consumer behavior that do create franchise value are those we have described in this chapter—habit, search costs, and switching costs—as leading to customer captivity. These may be encompassed by some definitions of brand behavior, but these definitions are so broad that they cannot compete with an examination of the direct sources of captivity.

Also, the value of brands is greatly enhanced by the presence of economies of scale. A sticker on a computer that says "Intel Inside" does little by itself to establish a strong brand, but when accompanied by powerful economies of scale in chip design and production, even a weak brand becomes an essential part of a powerful franchise. We get inside Intel in Chapter 7.

Chapter 6

A Wonderful Little Franchise
The Earnings Power of WD-40

Until it purchased the 3-IN-ONE brand from Reckitt and Colman, PLC, in December 1995, WD-40 had been a one-product company for over 40 years. WD-40, the product, is a lubricant that unfreezes sticky screws, removes rust, dissolves adhesives, stops squeaks, and comes to the aid of the home handyperson or machine shop professional whenever anything small needs to be lubricated or protected from rust. The name WD-40 means "water displacement, 40th attempt," suggesting the trials and effort that went into development. The familiar blue can is practically ubiquitous in homes, factories, and repair shops in the United States, the United Kingdom, and many other parts of the world. According to the company, four out of five American households have a can, and more people use WD-40 each week than use dental floss. While this may be good news for dentists, it leaves WD-40 with few untapped targets for new business in its domestic market.

WD-40 has been an extraordinarily profitable company: consistent and high operating margins (25–30%), net income margins (15–18%) and returns on equity (35–42%), even without adjusting for excess cash. But growth has been more difficult (see Table 6.1). After 1990, growth in sales fell from around 10 percent a year to slightly more than 5 percent. Net income, always a more variable figure, held up until after 1995, when it also tailed off.

WD-40 took three steps starting in 1995 to invigorate its growth. It

Table 6.1   WD-40 Annual Growth Rates

	Annual Growth Rates (%)			
	August 1985	*August 1990*	*August 1995*	*August 1999*
Sales	10.2	9.9	5.2	5.2
Income	1.1	11.7	9.8	3.4

Note: Percentages are for the five years prior to the dates shown.

bought 3-IN-ONE; it internally developed T.A.L.5, a more powerful lubricant that it sought, without success, to market to commercial users; and it purchased the Lava brand of hand soap from Block Drug in April 1999. Because it is still too early to say whether this effort will pay off—by which we mean growth in sales and income as well as maintaining the high level of profitability—we will focus on the financial numbers for the fiscal years ending with August 1998, before Lava entered the picture.

WD-40 contracts out the manufacture, packaging, and shipment of all these lubricants. In its fiscal year (FY) 1998, it needed only 167 employees to support $144 million in revenues. It is primarily a sales and marketing organization. It spends around 10 percent of its revenue on advertising and promotion. There is no secret formula for any of the lubricants, nothing that Dow, Dupont, Exxon, 3M, or any other firm with a modicum of competence in the chemical business could not duplicate. No patents protect these products. Yet WD-40 earns an exceptionally high rate of return however it is measured—as return on sales, return on assets, or return on equity. The company refers to WD-40 as a "fortress," and one of its goals is to extend the fortress beyond the U.S. and U.K. markets. When the company, in order to comply with environmental concerns, switched its aerosol propellant to CO_2, it was able to pass on the increased costs without blinking, meaning that it had been undercharging its customers. Every firm would love to have that kind of pricing power.

The balance sheets and income statements for the company for FY 1994 through FY 1998 are shown in Table 6.2. The extent of WD-40's profitability practically jumps off the page. In FY 1998 it earned almost $22 million; the book value of its equity at the end of the year was $55 million. That is a return on equity of almost 40 percent, accomplished with virtu-

Table 6.2   **WD-40 Financial Accounts**

	August 1994	August 1995	August 1996	August 1997	August 1998
Assets					
Cash and equivalents	22.7	24.3	6.9	10.9	14.7
Receivables—total (net)	14.9	17.1	21.4	22.6	27.0
Inventories—total	6.2	4.9	6.2	5.5	3.7
Current assets—other	1.5	3.3	3.2	3.4	4.3
Current assets—total	45.3	49.6	37.6	42.4	49.8
Plant, property, and equipment (net)	3.2	3.5	3.9	4.2	3.6
Low-income housing investments	4.7	4.4	4.0	3.7	3.4
Goodwill	0.0	0.0	14.4	13.4	12.5
Assets—other	1.7	2.2	1.7	1.8	1.7
Total Assets	54.9	59.6	61.7	65.4	70.9
Liabilities					
Accounts payable	4.3	4.7	5.8	6.7	6.9
Taxes payable	0.9	3.1	1.9	1.5	3.1
Debt (long-term) due in one year	0.6	0.7	0.7	0.8	0.8
Other current liabilities	2.4	2.6	2.7	2.4	3.1
Total current liabilities	8.2	11.1	11.1	11.4	13.9
Long term debt	3.8	3.1	2.4	1.7	0.9
Liabilities—other	0.8	0.9	1.0	1.0	1.1
Total liabilities	12.8	15.1	14.5	14.1	15.9
Total equity	42.1	44.5	47.2	51.3	55.0
Total liabilities and equity	54.9	59.6	61.7	65.4	70.9
Shares outstanding	15.39	15.41	15.42	15.51	15.66
Book value per share	2.74	2.89	3.06	3.31	3.51
Income Statement					
Sales (net)	112.2	116.8	130.9	137.9	144.4
Cost of goods sold	47.0	50.2	57.9	59.3	63.0
Selling, general, and administrative expenses	21.9	23.8	27.0	28.8	31.1
Advertising and sales promotion	10.6	11.0	12.2	13.8	14.8
Amortization	0.3	0.3	1.1	1.3	1.3
Total operating expenses	79.8	85.3	40.3	44.0	47.3
Earnings before interest and taxes	32.4	31.5	32.7	34.6	34.2
Interest income (net)	0.0	0.0	0.4	0.1	0.1
Other income (expense) (net)	(11.9)	1.2	0.3	(1.3)	(0.4)
Pretax income	20.5	32.7	33.4	33.4	33.8
Income taxes—total	7.8	12.2	12.1	12.0	12.4
Net income (loss)	12.7	20.5	21.3	21.4	21.9
Shares fully diluted	15.39	15.41	15.42	15.51	15.66
EPS per fully diluted share	0.82	1.33	1.38	1.38	1.40

Note: All figures are in millions of dollars except for book value per share and earnings per share, which are dollar amounts.

Table 6.3   WD-40 Return on Adjusted Equity

	August 1998	Change	Adjusted
Cash plus short-term investments	14.7	−12.7	2
Long-term investments	3.4	−3.4	0
Total debt	1.7	−1.7	0
Equity	55.0	−14.4	40.6
Income without interest income or tax benefit	21.1		
Adjusted equity	40.6		
Return on adjusted equity	52%		

Note: All figures are in millions of dollars except the return on adjusted equity.

ally no debt. Return on equity was even higher in the two prior years (see Table 6.3). If we eliminate the excess cash, marketable securities, and investments in low-income housing ($3.4 million in 1998) from its balance sheet, the returns are higher still. We estimate that the cash most businesses need to run their operations amounts to about 1 percent of sales; for WD-40, that is $1.4 million. It gets a modest tax benefit from the investment in low-income housing ($700,000 in 1998). To clean things up, we will adjust its assets and liabilities, paying off all the debt and keeping $2 million in cash to run the operation. To compensate for the loss of the tax shelter, we will reduce net income by $700,000. With all these adjustments in place, equity shrinks to $40.6 million (cash and investments down $16.1 million, partially offset by the elimination of $1.7 million in debt), and the return on the book value of the equity rises to 52 percent. As we said, WD-40 is very profitable.

Unlike Hudson General, where we focused on the hidden value of its assets, we will begin by looking at WD-40 as an earnings generation machine. We need to calculate its earnings power value (EPV); just as important, we need to understand its strategic position to see whether it will be able to sustain that level of profitability. Where are the competitors who should be entering its markets and stealing away customers or forcing WD-40 to lower its prices? If there is nothing magic in its lubricant elixir, what is it that keeps the challengers at bay?

Earnings Power Value

In Chapter 3 we defined the EPV of a firm as earnings after certain adjustments times $1/R$, with R representing the current cost of capital. The adjustments to earnings we mentioned were

1. Undoing accounting misrepresentations, such as frequent one-time charges that are supposedly unconnected to normal operations. The adjustment consists of finding the average ratio that these charges bear to reported earnings before adjustments, annually, and reducing the current year's reported earnings before adjustment proportionally.
2. Resolving discrepancies between depreciation and amortization, as reported by the accountants, and the actual amount of reinvestment the company needs to make in order to restore a firm's assets at the end of the year to their level at the start of the year. The adjustment adds or subtracts this difference.
3. Taking into account the business cycle and other transient effects. The adjustment reduces earnings reported at the peak of the cycle and raises them if the firm is currently in a cyclical trough.
4. Applying other modifications as are reasonable, depending on the specific situation.

The purpose of these adjustments is to arrive at a figure that represents *distributable cash flow*, or money the owners can extract from the firm and still leave its operations intact. There are two alternative ways of approaching this figure. One is to start at the bottom with net income; work up by adding back items, such as depreciation, that are not cash charges; and subtract cash outlays, such as capital expenditures, that do not figure into the income calculation. But this approach requires additional adjustments if the company has large income or expense items that depend on its capital structure—high interest payments if it carries a lot of debt or interest income on excess cash. Since neither of these relates directly to the operations of the firm, it is generally good practice to exclude them from the distributable cash flow calculation. And if there are gains or losses from investments outside the business, these also should be ignored on the same ground; they are not income that we can count on year in and year out.

Because of these concerns, we prefer the second approach, which is to start with operating income, or earnings before interest and taxes, and work down, calculating the taxes that would be paid on operating income and adjusting for depreciation, amortization, and capital expenditures. Other sources of income or expense are more or less ignored. Because we are assuming in this analysis that there is no growth in the distributable cash flow, we do not need to worry about any changes in working capital that might be required to support additional sales. And we need only charge the business for the capital expenditures necessary to sustain operations at their current level, or *maintenance capex*.

Starting with the first item in our adjustment list, we find nothing in WD-40's financial statements that points to the need to account for frequent "exceptional" charges. In 1994 the company paid out $12 million to former commissioned sales representatives who had sued it for wrongful termination. But that was truly a one-time charge and has not been repeated. Both operating income and net income as a percent of sales have been stable, except for that $12 million payment (pretax). Just to be safe, we will assume that WD-40 has a problem like this every ten years; we subtract $1.2 from EBIT for each year (see Table 6.4).

This table also answers the third issue: Do we need to adjust for cyclicality? Sales in 1991, which saw a recession for at least part of the year, were down slightly from 1990. But the difference was miniscule and did not find its way down to operating or net income. WD-40 and 3-IN-ONE are the kind of consumer staples not highly subject to swings in the overall economy. The squeaky wheel is going to get oiled, recession or not.

Amortization, depreciation, and capital expenditures do warrant adjustments. The amortization charge refers largely to the writing down of the goodwill stemming from the purchase of the 3-IN-ONE brand. The goodwill represents years of advertising and promotion to establish the public's favorable perception of the oil, plus money spent on developing the distribution channels. WD-40 will have to continue to support the brand with advertising and selling expenses to insure that the value of the

Table 6.4 WD-40 Sales, EBIT, Net Income, and Margins

	August 1990	August 1991	August 1992	August 1993	August 1994	August 1995	August 1996	August 1997	August 1998
Sales	91.0	89.8	100.0	109.0	112.2	116.8	130.9	137.9	144.4
EBIT	23.3	23.7	28.2	33.0	32.4	31.5	32.7	34.6	34.5
Less adjustment	(1.2)	(1.2)	(1.2)	(1.2)	(1.2)	(1.2)	(1.2)	(1.2)	(1.2)
EBIT adjusted	22.1	22.5	27.0	31.8	31.2	30.3	31.5	33.4	33.3
EBIT margin	24.3%	25.0%	27.0%	29.2%	27.8%	25.9%	24.0%	24.3%	23.1%
Net income	15.5	15.3	18.1	19.3	12.7	20.5	21.3	21.4	21.9
Net income margin	17.0%	17.0%	18.1%	17.7%	11.3%	17.5%	16.3%	15.5%	15.2%

Note: Figures are in millions of dollars, except for percentages.

Table 6.5 WD-40 Depreciation and Capital Expenditures

	August 1994	*August 1995*	*August 1996*	*August 1997*	*August 1998*
Depreciation	0.6	0.7	0.7	0.9	0.8
Maintenance capex	0.7	1.2	0.9	1.3	1.1
Difference	(0.1)	(0.6)	(0.2)	(0.4)	(0.3)

Note: Figures are in millions of dollars.

goodwill will not dissipate. Therefore, we are justified in adding the amortization charge back to net income. Amortization in 1998 amounted to $1.3 million, and the expense has another 12 years to run.

As shown in Table 6.5, the company's depreciation has been less by a small amount than the portion of its capital expenditures we calculate as necessary to maintain its operations.[1] The maintenance capital expenditure figures vary more than they should, probably because capital outlays come in lumps and our method for dividing the total into growth and maintenance capex produces only an inexact estimate for any single year. For our purposes here, however, the estimate is close enough. The difference between depreciation and maintenance capex is only $300,000 a year, on average, or about 1 percent of operating earnings.

---

[1] Companies generally report capital expenditures in their statement of cash flows. We assume that each year, a part of this outlay supports the business at its sales level for the prior year, and part is needed for whatever increase in sales it has achieved. Companies generally have a stable relationship between the level of sales and the amount of plant, property, and equipment (PPE), net of depreciation, that they report. We calculate the ratio of PPE to sales for each of the five prior years and find the average. We use this to indicate the dollars of PPE it takes to support each dollar of sales. We then multiply this ratio by the growth (or decrease) in sales dollars the company has achieved in the current year. The result of that calculation is growth capex. We then subtract it from total capex to arrive at maintenance capex.

In this case, WD-40 is spending more on maintenance capex than depreciation, suggesting that it is either not using its money wisely or that the cost of capital goods in its industry is increasing. Either way, the difference is insignificant.

Table 6.6 WD-40 Adjusted Earnings

	August 1994	August 1995	August 1996	August 1997	August 1998
EBIT adjusted	31.2	30.3	31.5	33.4	33.0
Tax rate	38%	37%	36%	36%	36%
EBIT after tax	19.3	19.1	20.2	21.4	21.1
Amortization	0.3	0.3	1.1	1.3	1.3
Depreciation	0.6	0.7	0.7	0.9	0.8
Maintenance capex	0.7	1.2	0.9	1.3	1.1
EBIT after tax adjusted	19.5	18.9	21.1	22.3	22.1
Net income	12.7	20.5	21.3	21.4	21.9

Note: Amounts are in millions of dollars, except for tax rate percentage.

Putting all our changes together, we get a figure for distributable cash flow of $22.1 million for 1998, and very similar numbers for the three previous years (see Table 6.6). None of them is materially different from the net income figure as reported. In the case of WD-40, the exercise proved unnecessary, but we only learn that after we have performed it.

We have completed the first step in arriving at an EPV for WD-40, which is to calculate distributable earnings for the company. Now we need to determine the appropriate cost of capital to use in the equation EPV = Adjusted Earnings × 1/R. Professional finance, as taught in schools of business and widely employed in practice, calls for a calculation of the weighted average cost of capital, known affectionately as the WACC. There are three steps:

1. Establish the appropriate ratio between debt and equity financing for this firm.
2. Estimate the interest cost that the firm will have to pay on its debt, after taxes, by comparing it with the interest costs paid by similar firms.
3. Estimate the cost of equity. The approved academic method for this task involves using something called the capital asset pricing model, in which the crucial variable is the volatility of the share price of the firm in question relative to the volatility of the stock

market as a whole, as represented by the Standard & Poor's 500. That measure is called beta, and as much as it is beloved by finance professors, it is viewed with skepticism by value investors.

An alternative approach is to begin with the definition of the cost of equity capital: what the firm must pay per dollar per year to induce equity investors voluntarily to provide funds. This definition makes determining the cost of equity equivalent to determining the cost of any other resource. The wage cost of labor, for example, is what employers must pay to attract that labor voluntarily. There is no need to be esoteric about how to calculate the cost of equity in practice. We could survey other fund-raisers to learn what they feel they must pay to attract funds. Venture capitalists in the late 1990s told us that they believed they had to offer at least 18 percent to attract funding. Venture investments are clearly more risky than those in WD-40; it is understandable that potential investors would demand higher returns. Alternatively, we could estimate the total returns—dividends plus projected capital gains—that investors expect to obtain from companies with characteristics similar to WD-40. This method, the details of which we avoid here, produces a cost of equity of around 10 percent. Because long term equity yields are about 12 percent per year, and because WD-40 has a much more stable earnings history than the average equity investment, 10 percent meets the reasonability test.

The riskier the investment, the higher the cost of capital should be, but to say a great deal more with both confidence and precision is presumptuous. Because value investors are attracted to companies that have steady and predictable income streams, it may be enough to use the federal bond rate and add a percentage point or two. We can test that against a back-of-the-envelope calculation of the WACC. For a company like WD-40, with stable earnings unaffected by the business cycle, a capital structure of 50 percent debt and 50 percent equity is reasonable. If the interest rate it has to pay is 9 percent, the after-tax cost becomes 6 percent. Again, because of the stability of its earnings and its share prices, we estimate that the equity cost will be 10 percent. Averaging the two gives us a WACC of 8 percent, which equals a federal bond rate of 6 percent plus 2 percent. Eight percent for the weighted average cost of capital seems reasonable.

Table 6.7   Earnings Power Value of WD-40 with Different Costs of Capital Rates (net income = $21.9 million)

Costs of Capital Rates	EPV	Per Share	Plus Cash-Debt Adjustment of $14	Per Share
6%	365	23.46	379	24.36
8%	274	17.61	288	18.51
10%	219	14.07	233	14.97
12%	183	11.76	197	12.66

Note: Figures are millions of dollars for EPV columns, dollars for per share columns.

Where does that put WD-40's EPV? At a cost of capital of 6 percent, the EPV is $365 million; if the cost of capital is 12 percent, the EPV falls to $183 million (see Table 6.7).

If we intend to compare the EPV to the market price, we need to make one final adjustment. The EPV assumes that all the capital is equity capital; it ignores both interest paid on debt and interest received on cash. If there is debt, it has to be subtracted from the EPV. If there is cash in excess of operating requirements, it should be added back. Only then can we compare the total EPV with the market price of the equity. For WD-40, this adjustment adds $14 million, or about $0.90 per share, to its value. At our preferred rate of 8 percent, a share would be worth $18.50.

The Value of the Assets

Even at our lowest estimate of $12.66 per share, WD-40's EPV is more than three times the size of its book value of $3.50. Provided our estimate of EPV is reasonably accurate, there are only two possible explanations for this divergence. Either the balance sheet understates the reproduction costs of the assets, or the company has an enormously valuable franchise. It may be that the discrepancy is not so large; the actual equity investment required to compete with WD-40 may be much more than the book value of $55 million. To make sure, we need to estimate the reproduction costs as precisely as possible. If a gap persists, we will have to examine the dimensions of the franchise.

At first glance, the adjustments to book value seem minor (see Table

Table 6.8 WD-40 Reproduction Cost of Assets

	August 1998	Adjustment	Reproduction
Assets			
Cash plus short-term investments	14.7	0	14.7
Accounts receivable	27.0	0.6	27.6
Inventory	3.7	0	3.7
Other current assets	4.3	0	4.3
Current assets	49.7	0.6	50.3
Plant, property, and equipment (net)	3.6	0	3.6
Long-term investments	3.4	0	3.4
Goodwill and intangibles	12.5	0	12.5
Other long-term assets	1.7	0	1.7
Total assets	70.9		71.5

Note: Amounts are in millions of dollars.

6.8). WD-40 has written off $0.6 million in receivables, so a competitor would likely have a similar experience. The inventories are its standard products, either ready for sale at the packaging contractor or in concentrate form at the company. They are not likely to go out of fashion, and the company is turning them over at more than 16 times per year. Its fixed assets are small, relative to sales and total assets, and are being depreciated over useful life. Whatever adjustment we might make would be about as trivial as the adjustment to receivables.

Goodwill is found on a company's balance sheet when it has purchased another firm and paid more for it than the fair market value of its assets. Goodwill is that additional amount. For WD-40, goodwill appears in 1996, after the company bought the 3-IN-ONE brand from Reckitt and Colman for $15 million in 1995. Though a small amount of inventory was included in the purchase, what WD-40 really acquired was the trademark and exclusive rights to sell 3-IN-ONE. For the moment, we will defer making any adjustment to this asset.

The obvious reason that WD-40 is so profitable is that consumers are willing to pay a lot more for its products than what it costs the company to make them. This loyalty does not come free. As we noted, each year WD-40 spends about 10 percent of sales on advertising and promotion. Under generally accepted accounting principles, advertising and promotion are expenses, appearing as a line on the income statement, even though the cumulative effect of all these messages may be to induce a consumer commitment that is more durable than a piece of heavy equipment that is treated as an asset and depreciated over five or seven years. A competitor would need to spend even more just to get into the game, so in assessing the reproduction costs of the assets, we cannot ignore advertising and promotion. It makes sense to consider them as off–balance sheet assets.

In a similar vein, a producer of consumer nondurables like WD-40 needs to develop channels of distribution through which to sell its wares. This also takes time and costs money. One reason for buying the 3-IN-ONE brand was that the company could expand the sales of WD-40, its flagship and more profitable lubricant, by using 3-IN-ONE's customer base. And its hopes for Lava largely depend on pushing the soap through its existing channels. So at least some portion of the selling, general, and administrative (SG&A) expense line should also be treated as a quasi asset.

If we consider advertising and promotion and SG&A as off–balance sheet assets—something a new entrant would have to spend to become a competitor—we still have to decide on how many years of expenses to include. This decision requires judgment based on experience in marketing consumer products: how long to build the brand and to develop the distribution pipeline. Let us estimate three years of both and include all of SG&A, even though some of it is pure overhead.[2] At $46 million per year, that would create a quasi-asset of around $140 million, which is exactly twice the size of all the other assets, both tangible and goodwill, put together (see Table 6.9). If we add that to our previous asset amount, we get a total asset value for the firm of $211.5 million. From this we can subtract the spontaneous liabilities—those interest-free advances the company gets from its suppliers, workers, and the tax collector—of $14.2 million. We can also deduct cash in excess of what the company needs to run its operations and its investment in low-income housing; together they amount to $16.1 million. That leaves a total of around $180 million, our estimate

[2] The goodwill from the purchase of 3-IN-ONE is precisely this kind of quasi-asset: money spent to develop the brand and the distribution infrastructure. We think a new entrant would have to match this spending in order to compete.

Table 6.9   WD-40 Reproduction Cost of Assets, Including Three Years Advertising, Promotion, and SG&A

	Reproduction Value
Total assets, as adjusted in Table 6.8	71.5
Three years advertising, promotion, and SG&A	140.0
Reproduction cost of all assets	211.5
Minus non-interest-bearing liabilities	−14.2
Minus excess cash and investment	−16.1
Total net reproduction cost	181.2

Note: Amounts are in millions of dollars.

of what it would cost a competitor to take on WD-40 for a share of its lucrative lubricant business.

The Value of the Franchise

Our work on the reproduction cost of the assets has increased that figure from a book value of $55 million to around $180 million. If we use a cost of capital rate of 8 percent, the EPV is $274 million. That leaves the franchise value of the firm at around $96 million. Is that amount defensible? To answer that question we need to look at the strategies that both WD-40 and its potential competitors might pursue.

Here is a likely scenario. For a company to take a substantial market share from WD-40, it would need not only to spend a fortune on advertising and distribution but also to price its products at a significant discount to WD-40. WD-40's products are small-ticket items, bought infrequently by consumers but with great loyalty. Making an inroad into WD-40's market means winning over thousands of individual customers, one at a time. A successful campaign costs money. And getting customers to switch means overcoming high search costs, as each consumer asks whether the new products will do everything WD-40 or 3-IN-ONE does, and as well.

What about price? Even at retail, WD-40 is hardly expensive. Small cans of it sell for less than $2.00, and an 11 oz. can, probably a lifetime supply for most users, can be bought for under $3.00. A competitive product priced at 10 percent less would hardly entice customers away from a

Table 6.10   Returns for WD-40 and a Potential Competitor under Different Assumptions Regarding Market Shares

	Each with 100% Current Market		Realistic Market Shares with Competition	
	WD-40	Competitor	WD-40	Competitor
Market share	100%	100%	75%	25%
Sales	144	130	97.5	32.5
COGS	63	63	39	13
Operating Expenses	47	47	47	47
EBIT	34	20	11.5	(27.5)
EBIT after tax	22	13	7.4	(17.8)
Investment	181	181	181	181
Return on investment	12%	7%	4%	−10%

Note: Amounts are in millions of dollars, except for return on investment.

brand they know and trust for a savings of 30 cents. But a 10 percent reduction in price would shrink the competitor's return on its investment enough to make the effort unappealing. That is what we see in Table 6.10 when we compare WD-40 to a competitor, assuming first that each has a 100 percent share of the current market for WD-40.

But that assumption is obviously self-contradictory. The more likely case is that the demand for WD-40 and its competitors does not grow, and the two firms divide the current market. The division, however, would favor WD-40. We put its share at 75 percent, which we think is conservative. If it chose to meet the competitor's price, as reported in the table, it would sell more units, thanks to customer loyalty. Because its advertising and other marketing expenses, which are fixed costs and do not vary with quantity sold, would be spread over more units, its total cost per unit would be lower and its profits higher. Under this scenario, competition could damage WD-40 and take an enormous chunk out of its returns. But the potential competitor would lose money on its investment. If would-be entrants are rational and can evaluate their prospects intelligently, which may be an enormous *if*, then WD-40 should relax.

There are barriers to entry that protect WD-40. Customer loyalty, built up over many years of advertising and consumer satisfaction, ensures that a competitor will have a difficult time persuading users to try something new.

The switching costs are high, at least relative to the price of the product and the low frequency of the purchases. Because these consumer costs are low, a competitor would have to sell its product at a substantially lower price in order to mount a challenge—so low that it would not be profitable. As we have said, however, it would still have to spend liberally on marketing and distribution and not be able to spread these costs over many units. That is the message of Table 6.10: Economies of scale make WD-40 more profitable and allow it, if the competition should turn nasty, to underprice its rivals and still make money. Finally, the whole enterprise is small. For the most likely new entrants—chemical companies like Dupont or Dow, and consumer product specialists like Proctor and Gamble or Unilever—the game isn't worth the effort. Even if they were willing to spend the money and drive WD-40 from the field—hardly a guaranteed result[3]—the victory would not repay the years of losses they would have to endure to achieve it. So the barriers work in part because the prize isn't large enough to merit the effort.

Because it seems so well defended against competitors, WD-40 may in fact have more pricing power than it utilizes. Just as offering its lubricant at a 10 percent discount is unlikely to win many converts for a new competitor, it is likely that only a few customers would be deterred if WD-40 raised its prices by a similar amount. Because all of this additional revenue would flow directly to pretax income, a 10 percent increase in revenue would raise net income by more than 40 percent. Even a 5 percent increase in revenue would result in a 20 percent boost to the bottom line and a similar increase to the EPV. In this case, that would put the intrinsic value of a share at $21.35 and of the company at $333 million.

Slow Growth Is Better than None

Getting back to valuation, there is a variant of the EPV approach that we should consider. WD-40 needs to reinvest very little to keep the business going; it pays out almost all of its earnings in dividends to shareholders.

---

[3] In fact, Dupont, GE, 3M, and Borden all did make efforts but abandoned them when the losses began to mount.

The dividend in 1998 was $1.28 per share, with an earnings per share of $1.40. It has paid dividends annually for at least the last quarter-century, and with a sporadic growth rate that has averaged 3 percent a year. Net income has increased at about the same rate. Because almost all the earnings are paid out as dividends, shareholders have not profited greatly from an increase in share price. In these circumstances, it is appropriate to use a dividend discount model to value the stock.

The relevant equation is $V = \text{Dividend} \times 1/R - G$, where R is cost of capital and G the growth rate of the dividend, which we know has averaged 3 percent over the last decade. If we use 8 percent as our cost of capital, then $1.28 \times 1/(.8 - .03) = 25.60. This is 45 percent more than the EPV with no growth.[4]

Together with its unused pricing power, WD-40's modest growth provides a margin of safety when the shares are selling at $18 or $19 dollars. At that price, WD-40 seems like a compelling investment; EPV supports the current valuation, and both growth and pricing power are free. In the decade of the 1990s, WD-40's share prices climbed unevenly from a low of $12.50 in 1991 to a high of around $32 in both 1997 and 1998. Share prices have declined since then, and at the end of 2000 sold for $19.50. With the genius of hindsight, it is easy to see that $32 was too optimistic, at least for the short term. At a price of $19.50, WD-40 seems to us to be fairly valued—a reasonable investment, but not a compelling bargain. Time will tell.

[4] In increasing dividends by 3 percent per year, we are assuming that the historical growth continues and also that WD-40 does not have to spend very much on current or fixed assets to support this growth. These assumptions are not always warranted. We examine the issue of profitable growth in Chapter 7.

Chapter 7

Inside Intel
The Value of Growth within the Franchise

Buying "Good" Companies

In recent years, it has been taken as axiomatic that the value approach, with its preference for tangible assets and current earnings power, prevents its adherents from investing in high-technology companies and other "growth" stocks. There is some truth in this thought, especially as it applies to more traditional Graham and Dodd investors, but it ignores some of the most significant innovations in valuation that modern value investors have developed. Warren Buffett and a number of other prominent value investors favor the shares of "good" companies, by which they mean firms like Coca-Cola—companies that grow. In this context, a good company— sometimes elevated to a "great" company—is one that can pay out cash to its investors even as it funds its growth. This is frequently not the case for companies with compelling stories about future revenues and earnings that attract many growth investors.

For value investors as a group, an investment based on a firm's prospects for growth must satisfy two requirements. First, they recognize that not all growth creates value. For most companies—or, more precisely, for the shareholders of most companies—growth is at best a break-even proposition. This sobering news applies to high-tech firms that expand by selling more gadgets as well as to restaurant franchisers that expand by opening more outlets. Growth creates value only when it takes place within the limits of a strong and sustainable company franchise, and these are rare. Second, not all growth—even growth that is worth something—can be appraised with enough precision to permit an accurate valuation. Because value investors demand a margin of safety, they will buy growth only at a discount from its estimated value large enough to make up for the greater uncertainty in valuation. The ideal price is zero: Pay in full for the current assets or earnings power and get the growth for free.

Keeping these two strenuous requirements in mind, that growth be both valuable and cheap, high-tech companies and other growth areas can be rich fields of opportunity for modern value investors. To illustrate the processes involved in making a growth investment that still meets value standards, we take a value investor's foray into the history of Intel Corporation, which since its inception has been a leading member of the growth and high-tech pantheon.

A Castle Built on Sand?

By any measure, Intel is one of the great success stories in business history. Founded in 1969, by January 2000 the company had a market capitalization of $275 billion. It placed eighth in the world in *Business Week*'s 1999 list of the Global 1,000. Its $29 billion in sales ranked it 39th on the Fortune 500 list of the biggest American companies. It stood at the pinnacle of the semiconductor industry, which was to the world economy in the last quarter of the twentieth century what the railroad was to the nineteenth century and what electricity and the automobile were to the first half of the twentieth: the great engine of growth and productivity. Its founding executives were legendary: Gordon Moore for his "law" that the capacity of memory chips would double every 18 to 24 months (later extended to refer to the processing power of logic chips), and Andrew Grove for elevating paranoia, which most people think of as a severe psychiatric disorder, into a theory of management.

Our interest in Intel is not actually on how it came to dominate the semiconductor industry or whether paranoia is an essential component of high-tech management. We will focus here on Intel from a value investor's perspective. With the advantage of hindsight, we can say unambiguously that an investment in Intel when it became a public company in 1971 would have been a stroke of genius. So would an investment ten years later, in 1981, and ten years after that, in 1991. Whether a purchase of shares in 2001 will be equally rewarding is a harder call. For five or six months during the year 2000, Intel finally received a valuation from the market that rewarded it for its years of stellar and profitable growth and then went on to project that growth into the distant future. By the start of 2001, the price of an Intel share had fallen 60 percent from its high, putting it back in range where some value investors might be tempted.

As we have said, value investors consider the three sources of intrinsic value to be the reproduction cost of the company's assets, the current earnings power of any franchise, and the value of its earnings growth within that franchise. An investor can have most confidence in his or her estimate of the reproduction cost of the assets; they exist in the present and can be measured with some precision. The value to put on current earnings power in excess of asset value is somewhat less certain. The earnings themselves, and the rate at which they should be discounted, are firm enough, but the value of those earnings depends on the company's continued success next year and for many years after that. Even the most established companies can lose their way, see their profit margins shrivel under pressure from new competitors, or find their services and products no longer in demand. So value investors are willing to buy companies based on their earnings power value only if there is an adequate margin of safety to cushion potential disappointments.

The most difficult aspect to value is the worth of future earnings growth, even though there are times when the market will pay for nothing else. The uncertainty has two sources. First, we need to assume that the company will grow at a specific rate in the future, for a number of years. Perhaps it will, perhaps it won't, but we cannot say with full confidence. Second, we also have to assume that that growth will be profitable—that is, growth within the franchise. After all, earnings rarely increase, at least not for very long, without a corresponding increase in sales. And sales hardly ever grow substantially without an increase in the amount of assets the company needs to employ. Assets require investments; investments need to be rewarded. Therefore, profitable growth as we define it here means growth in earnings in excess of the cost of the investments needed to pay for the assets that support that growth. Otherwise, the company is just breaking even, economically speaking, no matter how many new plants it builds, how many people it adds to the payroll, how much larger its sales figures are, and even how large its earnings per share swell.

There are not many companies that have been able to grow successfully within their franchises. Some of the most fundamental laws of market economies seem to be conspiring against them: declining marginal returns; creative destruction; the attraction of entrepreneurs to areas where investments have been earning an above-market return; the limited duration of patents, copyrights, and other formal barriers; and the loss of energy and hunger on the part of the now satiated leaders. Pushing against these limits are powerful resources that great companies possess: economies of scale that take advantage of R&D, production, marketing, and distribution; global brand recognition; cheaper access to capital; and support in the seats of political power. Despite these advantages, however, if it were easier for large companies to grow profitably (i.e., within their franchise), we would be looking at a world with more Microsofts and Coca-Colas, (both of which now seem somewhat tarnished) rather than having to wrack our brains to come up with additional names.

Intel's History: The Very Short Version

The series of events that gave birth to Intel read like a chapter from Genesis. In the beginning was Bell Labs. There, in the late 1940s, John Bardeen, Walter Brattain, and William Shockley invented the transistor, a solid state replacement for the vacuum tube that had been a key component of the ENIAC generation of computers. In 1956 the three earned the Nobel Prize for their efforts. In that year, Bell Labs begat Shockley Laboratories, as Shockley left to set up his own firm. One year later, eight of Shockley's best engineers departed to start a new firm with the financial backing of Sherman Fairchild. Thus Shockley Laboratories begat Fairchild Semiconductor. At Fairchild, Robert Noyce managed to combine multiple transistors on a single piece of silicon, inventing what became known as the integrated circuit. Fairchild, by contrast, began to disintegrate as talented employees began to strike out on their own. In 1967 Fairchild begat National Semiconductor when Charles Sporck left to found this new firm. One year later, Noyce and Gordon Moore, head of R&D, decided it was time for them to leave, frustrated that their most promising innovations seldom came to fruition. They made a telephone call to Arthur Rock, a venture capitalist before the term was invented, who raised enough money in two days for them to start on their own. Thus Fairchild Semiconductor begat Intel.

Intel's initial business was designing and manufacturing computer memory chips. Although it developed its first microprocessor, the 4004, in 1971, the company's bread and butter were integrated circuits that replaced magnetic core as the memory components of mainframe computers. The chips were smaller, faster, and cheaper than magnetic core. These three virtues, which became the dynamic behind continual innovation and growth in the computer and related industries, made the memory business very profitable for Intel. It had not discovered the particular technology that made that early generation of memory chips successful, nor was it the only company in the neighborhood—soon to be known as Silicon Valley—able to produce them. But it successfully combined product design, process engineering, and customer service to emerge quickly as the largest player in the memory chip game. Fairchild Semiconductor, from which both the engineers and the inventions had sprung, became less significant.

In 1971 Intel became a publicly traded company, when it raised $7.2 million by selling 307,000 shares in an IPO. It lost money on its operations in its first year (it did earn interest and nonoperating income), then began a succession of profitable years that lasted until 1985. The company flourished by turning silicon, an inexpensive raw material, into valuable and essential finished products: memory chips and later microprocessors. It accomplished this alchemy through the organized application of human capital in the form of scientific and engineering knowledge.

We will telescope the first three decades of Intel's history into a few sentences. It made a lot of money in the 1970s on memory chips, even though it often was neither the market leader nor the most efficient producer. Around 1980 one of its microprocessors, the 8088, was chosen by IBM to be the central processing unit of the IBM Personal Computer. At the same time that the PC revolution took off, Intel started to lose money on its memory chip business. Large Japanese conglomerates like Hitachi and Fujitsu beat Intel in every aspect of the dynamic random access memory (DRAM) game: They produced better chips (fewer duds) more cheaply, and then sold them for less to manufacturers with whom they had worked more closely.

After considerable soul searching—Intel's history was interwoven from birth with that of the memory chip—Gordon Moore and Robert Noyce decided in 1985 to leave the memory business. Since then, Intel has concentrated on microprocessors, both the original PC chip and its much more powerful successors, as well as a range of other processors for network, industrial, and computer uses. The company has been continually profitable since it came out of the memory loss period in the mid-1980s. It has continued to grow, although not at the rate it did in its early years when the silicon world was young. Throughout its history, Intel has invested heavily in developing its intellectual capital. Its R&D expenses averaged over 11 percent of sales for the period from 1971 to 1998. And Intel defended its intellectual capital. It used the courts repeatedly to contain rivals and former employees when it thought they were infringing on its patent-protected domains.

Intel's success in growing its business and keeping it profitable, with minor exceptions, is apparent from a few numbers and charts. In 1971 it had sales of $9 million. By 1998, these had grown to more than $26 billion. In 1972, its first profitable year, net income was slightly more than $1 million. In 1998, it reached $6 billion. Even if we ignore the first few years as a public company, which would give us a misleadingly low initial number on which to base growth figures, and start with Intel's results for 1975, we can see how enormous the firm's expansion has been. It had trouble in 1985, as it was leaving the DRAM business, but it recovered quickly. For the entire 24-year span, its sales grew on average 24 percent per year, and its net income grew by 28 percent. There are few companies in the history of the world that can match that record.

Table 7.1 and Figure 7.1 display these results. In the figure, the scale is logarithmic; each horizontal bar represents a ten-fold increase from the

Table 7.1   Intel Sales and Income Growth, 1975–1998

Year	Net Sales	Net Income
1975	$137	$16
1980	$855	$97
	44%	43%
1985	$1,365	$2
	10%	(56%)
1990	$3,921	$650
	23%	234%
1995	$16,202	$3,566
	33%	41%
1998	$26,273	$6,068
	13%	14%
1975–1988	24%	28%

Note: Percentages reflect changes per year. Dollar amounts are in millions.

bar below. Three messages stand out from the picture: Growth persists over three decades; Intel hit a rough patch in the mid-1980s; and exponential growth has been slowing as the company has gotten larger. It took around five years for sales to increase from $100 million to $1 billion; it has taken eleven years to grow from $2.9 to $29 billion. Climbing the hill gets

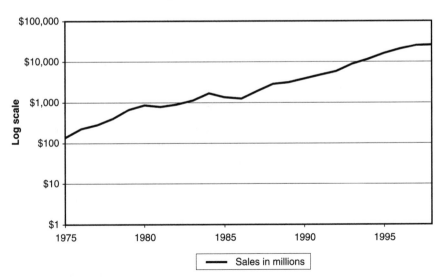

Figure 7.1   Intel Revenue Growth, 1975–1998

tougher as the burden (current sales) gets larger. Such are the labors of success.

Valuation I: Reproducing the Assets

Intel has been an extraordinary success by any measure. Our question here is whether a value investor, using the tools of valuation as we have developed them, would have bought the shares at some point in the history of the company. The decision has to be based on information that was available at the time; if hindsight is permitted, anyone can be a genius.

The first perspective on valuation focuses on the company's assets and what they are worth. As we said in Chapter 4, there are three basic ways to assess the assets. The most conservative is the net-net approach from Graham and Dodd: the current assets minus all the liabilities, putting no worth on plant, property, and equipment (PPE) or any other long-term assets. On any day, a screen of all publicly traded companies may come up with a few selling below their net-net valuation, but these are likely to be firms in serious difficulty, perhaps on the verge of bankruptcy. No profitable businesses can be bought at these liquidation prices.

The second valuation based on assets is to compare the price of the company's shares to the book value per share. The book value is the balance sheet entry for shareholder equity divided by the number of shares. Since equity by definition equals all the assets minus all the liabilities, book value can include the value of intangible assets such as goodwill and a number of other assets that may be worth considerably less than the balance sheet suggests. Buying stocks at a substantial discount to book value has been, as we have said, a successful investment strategy. No adjustment is made to the figures on the financial statement, which makes the strategy appropriate for investors who don't want to do a lot of work. Again, few successful businesses will be available for sale at book value, and even fewer at a discount sufficient to provide the margin of safety that the value investor seeks.

Just to be certain, Table 7.2 presents the book value and market value figures for Intel over five-year intervals starting in 1975. A graph of the

Table 7.2   Intel Book and Market Values, 1975–1998

	December 1975	December 1980	December 1985	December 1990	December 1995	December 1998
Book value	$74	$433	$1,421	$3,592	$12,865	$23,578
Market value	$503	$1,760	$3,447	$7,812	$50,167	$197,761
Market to book ratio	6.8	4.1	2.4	2.2	3.9	8.4

Note: Dollar amounts are in millions.

market to book ratio over the entire period, as shown in Figure 7.2, makes the relationship more apparent. For the years between 1980 and 1995, Intel traded at between two and four times the book value of its equity. These are all end-of-year numbers. During each year, Intel stock prices hit highs and lows that differed, sometimes significantly, from the price at year-end. Only in the general market run-up in the first half of 1987, however, did the company's market value exceed more than four times the value of its equity—until, that is, the end of 1995, when the investors decided that they could pay more than four times the book value for a company as successful as Intel and still make money.

The market-to-book analysis is quick and sometimes a bit muddy, if not downright dirty. To get a more precise take on what a competitor would

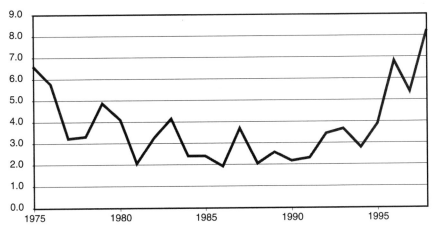

Figure 7.2   Intel Market to Book Ratio, 1975–1998

need to spend in order to get into the business, we have to look at the assets line by line and calculate—sometimes estimate—what their reproduction costs would be. We went through this exercise in Chapters 4 and 6, and the guidelines for adjustment remain the same. Table 7.3 presents Intel's assets as listed in its financial statements for 1975.

We have made virtually no adjustments to the assets as reported on the balance sheet. Intel did not use last in, first out (LIFO) accounting to value its inventory, and it had not purchased another company in a transaction that would have landed goodwill on its books. That leaves PPE as the account that needs scrutiny.

Intel owned chip factories (*fabs*, in industry parlance) in the Santa Clara region, and it had stocked them with the sophisticated equipment and clean rooms essential to turn out integrated circuits. It was a young company in 1975, so none of the plants or equipment would have been very old (although it did buy its first building, used, from Union Carbide).

Table 7.3   Intel Assets, 1975

Assets	Book Value	Adjustments to Arrive at Reproduction Costs	Adjustment Amount	Reproduction Cost
Current assets				
Cash	19.3	None	0.0	19.3
Accounts receivable (net)	29.9	Add bad debt allowances; adjust for collections	1.0	30.9
Inventories	20.1	Add LIFO reserve, if any; adjust for turnover	0.0	20.1
Prepaid expenses	0.0	None	0.0	0.0
Deferred taxes	0.0	Discount to present value	0.0	0.0
Other current assets	4.8		0.0	4.8
Total current assets	74.1		0.0	75.1
Property, plant, and equipment (net)	28.5	Original cost plus adjustment	0.0	28.5
Goodwill	0.0	Relate to product portfolio and R&D	0.0	0.0
Total assets	102.7		1.0	103.7

Note: Values are in millions of dollars.

On the other hand, the industry was changing rapidly, and the rate of obsolescence in semiconductor capital equipment may have been faster than the depreciation Intel was charging itself. A competitor might have been able to duplicate its facilities for less than the book value of its assets.

We can test how realistic the stated value of PPE is by comparing it with the actual capital expenditures Intel made (see Figure 7.3). For almost every year in the entire public history of the firm, Intel's net PPE has been more than the sum of its last four years of capital outlays and less than the sum of the last five years. Only if one thinks that a competitor could replicate Intel's entire production and research facilities with substantially less than four years' worth of its expenditures is the net PPE figure overstated. Conversely, if Intel's net PPE number understated the real (market) value of its fixed assets, Intel would not have needed to spend the equivalent sum every five years. The net PPE figure stands up as a reasonable amount when measured against capital outlays.

If there are assets that a competitor would have needed to produce to compete with Intel, they are not found on the balance sheet for 1975. That does not mean that they didn't exist. Intel, we should not forget, was a New

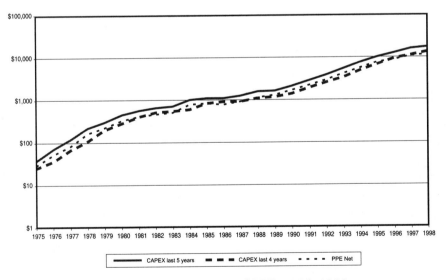

Figure 7.3   Intel Capital Expenditures and PPE, 1975–1998

Economy stock long before the New Economy had a name (at least in its post-1920s incarnation). As an early and major manufacturer of memory chips and then microprocessors, Intel invested in knowledge-based resources—the science and engineering skills needed to design and fabricate semiconductors—and supplied knowledge-enhancing products, which were the memory and brains of computers and industrial equipment, to its customers. But Intel's investments don't appear on the balance sheet because under accounting rules, R&D is generally treated as an annual expense rather than a capital expenditure. Unlike utility bills, computer paper, or real estate taxes, money spent wisely on R&D should continue to earn profits for the company long after the checks have been cut. The expertise essential to design and produce these chips—everything from Andrew Grove's 1967 book *The Physics and Technology of Semiconductor Devices* to the months of trial and error involved in increasing the yield on some stubborn manufacturing process—does not come cheaply; once purchased, it has lasting value. And not all of that knowledge is reflected in the R&D expense account; some of it no doubt disappears into the cost of goods sold as a manufacturing expense.

The investment in knowledge that does show up in Intel's income statement has been considerable. We wrote earlier that R&D averaged 11 percent of sales for the period from 1975 to 1998 (see Figure 7.4). Any company trying to compete with Intel would need to spend considerably to build up an equivalent expertise. How much would be enough? Some analysts have suggested treating R&D as a capital investment and depreciating it on a straight-line basis over five years. If we simplify and say that this past year's outlays should be fully valued as an asset, last year's at 80 percent, and so on, we can calculate the value of an off–balance sheet intangible asset that estimates what a competitor would need to spend just to get into the business. For Intel in 1975, that amount would have been $27 million. This would have increased the reproduction costs of the assets by 40 percent, and the book value of equity from $74 to $101 million, a gain of 37 percent.

There are other ways to gauge the costs of reproducing the knowledge base. If we used the sum of the last three years spent on R&D, the figure

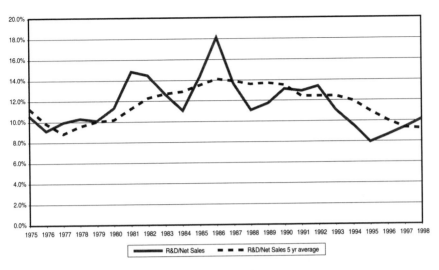

Figure 7.4   Intel R&D/Net Sales, 1975–1998

would be somewhat higher than our depreciated total; using the sum of the last two years would give us a slightly lower number. All of them might be understating the reproduction cost. Perhaps a competitor would need to spend five years' worth of R&D to become viable, or hire away some key Intel employs at a premium and then pay the court costs when Intel sued. We will use the five-year depreciated figure as a conservative estimate of the reproduction costs of Intel's storehouse of knowledge.

There is another nontangible, off–balance sheet asset a competitor would have to create in order to compete with Intel. Almost every company needs to spend money marketing its wares. In Intel's case, although it took several decades before the company started to spend serious money telling consumers about the advantages of "Intel Inside" their computers, from the start they sold highly technical products to a large number of sophisticated purchasers. This sales effort involved more than posting a list of specifications and prices for the semiconductors they offered. Sales executives had to work with customers to understand their needs and win contracts. Any new competitor would have had to develop a similar rapport with customers and understand their specific requirements to go head to head against Intel. All this effort costs money; it takes time to build the relationships with the engineers in the customer firms.

It is not possible to produce a hard figure for the magnitude of Intel's spending on marketing, which would include primarily the salaries and commissions of the sales staff as well as money spent on advertising and other forms of promotions. The amount for advertising is broken out, but until 1990 it never amounts to even 8 percent of the marketing, general, and administrative (MGA) expenses. To arrive at a reasonable number for what a competitor would have to spend in order to draw even with Intel requires making some estimates:

1. To even out the annual variations, we take the average of MGA as a percent of sales for the most recent five years and apply that to the current sales figure.
2. We assume that it would take three years of marketing expenses to get up to speed with Intel.
3. We set the share of MGA spent on running the business at half the total, leaving the other half for marketing.

Each of these assumptions can be challenged and refined; our aim is to arrive at a reasonable number to add to Intel's assets as an indication of the reproduction costs a new entrant would face. The amount is significant: slightly larger in most years than the R&D adjustment. (See Table 7.4 and Figure 7.5.)

When we include an adjustment for both R&D and marketing, we lower the market to book ratio for Intel by a considerable amount. There were several years in the period after 1975 when Intel could have been purchased at adjusted book value or slightly less. (Again, we are looking at year-end equity values and year-end prices. In some years, the interim prices were below the previous year-end.)

Starting in 1982, Intel began to invest in other companies, generally with the aim of advancing Intel's overall strategy, which was to encourage broad demand for microprocessors. Intel marked to the market the stock of publicly traded companies in this strategic portfolio; for privately owned companies, it valued the shares at its cost. We see no reason to challenge

Table 7.4   **Intel Adjusted Book Value, 1975–1998**

	December 1975	December 1980	December 1985	December 1990	December 1995	December 1998
Book value	$74	$433	$1,421	$3,592	$12,865	$23,578
R&D adjustment	$27	$190	$500	$1,149	$3,202	$6,377
Marketing adjustment	$39	$260	$698	$1,616	$4,822	$7,822
Book value adjusted	$141	$883	$2,620	$6,357	$20,889	$37,777
Market value	$503	$1,760	$3,447	$7,812	$50,167	$197,761
Market to adjusted book ratio	3.6	1.9	1.3	1.2	2.4	5.3

Note: Dollar amounts are in millions.

the company's practices here. Only if the privately owned shares had declined substantially since Intel's investments would it be necessary to adjust shareholder equity downward.

We have made no modifications to the liabilities on Intel's books. Over the years, the company did build up a sizeable deferred taxes account; if

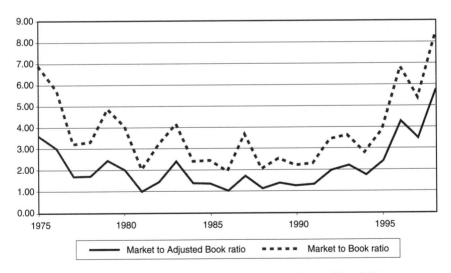

Figure 7.5   **Intel Market to Book and Market to Adjusted Book Ratios, 1974–1998**

that figure were discounted to the present, the liabilities would decline, and the equity would therefore rise. But the adjustment is minor and only becomes visible in the years after 1995, when the market value of Intel greatly outstripped the book value.

Measured against book or adjusted book value, the three best times in history to have purchased Intel shares would have been the following:

1. In January 1982, when the market value of the whole company fell briefly to around $925 million, compared with an adjusted book at year-end 1981 of just over $1 billion
2. In August 1986, when the market value was about $2 billion, versus an adjusted book value of $2.5 billion
3. At the end of 1988, when the adjusted book value of $3.9 billion was about even with the market value.

Had an investor been disciplined or fortunate enough to load up on Intel every time its market value came within hailing distance of its adjusted book, the results would have been excellent. At no time subsequent to the purchase would the value of the shares have been lower by any meaningful amount, and the gain over the next five years would have been substantial. Now, all of these dates occur within the extended bull market that began in August 1982 and persisted into the year 2000. The investor in Intel would have been sailing with the wind. Furthermore, purchasing shares at the start of 1982 and holding them into the one very rough period in Intel's history would still have provided a decent return, though slightly below the returns on the Standard & Poor's 500 index (see Table 7.5).

Valuation 2: Earnings Power Value

Our second swing at putting a value on Intel looks at earnings rather than assets. Here we will follow the approach we took in valuing WD-40 based on earnings power. The underlying assumptions are that the company will not grow, that its current earnings are sustainable for a long period of time, and that a shareholder, as an owner of the company, will receive as his or

Table 7.5   Intel Share Price Appreciation (selected periods)

Dates	Price at Start	Price at End	Compounded Annual Return	S&P 500 Comparison
1/82–1/87	$.47	$.895	13.8%	14.6%
8/86–8/91	$.82	$3.14	30.7%	6.5%
12/88–12/93	$1.48	$5.29	39.5%	17.5%

Note: Prices reflect subsequent share splits.

her return a proportionate share of the company's distributable earnings. The no-growth assumption works easily with WD-40, but it certainly does not fit Intel, a dynamic company in a rapidly changing and expanding industry. Therefore, it requires a considerable dose of strategic analysis to produce a reasonable estimate of Intel's constant earnings power in any particular year. Since the questions we want to answer are whether and when Intel shares presented an opportunity to investors adhering to the valuation criteria we have established, we can look only at information that would have been available at the time.

As we have seen, an estimate of the company's current intrinsic value on the basis of its earnings power requires two steps: first, adjustments to the reported earnings in order to arrive at a figure that represents the cash the investors can extract from the firm and still leave it functioning as before; second, selection of a discount rate that reflects both interest rates and the riskiness of the firm relative to other investment alternatives. Dividing the discount rate into the adjusted earnings gives us our earnings power value (EPV).

Adjusted Earnings: Special Charges, Business Cycles, R&D, and D&A

We will concentrate on the years from 1987 on, after Intel abandoned the memory chip business and just as the personal computer revolution began to hit its stride. As with WD-40, we begin with operating earnings and make our adjustments from there. The first adjustment concerns special charges. These are the write-offs that companies make when they revalue assets, such as inventory, equipment, or other investments they have made, or make provisions for layoffs, plant closings, and the like. The justification for keeping these charges separate from operating earnings is that they are singular events that do not effect the company's permanent earnings capacity. But in fact each of them represents the accumulation of real expenses that the company has incurred in the course of its business. If these charges persist from year to year, it means that the company is understating its true operating costs. To smooth out the erratic nature of these special charges, we take an average of the charges for the current and four prior years and deduct that from operating income.

Second, unlike WD-40, Intel's sales and earnings are not immune from cyclical swings. When Intel was involved in the memory chip business in the 1970s, its operating earnings margins were as high as 30 percent and as low as 20 percent. But in the microprocessor business, where there is less competition and the market is growing, it seems unlikely that the margins will vary as much. In the years 1987 through 1991, as sales grew rapidly, operating margins stabilized at somewhat more than 20 percent and even increased during the recession of 1990, so we think it is conservative to use 20 percent reported EBIT as a base for this period (see Table 7.6).

Third, for Intel, R&D is a major expense each year, averaging more than 12 percent of sales from 1987 through 1991, and hardly falling off after that. These were growth years for Intel, and we have to assume that some of that R&D was spent to support that growth. But in the fast-changing world of integrated circuits, a company will need a large R&D budget just to run in place. To get a more accurate picture of the earnings power with zero growth, we ought to add some of the R&D expense back to operating earnings. But how much? We can take the approach we used in calculating

Table 7.6   Intel Reported EBIT Margins, 1987–1991

	December 1987	December 1988	December 1989	December 1990	December 1991
Sales	$1,907	$2,875	$3,127	$3,921	$4,779
EBIT	$246	$594	$601	$858	$1,080
EBIT margin	12.9%	20.7%	19.2%	21.9%	22.6%

Note: Dollar amounts are in millions.

the reproduction cost of the assets, which was to treat R&D as a capital investment and depreciate that over five years. Each year's expense would be the depreciation charge, which is somewhat less than the actual R&D cost. A second method is to estimate a maintenance R&D on the same basis we estimated maintenance capex, by capitalizing R&D into an asset, finding a sales-to-asset ratio, and using that ratio times the dollars of additional sales to arrive at the growth portion of R&D. Maintenance R&D is simply the other portion. A third way is to look at the R&D spent by the closest competitor, in this case Advanced Micro Devices (AMD), and use that number as the necessary Intel expense. Finally, we can take a guess and say that at least a certain percent—we will use 25 percent—of Intel's R&D can be attributed to growth and therefore should be added back to EBIT. Having done all of these calculations, we are going to use the last one here. It is the most conservative in that it produces a smaller increase in current earnings than any of the alternative methods, and it is the simplest to implement.

Fourth, the adjustment for R&D can also be applied to selling, general, and administration (SG&A), a substantial part of which is spent on winning new business. We will add back 25 percent of the total—a rough estimate, but again a justifiable and conservative one.

Fifth, we can't escape taxes. For all these years we will assume a tax rate of 38 percent. This is higher than the accounting tax rate reported in Intel's audited financial statements, and it gives Intel no credit for whatever clever management of its tax liabilities it achieved. It is a good and conservative estimate of taxes on operating income.

Sixth, we need to adjust for depreciation, amortization, and maintenance capital expenditures. Here some knowledge of the industry helps. The cost of semiconductor capital equipment, the big and expensive machines that Intel uses to make its microprocessors, has declined over the years when improved capacity is taken into account. As a result, Intel's depreciation expense, which is based on the historical cost of its machinery, overstates the amount Intel would have to pay to keep its production capacity level. Rather than adding back all of depreciation and amortization (D&A) to EBIT after tax and then subtracting the maintenance portion of capital expenditure, we will simplify the calculations and add back 25 percent of D&A, assuming that the other 75 percent will be more than

Table 7.7　Intel Adjusted After-Tax Operating Earnings, 1987–1991

	December 1987	December 1988	December 1989	December 1990	Decemb 1991
Sales (net)	1,907	2,875	3,127	3,921	4,779
EBIT as reported	246	594	601	858	1,080
EBIT at 20% of sales	381	575	625	784	956
Special items average adjustment	(14)	(10)	(30)	(21)	(11)
Add back 25% of R&D	65	80	91	129	155
Add back 25% of SG&A	154	194	212	283	346
EBIT adjusted	587	838	899	1,176	1,445
EBIT adjusted margin	31%	29%	29%	30%	30
After tax of 38%	364	519	557	729	896
Add back 25% of D&A	43	53	59	73	105
Income as adjusted	227	572	616	802	1,000
Income as adjusted margin	12%	20%	20%	20%	21
Income as reported	248	453	391	650	819

Note: Amounts are in millions of dollars, except for percentages.

enough to cover maintenance capex. There is nothing magic about the 25 percent figure in all these calculations; we use it because it seems both rea-sonable and conservative.

Making all these adjustments gives us the adjusted and distributable operating earnings for Intel in the years 1987 to 1991, as shown in Table 7.7. After all that work, the differences between reported net income and adjusted and taxed operating income is not enormous, but that is only a rough check on the legitimacy of the estimations.

From Adjusted Earnings to Earnings Power Value

We have expressed skepticism at analysts' ability to derive with great pre-cision the rate at which the earnings of a company should be discounted to calculate the EPV. In this case, we are looking at Intel's earnings over a pe-riod in which long-term interest rates fell from around 12 percent to under 7 percent, and the risk-free rate fell from more than 13 percent to under 6 percent. Because the company rarely had any net debt on its books (i.e., debt left after deducting cash and short-term investments), its weighted average cost of capital would not have benefited from the fact that it costs less to borrow than to raise equity, especially after the deductibility of interest payments for tax purposes is taken into account. Surely there must be a simpler and more stable method for arriving at discount rate. For WD-40, we used a figure of 8 percent, made up of half debt at a cost of 6 percent, and half equity at a cost of 10 percent. Intel earnings, given their greater variability, should probably be discounted at a higher rate. We think 12 percent is a reasonable number—several percentages higher than the long-term return on the S&P 500 and probably a rate acceptable to most investors, at least before the great bull market of the 1990s.

With our earnings power (adjusted EBIT fully taxed) and discount rate in hand, we are almost ready to calculate an EPV for Intel. Before we compare that figure with the asset and market values, we will need to make one more set of adjustments. Both the asset value we calculated and the market value we are citing refer to the equity portion of Intel's capital and exclude the debt. By starting with book value and adding back adjustments, we in effect subtracted this debt from the reproduction value of Intel's assets to arrive at the asset value. To be consistent, we need to do the same thing here and reduce EPV by the amount of the debt outstanding. On the other hand, Intel has a lot of cash on its books in these years—substantially more than it needs to run the operations. When we did our asset valuation, we included this cash horde. Since we did not build this extra cash into the earnings power—operating earnings omit the interest on cash balances—we should add surplus cash to the EPV. This cash is definitely incorporated into the market value of the equity. Anyone buying the whole company would own this money along with all the other assets. Our cash-debt adjustments, which make all three values comparable, will be to subtract the book value of the interest-bearing debt and add back all cash in excess of 1 percent of sales, which is a general standard for the amount needed to operate the company.[1] With these last modifications, we arrive at the figures

[1] Since Intel had little debt in its capital structure, we have concentrated on the equity values of the assets and the earnings power. When a firm has significant financial leverage, the appropriate starting point is the enterprise value, which includes both debt and equity and then subtracts cash. Equity values are less stable because of the financial leverage. In Intel's case, the debt is insignificant.

Table 7.8   Intel EPV, Adjusted Book Value, and Market Value, 1987–1991

	December 1987	December 1988	December 1989	December 1990	December 1991
EPV at 12%	1,891	4,768	5,137	6,684	8,337
Less total interest bearing debt	(750)	(696)	(569)	(623)	(536)
Plus cash in excess of 1% of sales	600	842	1,058	1,746	2,229
Total EPV	1,741	5,013	5,626	7,807	10,030
Adjusted book value	2,755	3,893	4,781	6,357	7,671
Market value	4,779	4,285	6,513	7,812	10,240

Note: Amounts are in millions of dollars.

for Intel during the period 1987 to 1991 shown in Table 7.8. Figure 7.6 displays these values and extends them back and forward a few years to illustrate the transformation of Intel in this period.

We already knew that the mid-1980s were a tough time for Intel; its memory chip business was losing money, and its microprocessor business had not yet grown to make up the difference. In 1985 Intel's operating income was miniscule; in 1986 it was less than zero. But in 1987, Intel's earnings begin to improve dramatically, and with them the EPV. By 1988 it surpassed adjusted book value. After a brief halt in 1989, the gap between EPV and the reproduction cost of the assets continued to spread.

According to our analysis, if the EPV, accurately calculated, exceeds the reproduction costs of the assets for a considerable period, the company should enjoy sustained competitive advantages and be operating a franchise, protected by barriers to entry that keep competitors away or make them less successful than the incumbent if they should enter the field. In this case, Intel appears to benefit from the combination of demand advantages (i.e., consumer preferences) and powerful economies of scale. Its name had become synonymous with the IBM PC and all the clones that established positions in that industry. Intel set the standards for microprocessors operating first MS-DOS and then the Windows operating systems. Other companies, most notably AMD, offered computer manufacturers alternative products; for at least part of this period, these companies had to

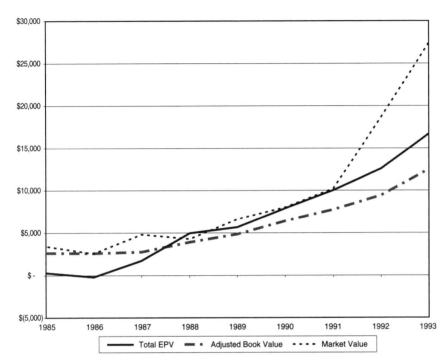

Figure 7.6   **Intel EPV, Adjusted Book Value, and Market Value, 1985–1993**

license the design from Intel. Especially after it initiated its "Intel Inside" advertising campaign, however, Intel dominated the minds, and hence the market, of PC buyers. Some PC makers did use AMD chips in their machines to reduce the prices they charged, and by 1998 the competition at the lower end—less powerful, less expensive chips—became intense. Still, for most PC manufacturers, the no-brainer has always been to stick with Intel. The company's volume in this segment of its business far exceeded those of its competitors.

The second element of Intel's competitive advantage is the existence of economies of scale. Microprocessors are the kind of product for which manufacturers enjoy economies of scale that extend over very large production quantities. Design of microprocessors, especially as they get faster and denser, is expensive. The more units of any design that are sold, the less

Table 7.9   Intel and AMD: Sales, R&D, and EBIT margins as adjusted

	Intel			Advanced Micro Devices		
	Sales	R&D	EBIT Margin	Sales	R&D	EBIT Margin
1988	2.88	0.32	29%	1.13	0.21	17%
1989	3.13	0.37	27%	1.10	0.20	17%
1990	3.92	0.52	31%	1.06	0.20	9%
1991	4.78	0.62	32%	1.23	0.21	22%
1992	5.84	0.78	36%	1.51	0.23	28%
1993	8.79	0.97	47%	1.65	0.26	30%
1994	11.52	1.11	40%	2.13	0.28	33%
1995	16.20	1.30	38%	2.43	0.40	26%
1996	20.85	1.81	42%	1.90	0.40	3%
1997	25.07	2.35	46%	2.30	0.47	11%
1998	26.27	2.67	40%	2.50	0.57	10%

Note: Figures for both Intel and AMD are firm-wide. Intel has a broader line of products and spends on R&D for products in which it does not compete with AMD, so this is not a perfect comparison. Amounts are in billions of dollars, except for percentages.

are the design costs per unit. From Table 7.9 we can see that Intel's total spending on R&D was much greater than that of AMD. But—and here is the economy of scale at work—AMD had to spend more R&D for each dollar of sales, almost twice as much over the entire period. Furthermore, the financial statement does not include additional R&D-type expenses posted to the cost of goods sold account every time a new fabrication line is put into operation and tinkered with until the output meets the company's standards.

These two features—more consumer demand and lower cost per unit at every level of sales—make Intel much more profitable than its competitors. After Intel established its dominance, its operating profit margins were double those of AMD. On a reported income basis, AMD lost money in 1996, 1997, 1998, and 1999. Intel, on the other hand, earned over $18 billion in the years 1996 through 1998, and another $7 billion in 1999. It hardly seems fair.

The strategic conclusion that after 1987 Intel enjoyed a significant and increasing competitive advantage confirms the picture painted by our asset value and EPV comparisons. From 1988 through 1991, EPV surpassed the asset value by an average of 25 percent each year. The difference between these two is the value of Intel's franchise. We can look at the franchise more directly to assess whether the additional earnings are sustainable given what we know about Intel's competitive advantages.

Without any competitive advantage, a company's earnings are equal to its cost of capital multiplied by its operating assets. We will call this amount free-entry earnings, indicating no special advantage. If it does enjoy a franchise, then the earnings attributable to that franchise are the actual EPV we calculated minus the free-entry earnings. We divide franchise earnings by sales to arrive at the franchise margin, which is the percent earned, after tax, on each dollar of sales that is attributable to the franchise. The higher the margin, the more valuable the franchise. We need to remember, however, that an extremely high margin is suspect on two counts. First, it may simply not be reasonable to accept the prediction that one company's assets, on a sustained basis, will generate much higher earnings than would similar assets in the hands of another company. Second, the more valuable the franchise, the more attractive it will be to potential competitors. At some point, we can be sure, some clever firm will breach the barriers to entry or reshape the market. In either case, the value of the original franchise will shrivel. To view the size of the franchise margin in pretax operating terms, we divide it by (1 – the tax rate). Table 7.10 presents these calculations for Intel from 1988 to 1991.

Like Mama Bear's porridge, Intel's operating franchise margin is not too hot to be unreasonable or unsustainable, and not too cold to be worthless. A portion of it can be traced directly to the economies of scale it en-

Table 7.10   Intel's Franchise Earnings and Margins, 1988–1991

	December 1988	December 1989	December 1990	December 1991
Cost of capital × operating assets	354	447	553	653
Operating earnings, after-tax	572	616	802	1,000
Franchise earnings	218	170	249	347
Franchise margin, after-tax	8%	5%	6%	7%
Operating franchise margin, pretax	12%	9%	10%	12%

Note: Amounts are in millions of dollars, except for percentages.

joys in its R&D spending. Compared with AMD, Intel spent considerably less on R&D per each dollar of sales than did its rival, even though its total was much higher. If AMD had wanted to match Intel's spending, it would have had to more than double its outlays, which already represented 18 percent of its sales. In these years, the scale advantage for Intel averaged 32 percent. With R&D at 12 percent of Intel's sales, that translates into a franchise margin of almost 4 percent. The rest can be attributed to similar scale economies in the other parts of the SG&A expenses. In these years, AMD spent 10 percent more than Intel here, for each dollar of sales.

Valuation 3: What Is Growth Worth?

Only within the franchise is growth worth anything. Growth requires investment; achieving more sales almost invariably requires more current and fixed assets. The purpose of these additional assets is to earn incremental returns that will add to the company's profits. If growth simply involves doing more of the same (i.e., the replication on a larger scale of all the functions of the existing business), then it is natural to assume that incremental returns on the additional assets will be equal to the returns already being earned, on average, by the investments in the existing business. In this simple example, if the company's return on capital has been 12 percent, then its returns on the investment necessary for growth should also be 12 percent. If that is the case, then new investments will be profitable for the firm only if the cost of the capital it needs to support the growth is less than 12 percent. If the company has to pay 15 percent to attract the additional investment, then it will lose 3 percent on each new dollar of capital. Thus, the principal determinant of the value of growth is the relationship between the return on the new capital required to fund the growth and the cost of that capital.

The reason why growth must be within the franchise to be profitable is that outside the franchise, there is no spread between the reproduction value of the assets and the EPV of the company. The cost of capital and the return on capital are identical thanks to the grinding competitive forces of a market economy. Only firms protected by barriers to entry can continue to earn excess returns—returns above the cost of capital—when challenged by new entrants who want to capture some of that excess for themselves. Profitable growth is subject to the same constraints; it needs to be protected by the same or equivalent barriers in order to earn more than the cost of capital.

There are some situations in which this kind of growth is possible. In Intel's case, the market for its primary products continued to grow, and even as it became international, Intel was still in the best position to supply microprocessors to manufacturers around the globe. So its competitive advantages, based on captive customers and economies of scale, were still operating and became even more formidable. Microsoft benefited from identical advantages with probably more extreme economies of scale, and it also locked in customers with high switching costs.

Most franchises do not expand so easily. Even Wal-Mart, for example, has been successful in some places but not in others. In areas like California, far from its core region, Wal-Mart enjoys no identifiable competitive advantages. If other retailers, such as Target, have dominant local market shares and the associated economies of scale, then Wal-Mart may find itself operating at a competitive disadvantage. Returns on incremental capital invested in these geographic areas will create little or no value for existing shareholders. When Wal-Mart expands closer to home, in the fringes of its core area, and can use its existing infrastructure, it may be able to capture some cost advantages. Though these will be smaller than the ones it has enjoyed in the heart of its core region, they may still be enough to allow it to earn returns from its incremental investments that are more than the cost of capital. In this case, growth on the fringe may create some value but be less than growth entirely within the franchise area.

Growth as the Margin of Safety

Only the most paranoid value investor will refuse to acknowledge that growth in Intel's CPU business will create value. The questions are how much and whether it is sufficient to provide an adequate margin of safety. We need to compare the value of this growth to the value of the current earnings power. The greater the amount by which the present value (PV) of the cash flows with growth tops the current EPV, the larger the margin of safety. We will use the ratio between the two as our measure of this margin.

$$PV/EPV = \text{margin of safety}$$

We know that the EPV of a company equals its earnings divided by the cost of capital (R). Its earnings are the product of the capital invested times the rate of return on that capital (ROC), so the equation becomes

$$EPV = \text{Capital} \times \text{ROC}/R, \text{ or } EPV = \text{Capital} \times (\text{ROC}/R)$$

In the appendix to this chapter we work out in detail the equation for the present value of a growing firm, which is

$$PV = \text{Capital} \times F = \text{Capital} \times (\text{ROC} - G)/(R - G)$$

where F is the growth factor. The only additional variable in the growth version is G, the rate of growth itself, and it has an important effect on the critical valuation factor of $(\text{ROC} - G)/(R - G)$. As long as ROC is larger than R, any increase in the growth rate raises the valuation factor. As the rate of growth approaches the cost of capital, the valuation factor accelerates. But there is a limit. When the rate of growth equals or exceeds the cost of capital, the valuation becomes infinite and thus absurd. These calculations make the simplifying assumptions that growth is constant over time and that it is balanced, meaning that each additional dollar of sales requires a fixed percentage increase in all the asset and liability accounts. No real company meets these conditions, but the model provides a basic yardstick that more or less matches many actual situations.

In general, the value created by growth depends on two factors. The first is the profitability of the incremental capital employed; the greater the amount by which incremental returns exceed the cost of capital, the greater will be the value created by each dollar invested. So our first variable is expressed as a ratio, ROC/R. The second factor is the amount of capital that can be employed to earn these franchise returns. That depends

Table 7.11   **The Growth Value Matrix**

		(A)	(B)	(C)	(D)	(E)
ROC/R		1.0	1.5	2.0	2.5	3.0
(1) G/R	25%	1.0	1.11	1.17	1.20	1.22
(2) G/R	50%	1.0	1.33	1.5	1.60	1.67
(3) G/R	75%	1.0	2.00	2.5	2.80	3.00

on how fast the franchise grows. The limits of sustainable growth are some fraction of the cost of capital. As we said, if growth equaled the cost of capital for any lengthy period, the return on capital would be infinite. We know that isn't possible, so we have to accept the fact that G/R will be less than one. We use 25 percent, 50 percent, and 75 percent as three standardized percentages.

Based on more algebra, which we have consigned to the appendix, we offer Table 7.11 to represent the relationship between the value of a business growing within a franchise and the value of the same business without growth, or PV/EPV. The number within each cell is the PV/EPV ratio for the appropriate values of ROC/R and G/R. In Column A, where the return on capital is the same as the cost of capital (ROC/R = 1), growth adds nothing to EPV; the ratio of PV/EPV remains 1. But as we move to Column B, where ROC/R = 1.5, growth starts to matter. If the growth rate is 25 percent of the cost of capital, then PV/EPV = 1.11. To flesh this out, if the return on incremental capital is 12 percent and the cost of capital is 8 percent, a business that grows 2 percent a year is worth 11 percent more than one with no growth. If it grows 4 percent a year, it is worth 33 percent more; if it grows at 6 percent, the value is twice that of its no-growth twin. At the extreme, a business with an incremental return of 24 percent, a cost of capital of 8 percent, and growth of 6 percent a year is worth three times as much as the business without growth.

The striking feature of Table 7.11 is how small the growth multiples are. It takes high returns on capital combined with high growth rates to move the multiple above 2. If a company without growth sells at a price to earnings ratio (P/E) of 16 (i.e., the EPV = 16 × the earnings), which is common today, then a company with a P/E of 48 (i.e., 3 × the EPV) ought to have a return on capital three times the cost of capital, and a growth rate of 75 percent of that cost. With a cost of capital of 12 percent, that would mean a ROC of 36 percent and a growth rate of 9 percent, not for the next year or two but for a long time into the future.

We can now apply our valuation matrix to Intel to see if we could have counted on growth within the franchise to provide our margin of safety, had we paid the full EPV price in 1990 or 1991. For that we need growth and profitability numbers, and here there are some choices we can make. We can look at growth in sales, growth in earnings, or both. From the vantage point of December 1990, it doesn't make much difference. Intel has grown fast enough over the last three years, on average, that with a cost of capital of 12 percent, we can easily fit it into the lowest row of Table 7.11, where growth is at least 75 percent of the cost of capital, or 9 percent.

The other variable required to complete the exercise is the relationship between return on capital and cost of capital. There are several measures of return on capital in everyday use. The easiest is return on equity (ROE), which is simply earnings per share divided by book value per share. This measure does not take into account the amount of debt the company carries or the surplus cash it may have accumulated. A measure favored by professionals is return on invested capital (ROIC), which uses operating earnings as the numerator and operating assets as the denominator. In Intel's case, this measure is considerably higher than ROE, reflecting the surplus cash and the company's small outstanding debt. Even if we choose the lower and less precise ROE figure, we have an average of over 18 percent for these years. With the cost of capital at 12 percent, the ratio is 1.5, landing Intel in Column B. The cell at the intersection of Column B and Row

Table 7.12   Intel's Growth and Return Variables, 1987–1990

	December 1987	December 1988	December 1989	December 1990
Growth in sales	51%	51%	9%	25%
Growth in adjusted EBIT	n.a.	152%	8%	30%
Return on equity	19%	22%	15%	18%
Return on invested capital	18%	40%	38%	40%

Note: n.a. = not applicable.

3 has a value of 2.00, meaning that Intel with growth should be worth twice the current EPV. Had we purchased Intel in this period at around its EPV, growth would have provided us a margin of safety of 50 percent.

All these calculations assume that the franchise is durable and that the spread between cost of capital and return on capital will persist. These are judgments about the future of the PC industry and Intel's place within it. Though not easy calls to make, at least prospectively, they demand much less than predicting the terminal value of the company a decade in the future and discounting that back to the present. Also, growth here is used as the margin of safety, not as the element essential to transform a company with miniscule revenues and negative cash flow into a world-class powerhouse.

We know now that the Intel investment would have paid off handsomely. As Figure 7.6 and earlier charts in this chapter illustrate, the market value of Intel continued its ascent after 1991, soon leaving behind the EPV. Perhaps growth within the franchise would have continued to provide a margin of safety for a few years after 1991, especially as we altered our model to take into account the higher operating earnings margins and returns on capital that Intel achieved in these years. At some point during the decade, the market exuberance, irrational or not, would have taken Intel off the table as a value investment. But there was a lengthy window of opportunity starting in the years after 1987, during which a modern value investor who grasped the power of Intel's franchise could have made a wonderful trade.

Appendix

Valuation Algebra: Return on Capital, Cost of Capital, and Growth

For some companies, growth creates wealth; for others, growth destroys it. To understand the reasons for this divergence, we will start with a simple case of a firm that grows forever at a constant rate in a balanced way. *Balanced* here means that as revenues increase by, say, 10 percent each year, every other item in the financial statements grows by the same percentage. The profit margins, both before and after taxes, remain constant. As a consequence, earnings before interest and taxes increase by the same 10 percent as sales, as does net income. The assets required to support revenue— from cash to plant, property, and equipment—expand proportionately, and so do the spontaneous liabilities. Since assets minus spontaneous liabilities equal the necessary capital that must be invested, that also has to grow by 10 percent. Put slightly differently, the ratio of every item to revenues remains unchanged.

The good news for this firm is that the growth in revenues and earnings each year makes the firm steadily more valuable. The bad news is that this growth has to be supported by additional investments in the same proportion; each year's infusion of new capital is 10 percent more than the previous year's. Growth is desirable if the good news (higher earnings) outweighs the bad (more investment required). How do we decide?

Return to our simple example (see Table 7.13). At the start of 1999, this company had $200 million in capital invested (capital is debt plus equity,

Table 7.13   **Balanced Growth**

	1999	2000	2001
Sales	$400	$440	$484
Net income	$32	$35	$39
Net profit margin	8%	8%	8%
Equity	$200	$220	$242
Return on equity	16%	16%	16%
Distributable to investors	$12	$13	$15

Note: Dollar amounts are in millions.

but to keep it really simple, this firm has only equity) to support anticipated sales of $400 million. We expect it to earn $32 million. The net profit margin is 8 percent; the return on equity is 16 percent. For our company to grow by 10 percent, it will need an additional investment of $20 million. That reduces to $12 million the money available to distribute to existing shareholders, so the bad news here is that growth needs the extra $20 million. The good news is that the available $12 million will continue to compound, in our simple scenario, by 10 percent each year. At some point in the future (roughly 12 years), it will increase beyond the original $32 million.

We still need to know whether this growth adds value. To determine that, we compare the present value of the cash flows available to investors in this growth illustration with those that would be available if there were no growth at all—if the sales, earnings, and capital required remained at the level for 1999. This zero growth case is nothing more or less than the EPV, so we will designate it (E)PV. Whenever cash flows increase at a constant rate, it is possible to calculate the present value (PV) of this stream with the following formula:

$$PV = \text{initial flow} \times 1/R - G$$

where R is the cost of capital and G is the rate of growth. If the cost of capital is 20 percent, then for zero growth the equation is

$$EPV = \$32 \times 1/(20\% - 0\%) = \$32/.2 = \$160.$$

The equation for the growing company is

$$PV = \$12 \times 1/(20\% - 10\%) = \$12/.1 = \$120.$$

The initial value is different because with no growth, the company can distribute all the earnings; growth requires additional investments. For this company, which is paying 20 percent for new capital, growth is a mistake. The present value of cash that will be available for shareholders is lower in the growth scenario than if sales and everything else were to remain constant.

The results are different if the company needs to pay only 14 percent for new capital. Then the equation for the static scenario becomes

$$\text{EPV} = \$32 \times 1/(14\% - 0\%) = \$32/.14 = \$229,$$

versus the growth scenario of

$$\text{PV} = \$12 \times 1/(14\% - 10\%) = \$12/.04 = \$300.$$

When the discount rate drops from 20 percent to 14 percent, growth adds value. Finally, if the discount rate is 16 percent, the static case equation is

$$\text{EPV} = \$32 \times 1/(16\% - 0\%) = \$32/.16 = \$200,$$

and the growth version is

$$\text{PV} = \$12 \times 1/(16\% - 10\%) = \$12/.06 = \$200.$$

Now growth neither adds nor destroys value.

Remember that this firm's return on capital is 16 percent. It is not a coincidence that growth is neutral when the discount rate, or cost of capital, is also 16 percent. To understand why, we need to present a few more equations.

The earnings (E) of $32 million equals the amount of capital (C) times the return on capital (ROC):

$$E = C \times \text{ROC}, \text{ which in this case is } \$32 = \$200 \times 16\%.$$

This is true by definition of the return on capital (ROC). The investment (I) needed to support annual growth of 10 percent is

$$I = C \times G, \text{ which in this case is } \$20 = \$200 \times 10\%.$$

This is the level of investment that enables our firm's capital to grow at the same 10 percent as sales.

The distributable cash flow (CF) equals the earnings minus the needed investment. Since $E = C \times ROC$ and $I = C \times G$, then

$$CF = (C \times ROC) - (C \times G) = C \times (ROC - G),$$

or in this case $12 = $200 \times (.16 - .10)$.

The present value of this growing distribution is

$$PV = CF \times 1/(R - G).$$

Since $CF = C \times (ROC - G)$, then $PV = C \times (ROC - G) \times 1/(R - G)$, which equals

$$C \times [(ROC - G)/(R - G)], \text{ or in this case}$$

$$\$200 = \$200 \times [(.16 - .1)/(.16 - .1)].$$

Embedded in this algebra are some intuitively understandable relationships. The present value of the distributable cash flow depends upon C, the amount of capital at the start, and the expression $(ROC - G)/(R - G)$, which we will call the growth factor (F). In our example, because the return on capital invested in the business and the cost of acquiring that capital are identical, $F = 1$. F always equals 1 when $ROC = R$, regardless of the rate of growth (G). If $ROC = 12\% = R$, then $F = (.12 - G)/(.12 - G) = 1$ for all values of growth. As long as the return on capital and the cost of capital are the same, growth never—no matter how fast or slow—adds value to the business.

We know why. Growth requires additional investment, and although this investment produces a return on capital, the financiers who supply it demand payment for the use of their funds, which is the cost of capital. In our example, ROC is constant, as is R. When $ROC = R$, the entire proceeds from the investment go to compensate the providers of the new funds; there is nothing left to pay to the existing owners of the firm. Therefore, no matter how much the new investment generates in increased revenue and earnings, the value of the firm to its existing owners does not change. This may be surprising to investors who have been drilled on the virtues of growth and are convinced that they should pay premiums for the stocks of rapidly growing companies. The implicit assumption behind this reasoning is that growth will require little new investment, leaving more cash available for distribution. Even for firms in the New Economy, however, that have substituted intellectual capital for bricks, mortar, and steel, growth without investment is a rarity.

Growth may be worse than neutral; it may actually destroy value. This occurs whenever the return on capital is less than the cost of capital. Returning to our growth value factor F, if ROC = .10, and R = .12, then F = (.10 – G)/(.12 – G). In this situation, F will (a) always be less than one no matter what the rate of growth, (b) get smaller as the rate of growth increases, and (c) fall to zero when G reaches 10 percent annual growth. As long as it costs us more for each dollar of new investment than that dollar will produce in increased earnings, growth destroys value. Higher growth rates require more investment and thus destroy value even faster.

Growth, it is now clear, only adds value when the return on capital is greater than the cost of capital (ROC > R). Using the growth value factor, if ROC = 20% and R = 10%, then F = (.20 – G)/(.10 – G), which (a) is always greater than one, and (b) increases as the rate of growth (G) increases, at least until G reaches 10 percent, at which point the denominator drops to zero and the value of the term spirals to infinity. This may be algebraically correct but is not something we are likely to see in practice.

Again the reason is straightforward. Each dollar invested earns $0.20, but only $0.10 must be paid to those who supply the funds. The other $0.10, per dollar and per year, is available to the original owners; this process does indeed create value. The faster the firm grows, the more dollars can be invested to earn $0.20 and cost only $0.10. Firms that expand in this fashion, earning more on their new investments than those investments cost, are the ones in which growth creates value.

What kind of businesses are these? The answer looks familiar. If a firm operates in an industry without competitive advantages, where there are no barriers to entry, returns above the cost of capital will attract new entrants whose competition will eliminate those higher rates of return. As we discussed in Chapter 5, without barriers to entry, sooner or later competition will force the rate of return downward until it equals the cost of capital. Since the most common competitive condition is a level playing field, for most firms return on capital will equal the cost of capital, and there will be no value created by growth. For these firms, growth adds zero to the current EPV. For firms that are on the wrong side of barriers to entry, outside and looking in, the cost of capital exceeds the return on capital, and growth destroys value. Only in markets where a company enjoys a sustainable competitive advantage, protected within its franchise by barriers to entry, will returns on capital be greater than the cost of capital. So the basic principle of growth valuation comes down to this: Only growth within the franchise reliably creates value.

For Intel, this means only growth within its basic market for CPU chips. Diversification into other markets—even other microprocessor markets—or ventures into products still further away from its core business, are as likely to destroy value as to create it. There are no barriers to entry protecting Intel in these markets; it is the new entrant. The best it can hope for is a level playing field. Leaving the franchise can be like forsaking Eden for Hobbes' vision of life in nature: solitary, poor, nasty, brutish, and short.

How much value does growth within the franchise actually create? To answer this question we compare the present value of the growing firm to its value without growth, which is the EPV. We will look at the proportional value that growth adds to the EPV, which we express as

$$M = PV/EPV,$$

with M defined as the growth-related value multiplier. In this expression,

$$PV = C \times (ROC - G)/(R - G) \text{ and}$$

$$EPV = C \times ROC/R = C \times (ROC/R).$$

Substitution from these two expressions into the definition of M and a little algebraic manipulation yield the equation

$$M = 1 - (G/R)(R/ROC)/1 - (G/R).$$

Table 7.11 The Growth Value Matrix

	(A)	(B)	(C)	(D)	(E)
ROC/R	1.0	1.5	2.0	2.5	3.0
(1) G/R 0.25	1.0	1.11	1.17	1.20	1.22
(2) G/R 0.50	1.0	1.33	1.5	1.60	1.67
(3) G/R 0.75	1.0	2.00	2.5	2.80	3.00

This expresses our growth-related value multiplier (M) in terms of two critical factors. The first is the ratio of the cost of obtaining that capital to the return on capital invested (i.e., R/ROC). The more profitable the investment is, the lower this ratio and the greater the value of growth become. The second factor is the ratio of the projected growth rate (G) to the maximum reasonable growth (R). (Remember that if G exceeds R, the value of the firm is infinite, so R is the realistic limit to the growth rate over the long term.) As long as ROC/R exceeds one (i.e., R/ROC is less than one), greater levels of growth will lead to a greater value for the company. The magnitudes of M (the growth-related value multiple) for a range of return on capital and growth rates are presented in Table 7.14. It takes both high rates of growth, relative to the maximum rate of R, and high levels of profitability, relative to the cost of capital R, to generate large levels of growth-related value.

So far we have discussed only growth that is balanced and takes place at a constant rate forever. Clearly these are artificial conditions. A more common situation is one in which a company grows very rapidly for some years and then slows down as it reaches maturity, at which point it grows at a slow but steady rate. In cases like this, the fundamental rules about growth and value still apply. Growth within the franchise creates value. Growth at a competitive disadvantage destroys value. Growth on a level playing field has no effect on value.

There are relatively uncomplicated methods for computing the value created by this type of growth. The simplest is to begin with an estimate of how many years the company will be able to grow at these heady rates, after which it becomes mature and has to settle for a second, much slower but still constant growth rate. Growth rates for each period are selected and used to project revenues. Standard ratios are applied to translate these sales figures into annual cash flows, with probably different ratios for the rapid growth and mature phases. Finally, a cost of capital is postulated for each period, and the net present value of cash flows is calculated from today to eternity, using the second period parameters to calculate a terminal value at the end of the period of rapid growth. This is a standard net present value analysis.

The trouble is that value estimates based on this kind of growth are likely to be highly unreliable in practice. A quick look at Microsoft will illustrate the difficulties. Microsoft is undoubtedly the greatest winner from the PC explosion, even more than Intel. In that world it has enjoyed and is likely to continue to enjoy a powerful franchise. For the years 1996 to 2000, its sales grew at around 30 percent per year, and its earnings per share grew at around 40 percent. In the year 2000, its stock traded at a heady multiple of earnings, from a low of 23 to a high of 70. The company pays no dividends, but it does accumulate substantial cash balances. Suppose we expect Microsoft to continue to grow both sales and earnings at 40 percent per year from 2000 through 2009. At the end of the period, its sales and earnings will be about 20 times their level today. Suppose as well that Microsoft were to distribute half of its earnings as dividends, starting in 2000, and that its cost of capital is 15 percent. The present value of these dividends received through 2009 would be around $22. That would represent less than 20 percent of the value of the shares at the high of $119. All the other returns that shareholders expect would depend on cash flows starting in the year 2010. Even at $50 a share, the price at which Microsoft was available around the end of 2000, almost 60 percent of the value still depends on results starting in 2010. The ability of even the best analysts in the year 2000 to forecast accurately Microsoft's earnings starting at 10 years in the future is likely to be limited. Under these circumstances, it is impossible to justify Microsoft as a value investment.

Chapter 8

Constructing the Portfolio
Risk, Diversification, and
Default Strategies

Our emphasis so far has been on the process of valuation, the techniques through which investors assay the intrinsic value of a business and compare that value with the market price. To be successful, however, money managers and private investors need to do more than identify undervalued securities. They have to combine these selections into a portfolio that should lessen the risk of owning only one security but still not cut unduly into the expected returns. Even the most energetic, skilled, and confident value investor knows that the best ideas can turn to dust or, at the least, fail to produce for discouragingly long periods. Diversification is inescapable. In his writing and his practice at Graham-Newman, Benjamin Graham explicitly endorsed the importance of diversification. But that still leaves wide differences regarding the principles with which a money manager diversifies a portfolio. Much depends on the conception of risk, on whether the manager has strategies to reduce risk in addition to diversification, on the willingness and ability to make use of alternatives to ordinary stock and bond investments, and on the expectations of the manager's clients.

Modern investment theory makes diversification one of the two central features of its approach to a proper investment strategy. Because, as the theory holds, it is possible to diversify away the risks of holding only one or a few securities, investors will not be rewarded for those risks that they assume in running narrow portfolios. The only risk that does earn a commensurate reward is the risk of volatility, or the risk that the diversified portfolio will move up and down at a greater rate than some even more broadly diversified benchmark, like the Standard & Poor's 500 index or the Wilshire 5000. The efficient market hypothesis—the idea that the market always incorporates the best estimate of the true value of a security—is embedded in this conception of risk and diversification; otherwise it might be possible for a clever investor to pick relatively few securities and be rewarded for these selections.

Value investors reject both parts of the theory. They think stock selection does matter, and they do not accept the definition of risk as simply relative volatility. So although no genuine value investor that we have heard about puts all his eggs in one basket, as a group they probably do run more concentrated portfolios than their non-value-oriented peers.[1] There are several reasons. First, value investors operate within the boundaries of their competence. The only securities they select are those they feel they understand, and their preferences are for those companies that can be reliably valued, with stable positions, a history of steady earnings, and businesses that are not vulnerable to sudden changes in technology or consumer taste. If these requirements exclude value investors from owning the alluring growth names in technology or other industries undergoing transformation, that is a restriction they have been willing to accept. Second, the margin of safety requirement provides a mechanism for reducing risk that is totally distinct from diversification. Buying a company for substantially less than tangible book value or the well-tested value of its earnings is already a low-risk strategy. Using a valuation based on assets as a check on a valuation based on earnings power, all the while refusing to pay much

---

[1] In the late 1990s, a fashion for more concentrated portfolios did emerge, even for growth-oriented investors. Mutual funds with the number "20" or "30" in their names started to appear, as did those dubbing themselves "focused." This may have been a result of the weakening hold of modern investment theory in the profession, or simply of the desire to increase returns by capitalizing on the "best ideas." After a decade and a half of a long bull market, the balance between fear and greed that regulates the levels of the markets may have shifted toward greed—a troubling sign, we believe.

if anything for the prospects of growth, further limits risk. If an ordinary portfolio (one not selected on value grounds) needs 20 or 30 names to be adequately diversified, then perhaps the margin of safety portfolio needs only 10 or 15.

Also, as we discussed in Chapter 1, volatility is not the only and perhaps not even the best measure of risk. Whenever the price of the security drops more than the comparable market index, its volatility increases, but so may the margin of safety now available to an investor. As Warren Buffett asked in reference to his investment in the Washington Post Company, if he could buy a company worth at least $400 million for $80 million, would that investment have been riskier had the price fallen to $40 million? If we think of risk as avoiding permanent loss of capital, then stock selection using the principles of valuation we have discussed, including the margin of safety, may be more important than diversification so extensive that nothing other than volatility is left as a source of return.

Diversification can also be measured by more than counting the number of positions in the portfolio or the number of industries represented. The task for all diversifiers is to find assets whose returns are not strongly correlated with one another, even assets with negatively correlated returns. The portfolio consisting of an umbrella maker and a sun-tan lotion manufacturer is the portfolio for all seasons expression of this idea. The hard part is to predict in advance how various assets will correlate with one another, no matter how trustworthy their past histories have been on this score. Prestigious investors have become notorious for betting the ranch on their ability to predict correlations. It did not help that they backed up the forecasts of their models with tons of borrowed money, insuring that if they were wrong for only a short time, the mistake would still be lethal.

Some value investors have diversified by taking advantage of the low correlation between the overall stock market and what we can call event-driven investments. Arbitrage positions, investments in companies being taken over or in newly spun-off divisions, investments in securities of companies in Chapter 11, investments in companies in the process of liquidation—all these can offer high returns that do not depend on or relate to the overall direction of the market. Investments in real estate or other hard assets can have the same maverick characteristics. Buying entire companies is one sure way of reducing the correlation between their returns and those of the overall market. Now the investor is the owner of a business, and the gains depend on how well the business does, not on what somebody else will pay for a fractional claim on that business. Berkshire Hathaway under Warren Buffett is the most well known example of direct business ownership by the most esteemed value investor.

Value investors also control risk by continually challenging their own judgments. Since many of their decisions run against the grain of prevailing Wall Street sentiment, they look for some credible confirmation of their opinions. For example, if knowledgeable insiders are buying the securities even as the market ignores the stock, the investor gains a measure of assurance. Though these insiders are not always right and they tend to be early in their purchases, no one outside the firm knows more about its prospects. A second confirmation comes from discovering that other highly respected investors are taking similar positions. Michael Price says that he learned early in the game not to be on the opposite side of a trade from someone like the Pritzkers or Thomas Mellon Evans. When they were buying what he was, he felt assured. Lastly, value investors often ask themselves what divine intervention has granted them this golden opportunity—that is, why, if it is such a screaming value, other investors have not piled in to move up the price. To answer this question, they review their analyses from the search strategy through all the valuation steps, trying to find where they have made an error. Does this situation look like others they have seen that turned out poorly? Is it the kind of value trap—the price gets cheap enough to buy and then stays cheap forever—that has snared them before? Still no iron-clad guarantee of infallibility, this exercise in self-examination is one more check on their wisdom.

Position limits are an additional safeguard. Investors establish policies that limit the amount of the portfolio they will commit to a single security. They can have one limit for the initial purchase and another standard for securities within the portfolio. If a position appreciates above those limits, it is a signal to trim back by selling into strength. This is certainly a form of diversification, but it is designed more to limit the exposure to any particular investment than to mimic the behavior of the broad market. Certain value investors use position limits from the opposite side. They will not buy a security if they are unwilling to invest a meaningful amount, say 5 percent, of their portfolio in it. The intent of this strategy is to insure that they will do all the work necessary to build the confidence they need to take a concentrated position. Not for them is the excuse that since Metapunt, Inc., represents such a small fraction of their assets, they can get by with cursory analysis.

There is another approach to risk management that most value investors avoid. There are short sellers in the money management business, and there are more hedge fund managers who run portfolios composed of long and short positions. At the extreme is a strategy called *market neutral*, in which a balance between long and short is maintained to immunize the portfolio from whatever the market does. The assumption behind all short selling is that the current price of a security is not sustainable, and that as the price falls, the investors will buy back the shares they have sold and make a profit. Short sellers and hedgers use technical, fundamental, and event-oriented analyses to make their selections. One might think that orthodox value investors, armed with their valuation methods, would be well equipped to spot overpriced securities and benefit as reality sets in. The problem is that no one can say with certainty when reality will set in. Benjamin Graham said that in the short run the market is a voting machine, in the long run a weighing machine. What he did not say was when the switch would be made. There are simply too many examples of securities overpriced by all measures of fundamental valuation that proceed to double or triple for a value investor to feel confident that he or she has called the top. And short positions are an added threat because the higher the price rises, the more significant a portion of the portfolio they become.

Finally, value managers are sometimes faced with the decision about what to do with the funds entrusted to them when they can find no more suitable places to put their money. In the worst case, the markets may be so extremely overpriced that there are no identifiable value opportunities. There are less extreme situations that also present challenges. Consider a value investment firm that has $100 million in assets. The portfolio managers have found enough value stocks or other investments to absorb $80 million, but everything else they look at seems either overpriced or too uncertain. What do they do with the last $20 million? One answer is to spread it among the existing investments. They may have decided against this course, either because they own full positions that they are reluctant to increase, or because the prices have risen to the point where, although they don't want to sell, perhaps because of the tax consequences, they won't buy any more either. For investment managers not of the value stripe, this problem may not emerge. They can live with a policy to be always fully invested, and they can at any time find securities that are "relatively" cheap or meet other comparative standards. Most value investors avoid the "relative" path.

The standard response of value investors has been expressed by Warren Buffett in his frequently cited baseball analogy. The investor can take pitches all day long and not have to swing because there are no called strikes in investing. Thus, it is reasonable to regard the paucity of new opportunities as a sign that the market as a whole is overvalued. This is not a market timing call made on the basis of a macroeconomic forecast or a broad valuation metric like the price to earnings ratio of the S&P 500. It is the result of a bottom up search for good investments that, at this moment, comes up empty. But the consequences may be identical. If the market is overvalued, it is a good time to hold cash, the risk-free asset, and wait until opportunities reappear. Cash for value investors has been the *default* default strategy; it may be the best place to keep the money, and the buildup of cash may serve, much like a miner's canary, as a sign that things are not right.

But in this investment climate, where they publish the scores every day, that may be a luxury that not all investment managers can afford. Had Berkshire Hathaway been an open-ended mutual fund rather than a corporation with publicly traded securities, many investors would have pulled money out after 1999 and into 2000, a period in which the company's stock declined by about half in the face of a rising market. In the last years of the 1990s, some value managers saw their asset base plummet as investors took their money out to pursue the higher returns being achieved in techno-growth funds or similar products. For nothing more elevated than career preservation purposes, some value managers may need a default strategy other than holding cash.

This brings us by a circuitous route back to modern investment theory and the efficient market hypothesis. Value investors would not be in business if they did not believe that fundamental analysis done from the value perspective can, in some but not all cases, identify an intrinsic value for a security that varies substantially from the price Mr. Market is quoting. Information and understanding do make a difference. But when the value investor's search for new ideas fails to turn up anything promising, then the default option may indeed be a broad-based index fund or some variant of it. If the manager is being measured against other equity managers, the option of sitting with large amounts of cash may not be wise. The justification for holding an index fund as a portion of the portfolio is straightforward. Historically, the stock market has outperformed bonds or cash over most five-year periods.[2] In the absence of particular knowledge or information, an index is indeed the best choice available. In fact, if the manager has no special insights at all, then the index is the choice for the entire portfolio, in which case the manager is superfluous. The case for active management of whatever persuasion only makes sense when the manager knows or understands more than the market. When that ceases to be the case, then it may be time to defer to Mr. Market.

[2] Between 1871 and 1992, stocks outperformed bonds in 71 percent of all five-year periods. They outperformed Treasury bills in 75 percent of the periods. See Siegel in References, Chapter 8.

PART III

VALUE INVESTING IN PRACTICE

Profiles of Eight Value Investors

In the chapters that follow, we turn from the economic foundations of value investing to look in detail at what some value investors actually do when they are at work. Our investors range in age from over 90 to under 35, providing evidence that not only is value investing as a discipline alive and well, but that choosing value investing as a discipline may make for a long life. Three of our investors worked for or with Benjamin Graham. Four attended Columbia Business School, taking courses with either Graham himself or his successors at that institution. Michael Price and Seth Klarman occupy a different branch on the value investing tree. Both worked with Max Heine, another legend in the field who was noted particularly for his expertise in bankruptcy investing and was a member of an informal network of value investors in New York City that also included Graham, Walter Schloss, and Robert Heilbrunn.

The world of value investing extends beyond this group portrait of people who, intellectually at least, may be considered cousins by training and affinity. Nevertheless, we do not need to leave the confines of this crowd to witness divergent styles of value investing. Some of the investors profiled here invest only in superior businesses that they intend to own for decades, if not forever. Others are looking for damaged goods that have been thrown on a rubbish heap, even though the assets or businesses are still worth something. Some investors run portfolios with six or eight stocks, others will own more than a hundred companies at any one time. Some of them buy the bonds of companies headed for or already in bankruptcy, thinking that either the bonds will be redeemed for more than their cost or that they will end up owning equity in a reorganized company as it emerges from bankruptcy. Some seek to avoid the crowd by concentrating on small and tiny companies; others prefer the stability and predictability of established firms with good businesses. Some try to buy shares in companies that they feel will command a premium from an industrial purchaser who wants to own the whole firm. Others play that role themselves and purchase the entire company.

There are many dimensions along which value investors differ from one another in how they select their companies: size, quality, growth prospects, asset backing, location (domestic only or more international), and so on. They also differ on how they assemble their portfolios: broadly diversified, industry-weighted to take advantage of a circle of competence, moderately concentrated, or tightly focused. We have located the eight investors profiled here, and a few additional ones, in the figure on the next page. This organization puts most emphasis on the "quality of company" dimension. The quality dimension entails preferences concerning valuation approaches (assets, earnings, growth), the breadth of the portfolio (better companies generally mean more concentration), and the expected time for holding the shares (for the deeply discounted stock, until they recover; for the great companies, forever).

The investors whose names are in italics are not profiled here. In addition to Benjamin Graham, they include the late Max Heine, manager of Mutual Shares; the advisory and brokerage firm of Tweedy, Browne, manager of Tweedy Browne American Value and Global Value mutual funds; John Neff, for many years the manager of the Windsor Fund; Charles Royce of Royce and Associates, managers of a stable of mutual funds; Joel Greenblatt, author of *You Can Be a Stock Market Genius: (Even If You're Not Too Smart)*; Martin Whitman, manager of the Third Avenue funds and author of *Value Investing: A Balanced Approach*; and William Ruane and Richard Cuniff, long-time managers of the Sequoia Fund.

The descriptive tags are intended to express some key elements of the investment approaches of each group of money managers. Knowledgeable readers may differ with many of these descriptions and categorizations. Placing the investors within these groups is a little like herding cats, and choosing the appropriate terms to describe each camp is a mug's game— that is, fruitless but still fun to play.

One final word of caution: Investing may not be neurosurgery or particle physics, but it isn't child's play either. The professionals we have profiled here, and many other skilled and dedicated money managers, spend years mastering their craft and hours each day practicing it. The easy availability of real-time security prices and inexpensive trading has convinced many otherwise sensible people that investing on their own will provide both enjoyment and profit. A barrage of advertisements shows us how simple it is to trade; it fails to mention how difficult it is to know what to trade. If the proponents of the efficient market hypothesis are correct, then *on average* no great harm will come from this enterprise. But tuitions are

APPROACHES TO VALUE INVESTING

CLASSIC	MIXED	CONTEMPORARY
Graham	*Gabelli*	**Buffett**
Tweedy, Browne	*Neff*	Greenberg
Schloss & Schloss	Price	*Ruane, Cuniff*
Heine	*Royce*	
Heilbrunn	*Greenblatt*	
Klarman	*Whitman*	
Sonkin		
Diversified portfolio	Replacement value	Concentrated portfolio
Tangible assets	Sufficient research	Intense research
Cursory research	Private market value	Franchise value
Unpresentable	Catalyst	Attractive but not sexy
"Wounded ducks"	Relative value	Owning the business
In the shadows	Bland	"Wounded eagles"
	Normalized earnings	Hiding in plain site
	Temporarily offstage	

paid and retirements are funded not on average but by specific people from particular accounts.

We think that direct and active investing is a dangerous game, not a trick one can do casually at home. After all, Mr. Market is merely the alias for the collectivity of investors. When Mr. Market creates opportunities for value investors by overreacting to information or otherwise lunging to an extreme, most participants are part of that herd, not the few standing to the side. To recall a piece of wisdom Warren Buffett frequently cites, if you have been in the poker game for thirty minutes and still don't know who the patsy is, you can be pretty certain the patsy is you.

Chapter 9

Warren Buffett
Investing Is Allocating Capital

Few will dispute the claim that Warren Buffett is the most illustrious investor, ever. The recognition he has earned rests both on the exceptional returns he has provided for his partners and shareholders over more than four decades and on his singular ability to explain the intricacies of his craft in a manner as long on clarity, modesty, and humor as it is short on pretense or self-exaltation. In the years he ran his limited partnerships, from 1956 through 1969, and beginning again in 1977 as chairman of Berkshire Hathaway, Buffett has written annual letters that report both the major choices he has made during the year and, of more permanent significance, the investment philosophy that has guided his actions. To say that these letters are a rich source of investment wisdom is to understate their true worth, as all the authors who collect royalties on books mined from this correspondence will attest.

While we have written the profiles on the other investors we discuss in this book, we thought it wiser to let Warren Buffett speak for himself. We have selected passages from the letters during the Berkshire Hathaway years and organized them to reveal what we consider the most significant elements of Buffett's approach to investing. The full text of these letters is available on request from Berkshire Hathaway and may be read and downloaded from the company's Web site. All the material is copyrighted by Warren Buffett, and it is quoted here with his permission.

In addition to the selection and organization of these excerpts, we will confine our contribution to three remarks about Buffett as an investor. First, as he himself says frequently in the letters, his association with his Berkshire partner Charlie Munger helped to move him away from an orthodox Benjamin Graham preference for buying assets at a deep discount to their value, no matter how miserable the company in which they were found, to buying good or excellent businesses at a reasonable price. While Buffett in the Berkshire years still speaks with reverence about Graham, he looks for companies that have impregnable franchises even though they may sell for multiples of their book value.

Second, while many investors say that they think of themselves as buying businesses rather than stocks or bonds, Buffett really means it. Berkshire Hathaway itself is a hybrid; it owns some businesses outright, including a number of insurance companies, and it has large investments in companies whose shares are still publicly traded. Carol Loomis, an observer and friend of Buffett for many years, wrote that

> the key point about the two Buffetts, the investor and the businessman, is that they look at the ownership of businesses in exactly the same way. The investor sees the chance to buy *portions* of a business in the stock market at a price below intrinsic value—that is, below what a rational buyer would pay to own the entire establishment. The manager sees the chance to buy the *whole* business at no more than intrinsic value.
>
> The kind of merchandise that Buffett wants is simply described also: "good businesses." To him that essentially means operations with strong franchises, above-average returns on equity, a relatively small need for capital investment, and the capacity therefore to throw off cash. That list may sound like motherhood and apple pie. But finding and buying such businesses isn't easy; Buffett likens the hunt to bagging "rare and fast-moving elephants."

Or, to say the same thing in somewhat different terms, no matter what he is buying, Buffett sees investing as allocating capital.

Finally, value investors share the conviction that they are most successful when they stay within their circle of competence. Buffett speaks repeatedly of looking for businesses that he can understand, and his avoidance of companies whose fortunes depend on their technological excellence is well chronicled. Operating within the confines of businesses that he definitely does understand, which include insurance, media companies, and consumer goods firms, he has earned a lot of money for himself and for those who have invested with him over the years. It may seem odd to claim that the greatest investor, ever, has made fortunes by following the humble precept of sticking to his knitting, and surely his superiority stems from more than adhering to this rule. Still, the gallery of investors is replete with geniuses who stumbled when they wandered away from their zones of excellence. Just as Coca-Cola discovered it was better at making and selling soft drinks than at producing films, Buffett has had the genius to recognize the boundaries of his own franchise.

General Principles

In 1996 Warren Buffett wrote and distributed "An Owner's Manual" in order to "explain Berkshire's broad economic principles of operation." Among these principles we find the following especially significant for understanding Buffett as a value investor:

Berkshire Hathaway as a Conduit

Although our form is corporate, our attitude is partnership. Charlie Munger and I think of our shareholders as owner-partners, and of ourselves as managing partners. (Because of the size of our shareholdings we are also, for better or worse, controlling partners.) We do not view the company itself as the ultimate owner of our business assets but instead view the company as a conduit through which our shareholders own the assets.

"We Eat Our Own Cooking"

In line with Berkshire's owner-orientation, most of our directors have a major portion of their net worth invested in the company. We eat our own cooking. . . . Charlie and I feel totally comfortable with this eggs-in-one-basket situation because Berkshire itself owns a wide variety of truly extraordinary businesses. Indeed, we believe that Berkshire is close to being unique in the quality and diversity of the businesses in which it owns either a controlling interest or a minority interest of significance.

Charlie and I cannot promise you results. But we can guarantee that your financial fortunes will move in lockstep with ours for whatever period of time you elect to be our partner.

Maximize Gain in Intrinsic Business Value

Our long-term economic goal (subject to some qualifications mentioned later) is to maximize Berkshire's average annual rate of gain in intrinsic business value on a per-share basis. We do not measure the economic significance or performance of Berkshire by its size; we measure by per-share progress. We are certain that the rate of per-share progress will diminish in the future—a greatly enlarged capital base will see to that. But we will be disappointed if our rate does not exceed that of the average large American corporation.

Definition of Intrinsic Value

Intrinsic value can be defined simply: It is the discounted value of the cash that can be taken out of a business during its remaining life. The calculation of intrinsic value, though, is not so simple. As our definition suggests, intrinsic value is an estimate rather than a precise figure, and it is additionally an estimate that must be changed if interest rates move or forecasts of future cash flows are revised. Two people looking at the same set of facts, moreover—and this would apply even to Charlie and me—will almost inevitably come up with at least slightly different intrinsic value figures. That is one reason we never give you our estimates of intrinsic value.

Control and Portfolio Investments Each Play a Part

Our preference would be to reach our goal by directly owning a diversified group of businesses that generate cash and consistently earn above-average returns on capital. Our second choice is to own parts of similar businesses, attained primarily through purchases of marketable common stocks by our insurance subsidiaries. The price and availability of businesses and the need for insurance capital determine any given year's capital allocation.

Additional principles can be found in the annual letters:

Equity Investment Strategy = Evaluate the Business in Its Entirety (from 1992 letter)

Our equity-investing strategy remains little changed from what it was fifteen years ago, when we said in the 1977 annual report: "We select our marketable equity securities in much the way we would evaluate a business for acquisition in its entirety. We want the business to be one (a) that we can understand; (b) with favorable long-term prospects; (c) operated by honest and competent people; and (d) available at a very attractive price." We have seen cause to make only one change in this creed: Because of both market conditions and our size, we now substitute "an attractive price" for "a very attractive price."

But how, you will ask, does one decide what's "attractive"? In answering this question, most analysts feel they must choose between two approaches customarily thought to be in opposition: "value" and "growth." Indeed, many investment professionals see any mixing of the two terms as a form of intellectual cross-dressing.

We view that as fuzzy thinking (in which, it must be confessed, I myself engaged some years ago). In our opinion, the two approaches are joined at the hip: Growth is always a component in the calculation of value, constituting a variable whose importance can range from negligible to enormous and whose impact can be negative as well as positive.

In addition, we think the very term "value investing" is redundant. What is "investing" if it is not the act of seeking value at least sufficient to justify the amount paid? Consciously paying more for a stock than its calculated value—in the hope that it can soon be sold for a still-higher price—should be labeled speculation (which is neither illegal, immoral, nor—in our view—financially fattening).

Whether appropriate or not, the term "value investing" is widely used. Typically, it connotes the purchase of stocks having attributes such as a low ratio of price to book value, a low price-earnings ratio, or a high dividend yield. Unfortunately, such characteristics, even if they appear in combination, are far from determinative as to whether an investor is indeed buying something for what it is worth and is therefore truly operating on the principle of obtaining value in his investments. Correspondingly, opposite characteristics—a high ratio of price to book value, a high price-earnings ratio, and a low dividend yield—are in no way inconsistent with a "value" purchase.

Similarly, business growth, per se, tells us little about value. It's true that growth often has a positive impact on value, sometimes one of spectacular proportions. But such an effect is far from certain. For example, investors have regularly poured money into the domestic airline business to finance profitless (or worse) growth. For these investors, it would have been far better if Orville had failed to get off the ground at Kitty Hawk: The more the industry has grown, the worse the disaster for owners.

Growth benefits investors only when the business in point can invest at incremental returns that are enticing—in other words, only when each dollar used to finance the growth creates over a dollar of long-term market value. In the case of a low-return business requiring incremental funds, growth hurts the investor.

In *The Theory of Investment Value*, written over 50 years ago, John Burr Williams set forth the equation for value, which we condense here: The value of any stock, bond or business today is determined by the cash inflows and outflows—discounted at an appropriate interest rate—that can be expected to occur during the remaining life of the asset. Note that the formula is the same for stocks as for bonds. Even so, there is an important, and difficult to deal with, difference between the two: A bond has a coupon and maturity date that define future cash flows; but in the case of equities, the investment analyst must himself estimate the future "coupons." Furthermore, the quality of management affects the bond coupon only rarely—chiefly when management is so inept or dishonest that payment of interest is suspended. In contrast, the ability of management can dramatically affect the equity "coupons."

The investment shown by the discounted-flows-of-cash calculation to be the cheapest is the one that the investor should purchase—irrespective of whether the business grows or doesn't, displays volatility or smoothness in its earnings, or carries a high price or low in relation to its current earnings and book value. Moreover, though the value equation has usually shown equities to be cheaper than bonds, that result is not inevitable: When bonds are calculated to be the more attractive investment, they should be bought.

Leaving the question of price aside, the best business to own is one that over an extended period can employ large amounts of incremental capital at very high rates of return. The worst business to own is one that must, or will, do the opposite—that is, consistently employ ever-greater amounts of capital at very low rates of return. Unfortunately, the first type of business is very hard to find: Most high-return businesses need relatively little capital. Shareholders of such a business usually will benefit if it pays out most of its earnings in dividends or makes significant stock repurchases.

Though the mathematical calculations required to evaluate equities are not difficult, an analyst—even one who is experienced and intelligent—can easily go wrong in estimating future "coupons." At Berkshire, we attempt to deal with this problem in two ways. First, we try to stick to businesses we believe we understand. That means they must be relatively simple and stable in character. If a business is complex or subject to constant change, we're not smart enough to predict future cash flows. Incidentally, that shortcoming doesn't bother us. What counts for most people in investing is not how much they know, but rather how realistically they define what they don't know. An investor needs to do very few things right as long as he or she avoids big mistakes.

Second, and equally important, we insist on a margin of safety in our purchase price. If we calculate the value of a common stock to be only slightly higher than its price, we're not interested in buying. We believe this margin-of-safety principle, so strongly emphasized by Ben Graham, to be the cornerstone of investment success.

Increasing Wealth is Not the Same as Increasing Size (from 1992 letter)

We have a firm policy about issuing shares of Berkshire, doing so only when we receive as much value as we give. Equal value, however, has not been easy to obtain, since we have always valued our shares highly. So be it: We wish to increase Berkshire's size only when doing that also increases the wealth of its owners.

Those two objectives do not necessarily go hand-in-hand as an amusing but value-destroying experience in our past illustrates. On that occasion, we had a significant investment in a bank whose management was hell-bent on expansion. (Aren't they all?) When our bank wooed a smaller bank, its owner demanded a stock swap on a basis that valued the acquiree's net worth and earning power at over twice that of the acquirer's. Our management—visibly in heat—quickly capitulated. The owner of the acquiree then insisted on one other condition: "You must promise me," he said in effect, "that once our merger is done and I have become a major shareholder, you'll never again make a deal this dumb."

Diversification and Concentration; Risk and Return (from 1993 letter)

The strategy we've adopted precludes our following standard diversification dogma. Many pundits would therefore say the strategy must be riskier than that employed by more conventional investors. We disagree. We believe that a policy of portfolio concentration may well decrease risk if it raises, as it should, both the intensity with which an investor thinks about a business and the comfort-level he must feel with its economic characteristics before buying into it. In stating this opinion, we define risk, using dictionary terms, as "the possibility of loss or injury."

Academics, however, like to define investment "risk" differently, averring that it is the relative volatility of a stock or portfolio of stocks—that is, their volatility as compared to that of a large universe of stocks. Employing data bases and statistical skills, these academics compute with precision the "beta" of a stock—its relative volatility in the past—and then build arcane investment and capital-allocation theories around this calculation. In their hunger for a single statistic to measure risk, however, they forget a fundamental principle: It is better to be approximately right than precisely wrong.

For owners of a business—and that's the way we think of shareholders—the academics' definition of risk is far off the mark, so much so that it produces absurdities. For example, under beta-based theory, a stock that has dropped very sharply compared to the market—as had Washington Post when we bought it in 1973—becomes "riskier" at the lower price than it was at the higher price. Would that description have then made any sense to someone who was offered the entire company at a vastly reduced price?

In fact, the true investor welcomes volatility. Ben Graham explained why in Chapter 8 of *The Intelligent Investor*. There he introduced "Mr. Market," an obliging fellow who shows up every day to either buy from you or sell to you, whichever you wish. The more manic-depressive this chap is, the greater the opportunities available to the investor. That's true because a wildly fluctuating market means that irrationally low prices will periodically be attached to solid businesses. It is impossible to see how the availability of such prices can be thought of as increasing the hazards for an investor who is totally free to either ignore the market or exploit its folly.

In assessing risk, a beta purist will disdain examining what a company produces, what its competitors are doing, or how much borrowed money the business employs. He may even prefer not to know the company's name. What he treasures is the price history of its stock. In contrast, we'll happily forgo knowing the price history and instead will seek whatever information will further our understanding of the company's business. After we buy a stock, consequently, we would not be disturbed if markets closed for a year or two. We don't need a daily quote on our 100% position in See's or H. H. Brown to validate our well-being. Why, then, should we need a quote on our 7% interest in Coke?

In our opinion, the real risk that an investor must assess is whether his aggregate after-tax receipts from an investment (including those he receives on sale) will, over his prospective holding period, give him at least as much purchasing power as he had to begin with, plus a modest rate of interest on that initial stake. Though this risk cannot be calculated with engineering precision, it can in some cases be judged with a degree of accuracy that is useful. The primary factors bearing upon this evaluation are:

1) The certainty with which the long-term economic characteristics of the business can be evaluated;

2) The certainty with which management can be evaluated, both as to its ability to realize the full potential of the business and to wisely employ its cash flows;

3) The certainty with which management can be counted on to channel the rewards from the business to the shareholders rather than to itself;

4) The purchase price of the business;

5) The levels of taxation and inflation that will be experienced and that will determine the degree by which an investor's purchasing-power return is reduced from his gross return.

These factors will probably strike many analysts as unbearably fuzzy, since they cannot be extracted from a data base of any kind. But the difficulty of precisely quantifying these matters does not negate their importance nor is it insuperable. Just as Justice Stewart found it impossible to formulate a test for obscenity but nevertheless asserted, "I know it when I see it," so also can investors—in an inexact but useful way—"see" the risks inherent in certain investments without reference to complex equations or price histories.

Acquisitions and Investments: Same Rules for Both (from 1978 letter)

We get excited enough to commit a big percentage of insurance company net worth to equities only when we find (1) businesses we can understand, (2) with favorable long-term prospects, (3) operated by honest and competent people, and (4) priced very attractively. We usually can identify a small number of potential investments meeting requirements (1), (2) and (3), but (4) often prevents action. For example, in 1971 our total common stock position at Berkshire's insurance subsidiaries amounted to only $10.7 million at cost, and $11.7 million at market. There were equities of identifiably excellent companies available—but very few at interesting prices. (An irresistible footnote: in 1971, pension fund managers invested a record 122% of net funds available in equities—at full prices they couldn't buy enough of them. In 1974, after the bottom had fallen out, they committed a then record low of 21% to stocks.)

The past few years have been a different story for us. At the end of 1975 our insurance subsidiaries held common equities with a market value exactly equal to cost of $39.3 million. At the end of 1978 this position had been increased to equities (including a convertible preferred) with a cost of $129.1 million and a market value of $216.5 million. During the intervening three years we also had realized pre-tax gains from common equities of approximately $24.7 million. Therefore, our overall unrealized and realized pre-tax gains in equities for the three year period came to approximately $112 million. During this same interval the Dow-Jones Industrial Average declined from 852 to 805. It was a marvelous period for the value-oriented equity buyer.

We continue to find for our insurance portfolios small portions of really outstanding businesses that are available, through the auction pricing mechanism of security markets, at prices dramatically cheaper than the valuations inferior businesses command on negotiated sales.

This program of acquisition of small fractions of businesses (common stocks) at bargain prices, for which little enthusiasm exists, contrasts sharply with general corporate acquisition activity, for which much enthusiasm exists. It seems quite clear to us that either corporations are making very significant mistakes in purchasing entire businesses at prices prevailing in negotiated transactions and takeover bids, or that we eventually are going to make considerable sums of money buying small portions of such businesses at the greatly discounted valuations prevailing in the stock market. (A second footnote: In 1978 pension managers, a group that logically should maintain the longest of investment perspectives, put only 9% of net available funds into equities—breaking the record low figure set in 1974 and tied in 1977.)

(same topic continued, from 1981 letter)

General Acquisition Behavior

As our history indicates, we are comfortable both with total ownership of businesses and with marketable securities representing small portions of businesses. We continually look for ways to employ large sums in each area. (But we try to avoid small commitments—"If something's not worth doing at all, it's not worth doing well.") Indeed, the liquidity requirements of our insurance and trading stamp businesses mandate major investments in marketable securities.

Our acquisition decisions will be aimed at maximizing real economic benefits, not at maximizing either managerial domain or reported numbers for accounting purposes. (In the long run, managements stressing accounting appearance over economic substance usually achieve little of either.)

Regardless of the impact upon immediately reportable earnings, we would rather buy 10% of Wonderful Business T at X per share than 100% of T at 2X per share. Most corporate managers prefer just the reverse, and have no shortage of stated rationales for their behavior.

However, we suspect three motivations—usually unspoken—to be, singly or in combination, the important ones in most high-premium takeovers:

1) Leaders, business or otherwise, seldom are deficient in animal spirits and often relish increased activity and challenge. At Berkshire, the corporate pulse never beats faster than when an acquisition is in prospect.

2) Most organizations, business or otherwise, measure themselves, are measured by others, and compensate their managers far more by the yardstick of size than by any other yardstick. (Ask a Fortune 500 manager where his corporation stands on that famous list and, invariably, the number responded will be from the list ranked by size of sales; he may well not even know where his corporation places on the list Fortune just as faithfully compiles ranking the same 500 corporations by profitability.)

3) Many managements apparently were overexposed in impressionable childhood years to the story in which the imprisoned handsome prince is released from a toad's body by a kiss from a beautiful princess. Consequently, they are certain their managerial kiss will do wonders for the profitability of Company T(arget).

Such optimism is essential. Absent that rosy view, why else should the shareholders of Company A(cquisitor) want to own an interest in T at the 2X takeover cost rather than at the X market price they would pay if they made direct purchases on their own?

In other words, investors can always buy toads at the going price for toads. If investors instead bankroll princesses who wish to pay double for the right to kiss the toad, those kisses had better pack some real dynamite. We've observed many kisses but very few miracles. Nevertheless, many managerial princesses remain serenely confident about the future potency of their kisses—even after their corporate backyards are knee-deep in unresponsive toads. . . .

Berkshire Acquisition Objectives

We will continue to seek the acquisition of businesses in their entirety at prices that will make sense, even should the future of the acquired enterprise develop much along the lines of its past. We may very well pay a fairly fancy price for a Category 1 business [those that can increase prices without fear of losing market share or unit volume] if we are reasonably confident of what we are getting. But we will not normally pay a lot in any purchase for what we are supposed to bring to the party—for we find that we ordinarily don't bring a lot.

During 1981 we came quite close to a major purchase involving both a business and a manager we liked very much. However, the price finally demanded, considering alternative uses for the funds involved, would have left our owners worse off than before the purchase. The empire would have been larger, but the citizenry would have been poorer.

Dividend Policy (from 1984 letter)

Dividend policy is often reported to shareholders, but seldom explained. A company will say something like, "Our goal is to pay out 40% to 50% of earnings and to increase dividends at a rate at least equal to the rise in the CPI." And that's it—no analysis will be supplied as to why that particular policy is best for the owners of the business. Yet, allocation of capital is crucial to business and investment management. Because it is, we believe managers and owners should think hard about the circumstances under which earnings should be retained and under which they should be distributed.

The first point to understand is that all earnings are not created equal. In many businesses, particularly those that have high asset/profit ratios, inflation causes some or all of the reported earnings to become ersatz. The ersatz portion—let's call these earnings "restricted"—cannot, if the business is to retain its economic position, be distributed as dividends. Were these earnings to be paid out, the business would lose ground in one or more of the following areas: its ability to maintain its unit volume of sales, its long-term competitive position, its financial strength. No matter how conservative its payout ratio, a company that consistently distributes restricted earnings is destined for oblivion unless equity capital is otherwise infused.

Restricted earnings are seldom valueless to owners, but they often must be discounted heavily. In effect, they are conscripted by the business, no matter how poor its economic potential. (This retention-no-matter-how-unattractive-the-return situation was communicated unwittingly in a marvelously ironic way by Consolidated Edison a decade ago. At the time, a punitive regulatory policy was a major factor causing the company's stock to sell as low as one-fourth of book value; i.e., every time a dollar of earnings was retained for reinvestment in the business, that dollar was transformed into only 25 cents of market value. But, despite this gold-into-lead process, most earnings were reinvested in the business rather than paid to owners. Meanwhile, at construction and maintenance sites throughout New York, signs proudly proclaimed the corporate slogan, "Dig We Must.")

Restricted earnings need not concern us further in this dividend discussion. Let's turn to the much-more-valued unrestricted variety. These earnings may, with equal feasibility, be retained or distributed. In our opinion, management should choose whichever course makes greater sense for the owners of the business.

This principle is not universally accepted. For a number of reasons managers like to withhold unrestricted, readily distributable earnings from shareholders—to expand the corporate empire over which the managers rule, to operate from a position of exceptional financial comfort, etc. But we believe there is only one valid reason for retention. Unrestricted earnings should be retained only when there is a reasonable prospect—backed preferably by historical evidence or, when appropriate, by a thoughtful analysis of the future—that for every dollar retained by the corporation, at least one dollar of market value will be created for owners. This will happen only if the capital retained produces incremental earnings equal to, or above, those generally available to investors. . . .

In judging whether managers should retain earnings, shareholders should not simply compare total incremental earnings in recent years to total incremental capital because that relationship may be distorted by what is going on in a core business. During an inflationary period, companies with a core business characterized by extraordinary economics can use small amounts of incremental capital in that business at very high rates of return (as was discussed in last year's section on Goodwill). But, unless they are experiencing tremendous unit growth, outstanding businesses by definition generate large amounts of excess cash. If a company sinks most of this money in other businesses that earn low returns, the company's overall return on retained capital may nevertheless appear excellent because of the extraordinary returns being earned by the portion of earnings incrementally invested in the core business. The situation is analogous to a Pro-Am golf event: Even if all of the amateurs are hopeless duffers, the team's best-ball score will be respectable because of the dominating skills of the professional.

Capital Allocation, Control Investment, and Taxes (from 1987 letter)

In making both control purchases and stock purchases, we try to buy not only good businesses, but ones run by high-grade, talented and likeable managers. If we make a mistake about the managers we link up with, the controlled company offers a certain advantage because we have the power to effect change. In practice, however, this advantage is somewhat illusory: Management changes, like marital changes, are painful, time-consuming and chancy. . . .

I would say that the controlled company offers two main advantages. First, when we control a company we get to allocate capital, whereas we are likely to have little or nothing to say about this process with marketable holdings. This point can be important because the heads of many companies are not skilled in capital allocation. Their inadequacy is not surprising. Most bosses rise to the top because they have excelled in an area such as marketing, production, engineering, administration or, sometimes, institutional politics.

Once they become CEOs, they face new responsibilities. They now must make capital allocation decisions, a critical job that they may have never tackled and that is not easily mastered. To stretch the point, it's as if the final step for a highly-talented musician was not to perform at Carnegie Hall but, instead, to be named Chairman of the Federal Reserve.

The lack of skill that many CEOs have at capital allocation is no small matter: After ten years on the job, a CEO whose company annually retains earnings equal to 10% of net worth will have been responsible for the deployment of more than 60% of all the capital at work in the business.

CEOs who recognize their lack of capital-allocation skills (which not all do) will often try to compensate by turning to their staffs, management consultants, or investment bankers. Charlie and I have frequently observed the consequences of such "help." On balance, we feel it is more likely to accentuate the capital-allocation problem than to solve it. . . .

The second advantage of a controlled company over a marketable security has to do with taxes. Berkshire, as a corporate holder, absorbs some significant tax costs through the ownership of partial positions that we do not when our ownership is 80%, or greater. Such tax disadvantages have long been with us, but changes in the tax code caused them to increase significantly during the past year. As a consequence, a given business result can now deliver Berkshire financial results that are as much as 50% better if they come from an 80%-or-greater holding rather than from a lesser holding.

The disadvantages of owning marketable securities are sometimes offset by a huge advantage: Occasionally the stock market offers us the chance to buy non-controlling pieces of extraordinary businesses at truly ridiculous prices—dramatically below those commanded in negotiated transactions that transfer control. For example, we purchased our Washington Post stock in 1973 at $5.63 per share, and per-share operating earnings in 1987 after taxes were $10.30. Similarly, our GEICO stock was purchased in 1976, 1979 and 1980 at an average of $6.67 per share, and after-tax operating earnings per share last year were $9.01. In cases such as these, Mr. Market has proven to be a mighty good friend.

Even Homer Nods, or Why Good Businesses Are Better than Poor Ones (from 1989 letter)

Mistakes of the First Twenty-Five Years (A Condensed Version)
To quote Robert Benchley, "Having a dog teaches a boy fidelity, perseverance, and to turn around three times before lying down." Such are the shortcomings of experience. Nevertheless, it's a good idea to review past mistakes before committing new ones. So let's take a quick look at the last 25 years.

• My first mistake, of course, was in buying control of Berkshire. Though I knew its business—textile manufacturing—to be unpromising, I was enticed to buy because the price looked cheap. Stock purchases of that kind had proved reasonably rewarding in my early years, though by the time Berkshire came along in 1965 I was becoming aware that the strategy was not ideal.

If you buy a stock at a sufficiently low price, there will usually be some hiccup in the fortunes of the business that gives you a chance to unload at a decent profit, even though the long-term performance of the business may be terrible. I call this the "cigar butt" approach to investing. A cigar butt found on the street that has only one puff left in it may not offer much of a smoke, but the "bargain purchase" will make that puff all profit.

Unless you are a liquidator, that kind of approach to buying businesses is foolish. First, the original "bargain" price probably will not turn out to be such a steal after all. In a difficult business, no sooner is one problem solved than another surfaces—never is there just one cockroach in the kitchen. Second, any initial advantage you secure will be quickly eroded by the low return that the business earns. For example, if you buy a business for $8 million that can be sold or liquidated for $10 million and promptly take either course, you can realize a high return. But the investment will disappoint if the business is sold for $10 million in ten years and in the interim has annually earned and distributed only a few percent on cost. Time is the friend of the wonderful business, the enemy of the mediocre.

You might think this principle is obvious, but I had to learn it the hard way—in fact, I had to learn it several times over. Shortly after purchasing Berkshire, I acquired a Baltimore department store, Hochschild Kohn, buying through a company called Diversified Retailing that later merged with Berkshire. I bought at a substantial discount from book value, the people were first-class, and the deal included some extras—unrecorded real estate values and a significant LIFO inventory cushion. How could I miss? So-o-o—three years later I was lucky to sell the business for about what I had paid. After ending our corporate marriage to Hochschild Kohn, I had memories like those of the husband in the country song, "My Wife Ran Away With My Best Friend and I Still Miss Him a Lot."

I could give you other personal examples of "bargain-purchase" folly but I'm sure you get the picture: It's far better to buy a wonderful company at a fair price than a fair company at a wonderful price. Charlie understood this early; I was a slow learner. But now, when buying companies or common stocks, we look for first-class businesses accompanied by first-class managements.

• That leads right into a related lesson: Good jockeys will do well on good horses, but not on broken-down nags. Both Berkshire's textile business and Hochschild Kohn had able and honest people running them. The same managers employed in a business with good economic characteristics would have achieved fine records. But they were never going to make any progress while running in quicksand.

I've said many times that when a management with a reputation for brilliance tackles a business with a reputation for bad economics, it is the reputation of the business that remains intact. I just wish I hadn't been so energetic in creating examples. My behavior has matched that admitted by Mae West: "I was Snow White, but I drifted."

• A further related lesson: Easy does it. After 25 years of buying and supervising a great variety of businesses, Charlie and I have not learned how to solve difficult business problems. What we have learned is to avoid them. To the extent we have been successful, it is because we concentrated on identifying one-foot hurdles that we could step over rather than because we acquired any ability to clear seven-footers. . . .

• My most surprising discovery: the overwhelming importance in business of an unseen force that we might call "the institutional impera-tive." In business school, I was given no hint of the imperative's existence and I did not intuitively understand it when I entered the business world. I thought then that decent, intelligent, and experienced managers would automatically make rational business decisions. But I learned over time that isn't so. Instead, rationality frequently wilts when the institutional im-perative comes into play.

For example: (1) As if governed by Newton's First Law of Motion, an institution will resist any change in its current direction; (2) Just as work expands to fill available time, corporate projects or acquisitions will mate-rialize to soak up available funds; (3) Any business craving of the leader, however foolish, will be quickly supported by detailed rate-of-return and strategic studies prepared by his troops; and (4) The behavior of peer com-panies, whether they are expanding, acquiring, setting executive compen-sation or whatever, will be mindlessly imitated.

Institutional dynamics, not venality or stupidity, set businesses on these courses, which are too often misguided. After making some expen-sive mistakes because I ignored the power of the imperative, I have tried to organize and manage Berkshire in ways that minimize its influence. Fur-thermore, Charlie and I have attempted to concentrate our investments in companies that appear alert to the problem. . . .

- Our consistently-conservative financial policies may appear to have been a mistake, but in my view were not. In retrospect, it is clear that sig-nificantly higher, though still conventional, leverage ratios at Berkshire would have produced considerably better returns on equity than the 23.8% we have actually averaged. Even in 1965, perhaps we could have judged there to be a 99% probability that higher leverage would lead to nothing but good. Correspondingly, we might have seen only a 1% chance that some shock factor, external or internal, would cause a conventional debt ratio to produce a result falling somewhere between temporary anguish and default.

We wouldn't have liked those 99:1 odds—and never will. A small chance of distress or disgrace cannot, in our view, be offset by a large chance of extra returns. If your actions are sensible, you are certain to get good results; in most such cases, leverage just moves things along faster.

Charlie and I have never been in a big hurry: We enjoy the process far more than the proceeds—though we have learned to live with those also.

Circles of Competence: Buffett's Areas of Expertise

Insurance (from 1977 letter)

It is comforting to be in a business where some mistakes can be made and yet a quite satisfactory overall performance can be achieved. In a sense, this is the opposite case from our textile business where even very good management probably can average only modest results. One of the lessons your management has learned—and, unfortunately, sometimes re-learned—is the importance of being in businesses where tailwinds prevail rather than headwinds.

In 1977 the winds in insurance underwriting were squarely behind us. Very large rate increases were effected throughout the industry in 1976 to offset the disastrous underwriting results of 1974 and 1975. But, because insurance policies typically are written for one-year periods, with pricing mistakes capable of correction only upon renewal, it was 1977 before the full impact was felt upon earnings of those earlier rate increases.

The pendulum now is beginning to swing the other way. We estimate that costs involved in the insurance areas in which we operate rise at close to 1% per month. This is due to continuous monetary inflation affecting the cost of repairing humans and property, as well as "social inflation," a broadening definition by society and juries of what is covered by insurance policies. Unless rates rise at a comparable 1% per month, underwriting profits must shrink. Recently the pace of rate increases has slowed dramatically, and it is our expectation that underwriting margins generally will be declining by the second half of the year. . . .

Insurance companies offer standardized policies which can be copied by anyone. Their only products are promises. It is not difficult to be licensed, and rates are an open book. There are no important advantages from trademarks, patents, location, corporate longevity, raw material sources, etc., and very little consumer differentiation to produce insulation from competition. It is commonplace, in corporate annual reports, to stress the difference that people make. Sometimes this is true and sometimes it isn't. But there is no question that the nature of the insurance business magnifies the effect which individual managers have on company performance. We are very fortunate to have the group of managers that are associated with us.

Insurance Continued (from 1979 letter)

The conventional wisdom is that insurance underwriting overall will be poor in 1980, but that rates will start to firm in a year or so, leading to a turn in the cycle some time in 1981. We disagree with this view. Present interest rates encourage the obtaining of business at underwriting loss levels formerly regarded as totally unacceptable. Managers decry the folly of underwriting at a loss to obtain investment income, but we believe that many will. Thus we expect that competition will create a new threshold of tolerance for underwriting losses, and that combined ratios will average higher in the future than in the past. . . .

Nevertheless, we believe that insurance can be a very good business. It tends to magnify, to an unusual degree, human managerial talent—or the lack of it. We have a number of managers whose talent is both proven and growing. (And, in addition, we have a very large indirect interest in two truly outstanding management groups through our investments in SAFECO and GEICO.) Thus we expect to do well in insurance over a period of years. However, the business has the potential for really terrible results in a single specific year. If accident frequency should turn around quickly in the auto field, we, along with others, are likely to experience such a year.

Insurance Continued (from 1980 letter)

We have written in past reports about the disappointments that usually result from purchase and operation of "turnaround" businesses. Literally hundreds of turnaround possibilities in dozens of industries have been described to us over the years and, either as participants or as observers, we have tracked performance against expectations. Our conclusion is that, with few exceptions, when a management with a reputation for brilliance tackles a business with a reputation for poor fundamental economics, it is the reputation of the business that remains intact.

GEICO may appear to be an exception, having been turned around from the very edge of bankruptcy in 1976. It certainly is true that managerial brilliance was needed for its resuscitation, and that Jack Byrne, upon arrival in that year, supplied that ingredient in abundance.

But it also is true that the fundamental business advantage that GEICO had enjoyed—an advantage that previously had produced staggering success—was still intact within the company, although submerged in a sea of financial and operating troubles.

GEICO was designed to be the low-cost operation in an enormous marketplace (auto insurance) populated largely by companies whose marketing structures restricted adaptation. Run as designed, it could offer unusual value to its customers while earning unusual returns for itself. For decades it had been run in just this manner. Its troubles in the mid-70s were not produced by any diminution or disappearance of this essential economic advantage.

GEICO's problems at that time put it in a position analogous to that of American Express in 1964 following the salad oil scandal. Both were one-of-a-kind companies, temporarily reeling from the effects of a fiscal blow that did not destroy their exceptional underlying economics. The GEICO and American Express situations, extraordinary business franchises with a localized excisable cancer (needing, to be sure, a skilled surgeon), should be distinguished from the true "turnaround" situation in which the managers expect—and need—to pull off a corporate Pygmalion. . . .

[A] largely unreported but particularly pernicious problem may well prolong and intensify the coming industry agony. It is not only likely to keep many insurers scrambling for business when underwriting losses hit record levels—it is likely to cause them at such a time to redouble their efforts.

This problem arises from the decline in bond prices and the insurance accounting convention that allows companies to carry bonds at amortized cost, regardless of market value. Many insurers own long-term bonds that, at amortized cost, amount to two to three times net worth. If the level is three times, of course, a one-third shrink from cost in bond prices—if it were to be recognized on the books—would wipe out net worth. And shrink they have. Some of the largest and best known property-casualty companies currently find themselves with nominal, or even negative, net worth when bond holdings are valued at market. Of course their bonds could rise in price, thereby partially, or conceivably even fully, restoring the integrity of stated net worth. Or they could fall further. (We believe that short-term forecasts of stock or bond prices are useless. The forecasts may tell you a great deal about the forecaster; they tell you nothing about the future.)

It might strike some as strange that an insurance company's survival is threatened when its stock portfolio falls sufficiently in price to reduce net worth significantly, but that an even greater decline in bond prices produces no reaction at all. The industry would respond by pointing out that, no matter what the current price, the bonds will be paid in full at maturity, thereby eventually eliminating any interim price decline. It may take twenty, thirty, or even forty years, this argument says, but, as long as the bonds don't have to be sold, in the end they'll all be worth face value. Of course, if they are sold—even if they are replaced with similar bonds offering better relative value—the loss must be booked immediately. And, just as promptly, published net worth must be adjusted downward by the amount of the loss.

Under such circumstances, a great many investment options disappear, perhaps for decades. For example, when large underwriting losses are in prospect, it may make excellent business logic for some insurers to shift from tax-exempt bonds into taxable bonds. Unwillingness to recognize major bond losses may be the sole factor that prevents such a sensible move.

But the full implications flowing from massive unrealized bond losses are far more serious than just the immobilization of investment intellect. For the source of funds to purchase and hold those bonds is a pool of money derived from policyholders and claimants (with changing faces)—money which, in effect, is temporarily on deposit with the insurer. As long as this pool retains its size, no bonds must be sold. If the pool of funds shrinks—which it will if the volume of business declines significantly—assets must be sold to pay off the liabilities. And if those assets consist of bonds with big unrealized losses, such losses will rapidly become realized, decimating net worth in the process.

Thus, an insurance company with a bond market value shrinkage approaching stated net worth (of which there are now many) and also faced with inadequate rate levels that are sure to deteriorate further has two options. One option for management is to tell the underwriters to keep pricing according to the exposure involved—"be sure to get a dollar of premium for every dollar of expense cost plus expectable loss cost."

The consequences of this directive are predictable: (a) with most business both price sensitive and renewable annually, many policies presently on the books will be lost to competitors in rather short order; (b) as premium volume shrinks significantly, there will be a lagged but corresponding decrease in liabilities (unearned premiums and claims payable); (c) assets (bonds) must be sold to match the decrease in liabilities; and (d) the formerly unrecognized disappearance of net worth will become partially recognized (depending upon the extent of such sales) in the insurer's published financial statements.

Variations of this depressing sequence involve a smaller penalty to stated net worth. The reaction of some companies at (c) would be to sell either stocks that are already carried at market values or recently purchased bonds involving less severe losses. This ostrich-like behavior—selling the better assets and keeping the biggest losers—while less painful in the short term, is unlikely to be a winner in the long term.

The second option is much simpler: just keep writing business regardless of rate levels and whopping prospective underwriting losses, thereby maintaining the present levels of premiums, assets and liabilities—and then pray for a better day, either for underwriting or for bond prices. There is much criticism in the trade press of "cash flow" underwriting; i.e., writing business regardless of prospective underwriting losses in order to obtain funds to invest at current high interest rates. This second option might properly be termed "asset maintenance" underwriting—the acceptance of terrible business just to keep the assets you now have.

Of course you know which option will be selected. And it also is clear that as long as many large insurers feel compelled to choose that second option, there will be no better day for underwriting. For if much of the industry feels it must maintain premium volume levels regardless of price adequacy, all insurers will have to come close to meeting those prices. Right behind having financial problems yourself, the next worst plight is to have a large group of competitors with financial problems that they can defer by a "sell-at-any-price" policy. . . .

Our own position in this respect is satisfactory. We believe our net worth, valuing bonds of all insurers at amortized cost, is the strongest relative to premium volume among all large property-casualty stockholder-owned groups. When bonds are valued at market, our relative strength becomes far more dramatic. (But lest we get too puffed up, we remind ourselves that our asset and liability maturities still are far more mismatched than we would wish and that we, too, lost important sums in bonds because your Chairman was talking when he should have been acting.)

Our abundant capital and investment flexibility will enable us to do whatever we think makes the most sense during the prospective extended period of inadequate pricing. But troubles for the industry mean troubles for us. Our financial strength doesn't remove us from the hostile pricing environment now enveloping the entire property-casualty insurance industry. It just gives us more staying power and more options.

Media Companies (from 1984 letter)

The economics of a dominant newspaper are excellent, among the very best in the business world. Owners, naturally, would like to believe that their wonderful profitability is achieved only because they unfailingly turn out a wonderful product. That comfortable theory wilts before an uncomfortable fact. While first-class newspapers make excellent profits, the profits of third-rate papers are as good or better—as long as either class of paper is dominant within its community. Of course, product quality may have been crucial to the paper in achieving dominance. We believe this was the case at the [Buffalo Evening] News, in very large part because of people such as Alfred Kirchhofer who preceded us.

Once dominant, the newspaper itself, not the marketplace, determines just how good or how bad the paper will be. Good or bad, it will prosper.

That is not true of most businesses: inferior quality generally produces in-ferior economics. But even a poor newspaper is a bargain to most citizens simply because of its "bulletin board" value. Other things being equal, a poor product will not achieve quite the level of readership achieved by a first-class product. A poor product, however, will still remain essential to most citizens, and what commands their attention will command the at-tention of advertisers.

Since high standards are not imposed by the marketplace, manage-ment must impose its own. Our commitment to an above-average expen-diture for news represents an important quantitative standard. We have confidence that Stan Lipsey and Murray Light will continue to apply the far-more important qualitative standards. Charlie and I believe that news-papers are very special institutions in society. We are proud of the News, and intend an even greater pride to be justified in the years ahead.

Media Continued (from 1990 letter)

Charlie and I were surprised at developments this past year in the media industry, including newspapers such as our Buffalo News. The business showed far more vulnerability to the early stages of a recession than has been the case in the past. The question is whether this erosion is just part of an aberrational cycle—to be fully made up in the next upturn—or whether the business has slipped in a way that permanently reduces in-trinsic business values.

Since I didn't predict what has happened, you may question the value of my prediction about what will happen. Nevertheless, I'll proffer a judg-ment: While many media businesses will remain economic marvels in comparison with American industry generally, they will prove consider-ably less marvelous than I, the industry, or lenders thought would be the case only a few years ago.

The reason media businesses have been so outstanding in the past was not physical growth, but rather the unusual pricing power that most par-ticipants wielded. Now, however, advertising dollars are growing slowly. In addition, retailers that do little or no media advertising (though they sometimes use the Postal Service) have gradually taken market share in certain merchandise categories. Most important of all, the number of both print and electronic advertising channels has substantially increased. As a consequence, advertising dollars are more widely dispersed and the pricing power of ad vendors has diminished. These circumstances materially reduce the intrinsic value of our major media investments and also the value of our operating unit, Buffalo News—though all remain fine businesses.

Media Continued (from 1991 letter)

A Change in Media Economics and Some Valuation Math
In last year's report, I stated my opinion that the decline in the profitability of media companies reflected secular as well as cyclical factors. The events of 1991 have fortified that case: The economic strength of once-mighty media enterprises continues to erode as retailing patterns change and advertising and entertainment choices proliferate. In the business world, unfortunately, the rear-view mirror is always clearer than the windshield: A few years back no one linked to the media business—neither lenders, owners nor financial analysts—saw the economic deterioration that was in store for the industry. (But give me a few years and I'll probably convince myself that I did.)

The fact is that newspaper, television, and magazine properties have begun to resemble businesses more than franchises in their economic behavior. Let's take a quick look at the characteristics separating these two classes of enterprise, keeping in mind, however, that many operations fall in some middle ground and can best be described as weak franchises or strong businesses.

An economic franchise arises from a product or service that: (1) is needed or desired; (2) is thought by its customers to have no close substitute and; (3) is not subject to price regulation. The existence of all three conditions will be demonstrated by a company's ability to regularly price its product or service aggressively and thereby to earn high rates of return on capital. Moreover, franchises can tolerate mis-management. Inept managers may diminish a franchise's profitability, but they cannot inflict mortal damage.

In contrast, "a business" earns exceptional profits only if it is the low-cost operator or if supply of its product or service is tight. Tightness in supply usually does not last long. With superior management, a company may maintain its status as a low-cost operator for a much longer time, but even then unceasingly faces the possibility of competitive attack. And a business, unlike a franchise, can be killed by poor management.

Until recently, media properties possessed the three characteristics of a franchise and consequently could both price aggressively and be managed loosely. Now, however, consumers looking for information and entertainment (their primary interest being the latter) enjoy greatly broadened choices as to where to find them. Unfortunately, demand can't expand in response to this new supply: 500 million American eyeballs and a 24-hour day are all that's available. The result is that competition has intensified, markets have fragmented, and the media industry has lost some—though far from all—of its franchise strength.

Consumer Goods Companies (from 1990 letter)

Twenty Years in a Candy Store
We've just passed a milestone: Twenty years ago, on January 3, 1972, Blue Chip Stamps (then an affiliate of Berkshire and later merged into it) bought control of See's Candy Shops, a West Coast manufacturer and retailer of boxed chocolates. The nominal price that the sellers were asking—calculated on the 100% ownership we ultimately attained—was $40 million. But the company had $10 million of excess cash, and therefore the true offering price was $30 million. Charlie and I, not yet fully appreciative of the value of an economic franchise, looked at the company's mere $7 million of tangible net worth and said $25 million was as high as we would go (and we meant it). Fortunately, the sellers accepted our offer.

The sales of trading stamps by Blue Chip thereafter declined from $102.5 million in 1972 to $1.2 million in 1991. But See's candy sales in the same period increased from $29 million to $196 million. Moreover, profits at See's grew even faster than sales, from $4.2 million pre-tax in 1972 to $42.4 million last year.

For an increase in profits to be evaluated properly, it must be compared with the incremental capital investment required to produce it. On this score, See's has been astounding: The company now operates comfortably with only $25 million of net worth, which means that our beginning base of $7 million has had to be supplemented by only $18 million of reinvested earnings. Meanwhile, See's remaining pre-tax profits of $410 million were distributed to Blue Chip/Berkshire during the 20 years for these companies to deploy (after payment of taxes) in whatever way made most sense.

In our See's purchase, Charlie and I had one important insight: We saw that the business had untapped pricing power. Otherwise, we were lucky twice over. First, the transaction was not derailed by our dumb insistence on a $25 million price. Second, we found Chuck Huggins, then See's executive vice president, whom we instantly put in charge. Both our business and personal experiences with Chuck have been outstanding. One example: When the purchase was made, we shook hands with Chuck on a compensation arrangement—conceived in about five minutes and never reduced to a written contract—that remains unchanged to this day.

Bonds as Businesses (from 1984 letter)

Washington Public Power Supply System
From October, 1983 through June, 1984 Berkshire's insurance subsidiaries continuously purchased large quantities of bonds of Projects 1, 2, and 3 of Washington Public Power Supply System ("WPPSS"). This is the same entity that, on July 1, 1983, defaulted on $2.2 billion of bonds issued to finance partial construction of the now-abandoned Projects 4 and 5. While there are material differences in the obligors, promises, and properties underlying the two categories of bonds, the problems of Projects 4 and 5 have cast a major cloud over Projects 1, 2, and 3, and might possibly cause serious problems for the latter issues. In addition, there have been a multitude of problems related directly to Projects 1, 2, and 3 that could weaken or destroy an otherwise strong credit position arising from guarantees by Bonneville Power Administration.

Despite these important negatives, Charlie and I judged the risks at the time we purchased the bonds and at the prices Berkshire paid (much lower than present prices) to be considerably more than compensated for by prospects of profit.

As you know, we buy marketable stocks for our insurance companies based upon the criteria we would apply in the purchase of an entire business. This business-valuation approach is not widespread among professional money managers and is scorned by many academics. Nevertheless, it has served its followers well (to which the academics seem to say, "Well, it may be all right in practice, but it will never work in theory"). Simply put, we feel that if we can buy small pieces of businesses with satisfactory underlying economics at a fraction of the per-share value of the entire business, something good is likely to happen to us—particularly if we own a group of such securities.

We extend this business-valuation approach even to bond purchases such as WPPSS. We compare the $139 million cost of our yearend investment in WPPSS to a similar $139 million investment in an operating business. In the case of WPPSS, the "business" contractually earns $22.7 million after tax (via the interest paid on the bonds), and those earnings are available to us currently in cash. We are unable to buy operating businesses with economics close to these. Only a relatively few businesses earn the 16.3% after tax on unleveraged capital that our WPPSS investment does and those businesses, when available for purchase, sell at large premiums to that capital. In the average negotiated business transaction, unleveraged corporate earnings of $22.7 million after-tax (equivalent to about $45 million pre-tax) might command a price of $250–$300 million (or sometimes far more). For a business we understand well and strongly like, we will gladly pay that much. But it is double the price we paid to realize the same earnings from WPPSS bonds.

However, in the case of WPPSS, there is what we view to be a very slight risk that the "business" could be worth nothing within a year or two. There also is the risk that interest payments might be interrupted for a considerable period of time. Furthermore, the most that the "business" could be worth is about the $205 million face value of the bonds that we own, an amount only 48% higher than the price we paid.

This ceiling on upside potential is an important minus. It should be realized, however, that the great majority of operating businesses have a limited upside potential also unless more capital is continuously invested in them. That is so because most businesses are unable to significantly improve their average returns on equity—even under inflationary conditions, though these were once thought to automatically raise returns.

(Let's push our bond-as-a-business example one notch further: If you elect to "retain" the annual earnings of a 12% bond by using the proceeds from coupons to buy more bonds, earnings of that bond "business" will grow at a rate comparable to that of most operating businesses that similarly reinvest all earnings. In the first instance, a 30-year, zero-coupon, 12% bond purchased today for $10 million will be worth $300 million in 2015. In the second, a $10 million business that regularly earns 12% on equity and retains all earnings to grow, will also end up with $300 million of capital in 2015. Both the business and the bond will earn over $32 million in the final year.)

Our approach to bond investment—treating it as an unusual sort of "business" with special advantages and disadvantages—may strike you as a bit quirky. However, we believe that many staggering errors by investors could have been avoided if they had viewed bond investment with a businessman's perspective. For example, in 1946, 20-year AAA tax-exempt bonds traded at slightly below a 1% yield. In effect, the buyer of those bonds at that time bought a "business" that earned about 1% on "book value" (and that, moreover, could never earn a dime more than 1% on book), and paid 100 cents on the dollar for that abominable business.

If an investor had been business-minded enough to think in those terms—and that was the precise reality of the bargain struck—he would have laughed at the proposition and walked away. For, at the same time, businesses with excellent future prospects could have been bought at, or close to, book value while earning 10%, 12%, or 15% after tax on book. Probably no business in America changed hands in 1946 at book value that the buyer believed lacked the ability to earn more than 1% on book. But investors with bond-buying habits eagerly made economic commitments throughout the year on just that basis. Similar, although less extreme, conditions prevailed for the next two decades as bond investors happily signed up for twenty or thirty years on terms outrageously inadequate by business standards. (In what I think is by far the best book on investing ever written—*The Intelligent Investor*, by Ben Graham—the last section of the last chapter begins with, "Investment is most intelligent when it is most businesslike." This section is called "A Final Word," and it is appropriately titled.)

We will emphasize again that there is unquestionably some risk in the WPPSS commitment. It is also the sort of risk that is difficult to evaluate. Were Charlie and I to deal with 50 similar evaluations over a lifetime, we would expect our judgment to prove reasonably satisfactory. But we do not get the chance to make 50 or even 5 such decisions in a single year. Even though our long-term results may turn out fine, in any given year we run a risk that we will look extraordinarily foolish. (That's why all of these sentences say "Charlie and I," or "we.")

Most managers have very little incentive to make the intelligent-but-with-some-chance-of-looking-like-an-idiot decision. Their personal gain/loss ratio is all too obvious: if an unconventional decision works out well, they get a pat on the back and, if it works out poorly, they get a pink slip. (Failing conventionally is the route to go; as a group, lemmings may have a rotten image, but no individual lemming has ever received bad press.)

Swimming against the Tide: When Nothing Works (from 1985 letter)

Shutdown of Textile Business

In July we decided to close our textile operation, and by yearend this unpleasant job was largely completed. The history of this business is instructive.

When Buffett Partnership, Ltd., an investment partnership of which I was general partner, bought control of Berkshire Hathaway 21 years ago, it had an accounting net worth of $22 million, all devoted to the textile business. The company's intrinsic business value, however, was considerably less because the textile assets were unable to earn returns commensurate with their accounting value. Indeed, during the previous nine years (the period in which Berkshire and Hathaway operated as a merged company) aggregate sales of $530 million had produced an aggregate loss of $10 million. Profits had been reported from time to time but the net effect was always one step forward, two steps back.

At the time we made our purchase, southern textile plants—largely non-union—were believed to have an important competitive advantage. Most northern textile operations had closed and many people thought we would liquidate our business as well.

We felt, however, that the business would be run much better by a long-time employee whom we immediately selected to be president, Ken Chace. In this respect we were 100% correct: Ken and his recent successor, Garry Morrison, have been excellent managers, every bit the equal of managers at our more profitable businesses.

In early 1967 cash generated by the textile operation was used to fund our entry into insurance via the purchase of National Indemnity Company. Some of the money came from earnings and some from reduced investment in textile inventories, receivables, and fixed assets. This pullback proved wise: although much improved by Ken's management, the textile business never became a good earner, not even in cyclical upturns.

Further diversification for Berkshire followed, and gradually the textile operation's depressing effect on our overall return diminished as the business became a progressively smaller portion of the corporation. We remained in the business for reasons that I stated in the 1978 annual report (and summarized at other times also): "(1) our textile businesses are very important employers in their communities, (2) management has been straightforward in reporting on problems and energetic in attacking them, (3) labor has been cooperative and understanding in facing our common problems, and (4) the business should average modest cash returns relative to investment." I further said, "As long as these conditions prevail—and we expect that they will—we intend to continue to support our textile business despite more attractive alternative uses for capital."

It turned out that I was very wrong about (4). Though 1979 was moderately profitable, the business thereafter consumed major amounts of cash. By mid-1985 it became clear, even to me, that this condition was almost sure to continue. Could we have found a buyer who would continue operations, I would have certainly preferred to sell the business rather than liquidate it, even if that meant somewhat lower proceeds for us. But the economics that were finally obvious to me were also obvious to others, and interest was nil.

I won't close down businesses of sub-normal profitability merely to add a fraction of a point to our corporate rate of return. However, I also feel it inappropriate for even an exceptionally profitable company to fund an operation once it appears to have unending losses in prospect. Adam Smith would disagree with my first proposition, and Karl Marx would disagree with my second; the middle ground is the only position that leaves me comfortable.

I should reemphasize that Ken and Garry have been resourceful, energetic and imaginative in attempting to make our textile operation a success. Trying to achieve sustainable profitability, they reworked product lines, machinery configurations and distribution arrangements. We also made a major acquisition, Waumbec Mills, with the expectation of important synergy (a term widely used in business to explain an acquisition that otherwise makes no sense). But in the end nothing worked and I should be faulted for not quitting sooner. A recent *Business Week* article stated that 250 textile mills have closed since 1980. Their owners were not privy to any information that was unknown to me; they simply processed it more objectively. I ignored Comte's advice—"the intellect should be the servant of the heart, but not its slave"—and believed what I preferred to believe.

The domestic textile industry operates in a commodity business, competing in a world market in which substantial excess capacity exists. Much of the trouble we experienced was attributable, both directly and indirectly, to competition from foreign countries whose workers are paid a small fraction of the U.S. minimum wage. But that in no way means that our labor force deserves any blame for our closing. In fact, in comparison with employees of American industry generally, our workers were poorly paid, as has been the case throughout the textile business. In contract negotiations, union leaders and members were sensitive to our disadvantageous cost position and did not push for unrealistic wage increases or unproductive work practices. To the contrary, they tried just as hard as we did to keep us competitive. Even during our liquidation period they performed superbly. (Ironically, we would have been better off financially if our union had behaved unreasonably some years ago; we then would have recognized the impossible future that we faced, promptly closed down, and avoided significant future losses.)

Over the years, we had the option of making large capital expenditures in the textile operation that would have allowed us to somewhat reduce variable costs. Each proposal to do so looked like an immediate winner. Measured by standard return-on-investment tests, in fact, these proposals usually promised greater economic benefits than would have resulted from comparable expenditures in our highly profitable candy and newspaper businesses.

But the promised benefits from these textile investments were illusory. Many of our competitors, both domestic and foreign, were stepping up to the same kind of expenditures and, once enough companies did so, their reduced costs became the baseline for reduced prices industrywide. Viewed individually, each company's capital investment decision appeared cost-effective and rational; viewed collectively, the decisions neutralized each other and were irrational (just as happens when each person watching a parade decides he can see a little better if he stands on tiptoes). After each round of investment, all the players had more money in the game and returns remained anemic.

Thus, we faced a miserable choice: huge capital investment would have helped to keep our textile business alive, but would have left us with terrible returns on ever-growing amounts of capital. After the investment, moreover, the foreign competition would still have retained a major, continuing advantage in labor costs. A refusal to invest, however, would make us increasingly non-competitive, even measured against domestic textile manufacturers. I always thought myself in the position described by Woody Allen in one of his movies: "More than any other time in history, mankind faces a crossroads. One path leads to despair and utter hopelessness, the other to total extinction. Let us pray we have the wisdom to choose correctly."

For an understanding of how the to-invest-or-not-to-invest dilemma plays out in a commodity business, it is instructive to look at Burlington Industries, by far the largest U.S. textile company both 21 years ago and now. In 1964 Burlington had sales of $1.2 billion against our $50 million. It had strengths in both distribution and production that we could never hope to match and also, of course, had an earnings record far superior to ours. Its stock sold at 60 at the end of 1964; ours was 13.

Burlington made a decision to stick to the textile business, and in 1985 had sales of about $2.8 billion. During the 1964–85 period, the company made capital expenditures of about $3 billion, far more than any other U.S. textile company and more than $200 per share on that $60 stock. A very large part of the expenditures, I am sure, was devoted to cost improvement and expansion. Given Burlington's basic commitment to stay in textiles, I would also surmise that the company's capital decisions were quite rational.

Nevertheless, Burlington has lost sales volume in real dollars and has far lower returns on sales and equity now than 20 years ago. Split 2-for-1 in 1965, the stock now sells at 34—on an adjusted basis, just a little over its $60 price in 1964. Meanwhile, the CPI has more than tripled. Therefore, each share commands about one-third the purchasing power it did at the end of 1964. Regular dividends have been paid but they, too, have shrunk significantly in purchasing power.

This devastating outcome for the shareholders indicates what can happen when much brain power and energy are applied to a faulty premise. The situation is suggestive of Samuel Johnson's horse: "A horse that can count to ten is a remarkable horse—not a remarkable mathematician." Likewise, a textile company that allocates capital brilliantly within its industry is a remarkable textile company—but not a remarkable business.

My conclusion from my own experiences and from much observation of other businesses is that a good managerial record (measured by economic returns) is far more a function of what business boat you get into than it is of how effectively you row (though intelligence and effort help considerably, of course, in any business, good or bad). Some years ago I wrote: "When a management with a reputation for brilliance tackles a business with a reputation for poor fundamental economics, it is the reputation of the business that remains intact." Nothing has since changed my point of view on that matter. Should you find yourself in a chronically leaking boat, energy devoted to changing vessels is likely to be more productive than energy devoted to patching leaks.

Chapter 10

Mario Gabelli

Discovering and Unlocking the Private Market Value

Mario Gabelli graduated from Columbia Business School in 1967, where he had been introduced to value investing by Roger Murray, a coauthor of the fifth edition of *Security Analysis*. Moving directly to Wall Street, Gabelli worked as a sell-side analyst for a decade, specializing first in the automotive and then in the entertainment industries. In 1977 he founded Gabelli Asset Management; by 2000 this firm had grown to manage more than $20 billion in mutual funds, separate accounts for individuals and institutions, and private investment partnerships. The company went public in early 1999 and is listed on the New York Stock Exchange under the symbol GBL. Gabelli himself is a regular member of the *Barron's* annual investment roundtable and makes frequent appearances on television, which is fitting for someone who has been as successful as he has with investments in media stocks. In addition to making great picks, he tells a great stock story.

For a value investor like Mario Gabelli, schooled in the Benjamin Graham tradition, the current form of the question he has had to address over the course of his career is this: Has the Internet done away with the net-net stock? When Graham examined stacks of financial statements, searching for his net-nets, he and the people he hired did it the old-fashioned way, by hand. If they were not alone in this quest, they certainly did not have much company. Now Graham's secret has been out for many decades.

More to the point, modern electronic information systems, including the Internet but certainly not confined to it, make it child's play to screen databases for companies selling below the value of their net working capital or some other rock-bottom measure of value. If fish were this easy to catch, all the oceans would be barren and we would be the hungrier. So one of the challenges value investors face in an age when information is no longer a scarce resource is to find some value metric that is less easily uncovered than net-net but no less discriminating in its ability to identify underpriced securities.

Private Market Value Defined

Probably no contemporary value investor is so closely identified with a modern variant of net-net as Mario Gabelli is with private market value (PMV), his potent contribution to the arsenal of value investing. Private here does not mean personal, individual, or secret. Gabelli defines PMV as "the value an informed industrialist would pay to purchase assets with similar characteristics" (Gabelli's Web site, www.gabelli.com, Value Investing—US). This succinct definition needs some elaboration.

The PMV contrasts with the value that the stock market is placing on the equity of the firm. In the market, the last trade determines the value. All the players who make up the market—Mr. Market, as we have called this collectivity—have an equal say in what that price should be. They trade shares back and forth, some motivated by their sense of what the company is worth, others by the prior movement of the stock price itself. Over the course of a day, a month, or a year, the price can move one way or another without any fundamental changes to the business of the company or even, on a larger scale, to the outlook for the economy as a whole. Certainly there are moments when the market price is a good reflection of the intrinsic value of the company, but if that were constantly true, the price would not fluctuate so dramatically. The industrial buyer, concerned with the worth of business and the cash it can generate, has a less frantic disposition than the market and regards sharp declines in price as an opportunity, not as a cause for panic. In this sense, the PMV is little more than the intrinsic value as determined by the buyer of a firm who is more knowl-edgeable than the market about what the firm is really worth.

But PMV as an investment strategy has three additional features that make it a genuine innovation. First, as Roger Murray commented to Gabelli, PMV equals intrinsic value plus a premium for control. Unlike the passive investor who buys a security and hopes the company exceeds ex-pectations, the industrial buyer is in a position to change the underlying business. He or she can fire incompetent management, dispose of unpro-ductive assets, consolidate the operations with those of another firm, re-structure the balance sheet, and do a host of other things to make the as-sets more productive and swell the cash flow. Because this buyer is probably familiar with the industry, it will not take long to turn things around. Be-cause they can do more with the company than can the passive portfolio investor, they may be willing to pay more for it than the current market price. That extra amount is the premium for control. The payoff for port-folio investors such as Gabelli is that if they can identify firms selling sub-stantially below their PMV, they can buy the shares and capture that con-trol premium when the industrial buyer moves on the company.

The second innovative feature of PMV consists of the analytical tools that Gabelli and his associates have developed to allow them to estimate the PMV of the firms they follow. Like many value investors, they are look-ing for gaps in GAAP—that is, either assets or earnings power that are masked by generally accepted accounting principles and thus not revealed in standard financial statements. Some of these may be the old standbys: assets not reported at all on the balance sheet or carried at cost rather than current market value; operating income not disclosed on the profit and loss statement thanks to some unusual financial structure or the consolidation of profitable divisions with those that are losing money. Certainly the in-dustrial buyer will not be blind to these values. If the Gabelli firm can dis-cover them first, it stands to gain.

The other and more novel approach to exposing a PMV different from the share price is to move beyond financial data and focus on operating sta-tistics. Many of the companies that have been in Gabelli portfolios are somewhere in the communications business, broadly considered: tele-phone companies, both fixed and mobile; cable and broadcast television companies; radio operators; and magazine and newspaper publishers. What these companies have in common are subscribers who pay for the services that the companies provide. The number of subscribers is an operating statistic. Knowing the number of subscribers helps the financial analyst compare the performance of different firms in the same industry: what their revenues or operating earnings per subscriber are. It also permits the analyst, on the basis of recent sales of firms within the industry, to see how much the industrial buyer was willing to pay per subscriber. If one wireless telephone company with 500,000 subscribers has just been bought out for $300 million, that suggests a per-subscriber price of $6,000, and it becomes the starting point for establishing the value of another wireless company. Certainly additional analysis is necessary, and adjustments must be made, but the approach to valuation begins with a PMV transaction—an industrial buyer paying so much for each unit of a revenue stream. It is a short step from here to a valuation of the entire company, which then can be compared with the current market value. A substantial difference suggests an investment opportunity. Other useful operating statistics are the number of hotel rooms, the population reached by a broadcaster, the number of square feet of marketing space, and the acreage in timber. In all these cases, the resource represents a stream of revenue that some industrial buyer has recently priced.

The third feature of PMV as an investment strategy is the recognition that it takes something—an event, a person, a change in perception—to narrow the spread between the market price and PMV. Gabelli calls this agent a *catalyst*, and the term has become widely adopted in the investment world to signify the source of a change. All investment strategies require a catalyst to make them pay off. Even the most patient investor wants the value of the investment to rise within a reasonable—meaning relatively short—period; the longer the wait, the lower the annualized return. In most cases, the catalyst is left unspecified, which means that it is simply left to the market to recognize that the price of the shares should be higher. Beating earnings expectations is this kind of catalyst, something dependent not only on the performance of the company but also on its ability to surprise the analysts who cover it. Value investors in general, and PMV investors in particular, would prefer not to rely on such an amorphous and fickle instrument.

There are two kinds of catalysts: specific and environmental. Specific catalysts are those changes, either anticipated or recently occurring, that alter the prospects of a particular company. The grimly labeled "death watch" stocks are attractive to investors who believe that the departure of the CEO or a large shareholder will allow the company, once freed from restraints, either to improve its performance or to restructure itself, including here selling the whole thing. Gabelli invested in the supermarket chain Giant Foods after the founder died, anticipating either an increase in earnings or the sale of the company. The sale did occur, at a 50 percent premium to Gabelli's cost, but it took three years to complete. The slower-than-anticipated unfolding of the catalyst resulted in a somewhat lower annualized return on his investment. Other company-specific catalysts include all types of financial or operational restructurings, such as the spin-off of a division or a significant repurchase of shares, a change in management, and investments in new business developments. Changes like these stir the pot and reward investors who understand the company and can see, before the market, that improved earnings are on the way.

Environmental catalysts are disruptive shifts in the world in which businesses operate. We refer not only to global warming, which is obviously an environmental catalyst however one uses the term, but to changes in the political, social, and economic climates as well. For example, the destruction of the Berlin Wall in 1989 was the symbolic representation of a major catalyst for change in the years ahead. With the end of the Cold War, firms in the west such as Boeing, General Electric, Coca-Cola, Siemens, and a host of others would be able to sell their wares in the former Soviet Union and its previous allies. At the same time, the end of the Cold War held out the prospects that defense budgets would shrink—bad news for those firms heavily dependent on military contracts. One should have predicted that there would be consolidation in the defense industry, although deciding ahead of time who would be taken over and at what price may have been more difficult.

In many instances, the environment in question is the government, in its legislative, administrative, and regulatory roles. Even in the most free market of countries, governments cast enormous shadows over the economy and the companies operating within it. Changes in laws, regulations, and tax rulings, as well as other administrative decisions like monetary policy and contracting standards—all of these can alter the rules and modify the rewards that shape business decisions. The passing of the Telecommunications Act of 1996 has allowed new entrants to compete against the incumbent local exchange carriers in their local markets. Various additional pieces of legislation, along with judicial and regulatory decisions, have promoted the radical restructuring of the telecommunications industry in both the United States and abroad. Companies that didn't exist five years ago now have market values in the billions and are bought, sold, merged, or transformed every week. Again, for the astute investor who has the ability and the tools to grasp the implications of these governmentally induced changes, opportunities abound.

Other environmental catalysts emerge as the consequences of disruptive shifts in technology that facilitate the reorganization of whole industries. The most unavoidable one in our time is the Internet and all the related changes that flow from breaching the protective barriers of time and space. Although it is far from clear at this moment which kinds of firms and which industries will profit from the corrosive impact of faster and deeper communications, what is certain is that there will be losers and winners, and that the landscape of many industries will be redrawn.

Consolidation is one result of many of these environmental catalysts: Big companies buy up smaller ones (sometimes the other way around) to take advantage of new opportunities that are suddenly legally permissible or commercially feasible. By knocking over some of the barriers of space and time, the Internet and other advances in telecommunications are some of the forces behind "globalization," meaning here the spread of firms beyond their national boundaries on an unprecedented scale. "Want to be a global heavyweight in the telecommunications game? Better buy that small wireless company in Indiana to expand your footprint and fill in your service area." Whatever the motivations, consolidations advance on many fronts. And there is nothing that brings PMV to the surface as quickly as whole industries in the throes of a consolidation frenzy. For Gabelli, prepared with techniques for appraising PMV and adept at spotting catalysts, it is a heady time.

Aside from a few specific international funds, the Gabelli firm confines its universe to domestic, cash-generating franchise business. It defines cash generating as operating earnings plus depreciation and amortization less capital expenditures for the maintenance of the franchise (EBITDA – capex). Its approach is one stock at a time, bottom up, which is typical of most value investors. It does try to identify large-scale trends—economic, demographic, political, or cultural—that will help or impede the earnings of the company moving forward. In 1999 trends that influenced the firm's thinking were working women (leading to the idea that cats would become the pet of choice and increase the demand for kitty litter), speed, the digital revolution, globalization, aging populations, free flow of capital and ideas, education, entertainment, and Euroland as a place of opportunity. But these themes merely identify potentially rich fishing grounds; they need to be supplemented with the valuation tools before the company makes a purchase decision.

Private Market Value in Practice: General Housewares Corporation

How does globalization affect a company that makes kitchen gear and other small household goods? In 1994 General Housewares designed and produced about 75 percent of the products it sold. By 1998 it was in the process of contracting out both design and manufacturing for the same percentage of its sales. The manufacturing facilities were located in foreign countries with lower labor costs. The company was also shifting its capital spending from upgrading old plants to automating its distribution centers. Table 10.1 shows the firm's financial performance for these years and reveals a company in transition, with sizeable year-to-year fluctuations in sales and various measures of income, especially for a company in the domestic housewares business.

The operating results of the company are masked in this table by interest expenses, taxes, and obscure items such as adjustments to the pension liability and losses in foreign currency transactions. If we look at only those items that Gabelli focuses on, we get a somewhat clearer picture, as shown in Table 10.2.

Using this measure of operating cash flow, General Housewares had

Table 10.1   General Housewares Income Statements, 1994–1998

	December 1994	December 1995	December 1996	December 1997	December 1998
Net Sales	96.5	119.3	105.5	104.5	97.0
Cost of goods sold	61.5	79.0	68.3	62.1	54.5
Selling, general, and administrative	28.4	33.2	37.3	38.0	39.4
Operating income	6.6	7.1	(0.1)	4.5	3.1
Interest expense	1.7	3.1	2.8	2.7	2.3
Income before taxes and extraordinary item	4.9	1.7	(2.9)	1.7	0.8
Income tax expense	2.2	4.0	(0.8)	1.1	0.7
Extraordinary item, net of tax benefit	0.0	0.0	(2.0)	0.0	0.0
Net operating income	2.8	2.3	(0.6)	0.7	0.0
Net income	2.8	2.3	(2.6)	0.7	0.0
Foreign currency adjustments			(0.1)	(0.2)	(0.5)
Pension liability adjustments			0.1	0.4	0.0
Comprehensive income	2.8	2.3	(2.6)	0.8	(0.4)
Shares outstanding	3.4	3.8	3.8	3.8	4.0
Earnings per share	$0.80	$0.61	$(0.69)	$0.21	$(0.11)

Note: Figures are in millions of dollars, except for earnings per share.

Table 10.2   General Housewares Cash Flow

	December 1994	December 1995	December 1996	December 1997	December 1998
EBIT	6.6	7.1	(0.1)	4.5	3.1
Depreciation and amortization	3.6	4.5	4.9	5.4	4.9
Capex	2.5	4.3	4.2	2.6	3.7
EBITDA less capex	7.8	7.3	0.5	7.2	4.2
Debt + equity – surplus cash	78.1	69.5	68.6	71.2	68.6
Capitalization rate	9.9%	10.5%	0.7%	10.1%	6.1%

Note: Figures are in millions of dollars, except for percentages.

Table 10.3   Operating Segments of General Housewares

	K&HT	PCT	CUT	COOK	RET	Other	Total
Net sales	38.4	18.7	28.0	2.4	7.1	2.3	97.0
EBIT	12.1	7.5	7.4	0.2	1.5	0.2	28.8
Depreciation and							
amortization	1.1	0.4	1.9	0.2	0.3	0.0	4.0
Identifiable capex	2.4	0.1	0.8	0.0	0.0	0.1	3.5
Total identifiable assets	11.0	10.9	26.2	0.0	1.7	1.1	50.9

Note: Figures are in millions of dollars.

one awful, one mediocre, and three decent years during this period. But would we, or an industrial buyer, want to purchase the company to get our hands on this cash flow? That depends, as always, on the price. If we are buying the operating cash flow, the standard comparison is to the *enterprise value*, which means the market value of the equity plus all the debt, minus cash in excess of the amount needed to run the business. Operating cash flow divided by the enterprise value gives us a *capitalization rate*, which is the pretax earnings on the entire investment. Because it includes both debt and the market value of the equity and uses earnings before interest payments, the cap rate allows comparison between companies with very different capital (debt and equity) structures. The numbers for General Housewares for these years are not enticing. Unless there is some value masked by these financial figures, we would pass on the company.

In its annual reports, General Housewares broke its business up into six operating segments and provided summary financial information for each. Table 10.3 illustrates these results for 1998. Three observations stand out from this table. First, three of the six segments account for about 90 percent of sales and operating earnings. Second, the segments as a group have an enormously high return on operating (identifiable) assets: 57%. Third, since the operating earnings for the whole corporation were only $3.1 million, compared with $29 million for all the segments, a great deal of money is being spent at the corporate level that is not directly connected to the operating segments. The report in Table 10.4 confirms this. Operating income generated by the divisions is almost entirely consumed by overhead at the corporate level.

Table 10.4   Corporate Overhead and Interest Expenses

Divisional operating income	28.8
Unallocated corporate selling, general, and administrative	25.7
EBIT	3.1
Unallocated interest expense	2.3
Pretax income	0.769

Note: Figures are in millions of dollars.

The question any industrial purchaser has to ask is whether this overhead is fat or muscle—an expense that can be trimmed severely without impairing the earnings or functions vital to the success of the company. Gabelli assumed that the right buyer, probably a firm already in the same businesses, could drastically shrink corporate overhead. If so, then the PMV of the firm was considerably more than its market price. Here are the calculations, back-of-the-envelope style:

There are four million shares outstanding, selling at $11	$44.
The company had debt of	$24,
making the enterprise value equal	$68.
The three largest divisions have operating income of	$27.
Corporate overhead required	$2,
leaving adjusted operating earnings of	$25.
The rate of return, pretax, on $68 is	37%.

This is an extraordinary cap rate, especially for a company selling nothing more exotic than kitchen tools.

The story had a swift denouement. A catalyst for the sale of the entire company was already present in the form of a corporate raider who had gained a seat on the board of directors. All that was necessary was the industrial buyer, tempted by the low enterprise value and the high rate of return. In Spring 1999 a third party offered $11 per share to buy the entire company. General Housewares then hired an investment bank to find a better deal. By the end of July, they had secured three offers, including one from a buyout firm that had already acquired the home products division of Corning and which eventually bought General Housewares for $28.75 a share. If we change the equity line in our previous calculation to $115, we still get a rate of return, pretax, of 18.1 percent on the entire investment. That return is more than decent, and although it does assume a major reduction in corporate overhead, it does not factor in the expanded sales that might ensue with General Housewares now promoted by a larger company with complementary product lines, nor does it reduce the cost of the investment by whatever the buyer would have been able to fetch for the smaller divisions. Also, the presence of so much fat at the corporate level suggests that the divisions themselves could have had their expenses cut. The PMV turned out to be considerably more than the price the public market had set.

Private Market Value in Practice: Telephone and Data Systems

In April 1999 Gabelli & Company issued a report on Telephone and Data Systems (TDS). TDS, the report began, "provides local, long distance, cellular and PCS services to about 3 million customers in 35 states. TDS currently owns 81% of United States Cellular Corporation (USM—$44⁵⁄₁₆—NYSE) and 82.3% of Aerial Communications, Inc. (AERL—$7⁵⁄₁₆—OTC)." In January 2000 its updated report began with exactly the same information. The only difference was that by January 2000 USM was selling at $98 a share, up from $44⁵⁄₁₆, and AERL had risen to $51½, up from $7⁵⁄₁₆. Naturally the price of TDS had shot up as well, from $57⅛ to $115⅞. The first few months of 2000 were a heady time for technology and telecommunications stocks, and some of the lift in TDS's price may have been the animal spirits infecting the entire sector. But part of the rise may have been due to a realization that, in most instances, the whole should not be worth less than the sum of the parts.

As of the date of the report, a buyer of a share of TDS would own $112.70 worth of stock in USM and $49.56 of stock in AERL (see Table 10.5). Taken together, the total was substantially more than the cost of a TDS share. But the situation for a TDS shareholder was even better than it looked. At the time of the report, VoiceStream was in the process of buy-

Table 10.5   **TDS's Stake in Other Companies**

	TDS	USM	AERL	VSTR Addtitional	Other Companies	Total Other Stock
Price	$115.88	$98.00	$51.50			
Shares	61.4	87.8	71.8			
Percentage TDS ownership	100%	81%	82%			
Shares per TDS share	1	1.15	0.96			
Market value	$115.88	$112.70	$49.56	$18.00	$11.30	$191.56

Note: Shares and market value are in millions.

ing Aerial for stock. Based on current market prices, the VoiceStream stock that TDS would own upon completion of the deal was worth $68 per share of TDS, $18 more than the current value of a Aerial share. To that one had to add an additional $11.30 per share of publicly traded stock in other companies. Counting only its ownership of stock in all these other companies, a share of TDS had assets worth $192. Subtracting its debt of around $30 per share leaves the equity value at $162 compared with a market price of $116, a margin of safety of almost 30 percent.

After the second TDS report was written, VoiceStream completed acquisition of Aerial. TDS ended up with 35.6 million shares of Voice-Stream, valued at the closing at $69.20 per TDS share. The consolidation wave then swept over VoiceStream; Deutsche Telecom (DT) offered 3.2 shares plus $30 in cash for each VoiceStream share. Even in the widespread carnage for telecom stocks at the end of 2000, with DT shares down by two thirds from their high, this put a value on each share of VoiceStream of $133, which translates into $76.50 for each TDS share.

There are a number of reasons why companies own shares in other firms, and not all of them benefit the stockholders. Managers may decide that they are better at investing than running their business—some probably are—or they may have other dreams of glory. The shareholder would like to benefit from the increasing value of these embedded shares, but it is not always clear how. For TDS shareholders, this was not a problem. First, management owned about half of TDS, meaning that their interests and the interests of ordinary shareholders were pretty well aligned. Also, they had sold the large stake in Aerial to VoiceStream, a sure sign that they were concerned with shareholder value. There was no reason to believe that they would treat the other assets any differently.

This arbitrage valuation is only the start of the analysis. TDS Telecom was a real telephone company as well as an investor in the shares of other firms. In 1999 it had operating cash flows of $240 million from revenues of $550. These were growing, and profit margins were improving. In each of its three lines of business, it had a definite number of subscribers buying specific kinds of telecommunication services. Because of all the transactions in the telecommunications industry during an era of deregulation, technological innovation, and massive restructuring, a private market price existed, at least within a reasonable range, for all of these units. Expressed as dollars per subscriber or as a multiple of sales or EBITDA, the valuation is clearly comparative. Private market purchasers can always decide to lower their bid price for comparable businesses.

Still, the approach is based on current comparable values, realized in arm's-length transactions among knowledgeable buyers and sellers, and not based on discounted cash flows from many years in the future. Used in conjunction with the valuation of TDS's publicly traded shares, the private market valuation of operating businesses is the icing on the cake. For the year 2000, the Gabelli firm put the private market value of the entire company, including all of its interests in publicly traded companies, at $226 per share. Though the stock traded down during 2000 from its price when the report was issued, the purpose of the valuation is not to predict fluctuations in the market but to give the Gabelli firm and its clients an intrinsic value against which they can compare the current market price. It is one more useful wrench in the tool kit of valuation techniques.

Chapter 11

Glenn Greenberg
Investigate, Concentrate, and—Watch That Basket

Glenn Greenberg does not claim to have bought his first stock while still in the stroller, nor to have paid for his introductory subscription to the *Wall Street Journal* with money earned on his paper route. In college he studied English literature, not the standard preparation for someone intending to spend more time reading financial statements than Dickens, Lawrence, or Joyce. Still, there is a frequently cited bit of wisdom that Mark Twain recorded in Pudd'nhead Wilson's calendar that describes a select few investors, Glenn Greenberg among them:

> Behold, the fool saith, "Put not all thine eggs in the one basket"— which is but a manner of saying, "Scatter your money and your attention"; but the wise man saith, "Put all your eggs in the one basket and—watch that basket!"

Greenberg doesn't maintain that everything he learned about investing he picked up in an American literature course, but somewhere along the line he did learn to concentrate both his attention and his investments.

His first job after graduation from college was teaching school, initially at the elementary school level, then in a high school where he also served as principal. By the end of three years, he realized that teaching was not the calling for which he was intended. His greatest satisfaction came from managing the high school, and when his boss suggested that he might like to try business school, Greenberg regarded this not as a reproach but as an opportunity. He applied to Columbia Business School because it operated on a year-round system and he would be able to start without having to wait until the following fall. In the MBA program, he found that he most enjoyed the courses in finance. He took one in which students were assigned a company to analyze from the perspective of a potential investor. His company was TWA, and his recommendation was not to invest, a promising start for his incipient career. He also wrote a long analysis of his family's business, Gimbel Brothers (which also owned Saks Fifth Avenue), in which he faulted their planning process from top to bottom. His uncle, the CEO, was furious. The company nearly went bankrupt within the next year and then was sold to British American Tobacco as part of its ill-fated venture into the retail trade. Although Greenberg interviewed for jobs in consulting and investment banking, he decided to take a position with J.P. Morgan, at the time the largest money management firm in the country.

Glenn Greenberg alleges that during his five years in this position he worked as a money *mis*manager. When he started in 1973, his firm's primary concern was that it would not be able to buy enough Avon or Polaroid shares, at 100 times earnings, to satisfy the needs of its clients. As some readers may recall, Avon and Polaroid were charter members of the so called Nifty-Fifty group of stocks, much beloved by institutional investors during this period because they were "one-decision" securities: You buy them and hold them forever. It became apparent soon enough that they would not be rewarded for this insight. The Dow-Jones average dropped from around 1,000 at the start of 1973 to a low of 570 toward the end of 1974, a decline of over 40 percent. This is the kind of experience that indelibly stamps itself on someone getting started in the business and emphasizes the threat of risk and the pain of loss that are always present in investment markets, especially in times of euphoria.

The lesson also taught Greenberg to be skeptical of prevailing wisdom and to make sure that he personally understood why he bought every stock he chose. He recounts going into a meeting with his peers at the investment firm to talk about the positions they held in their portfolios. It became dismayingly clear to him during the discussion that no one knew anything about the companies they owned and could offer no reason for holding the shares. Somehow that crucial part of an investment manager's responsibilities had gotten lost over time; it was also made impossible by the large number of stocks in each portfolio. After five years at Morgan, Greenberg left to join a smaller firm that put him through the basic training that had so far been denied him. His new employer believed that, at least in the investment world, anyone could comprehend anything with enough study. Greenberg's first assignment was to master the intricacies of the Penn Central bankruptcy reorganization. He quickly became a believer in the merits of attention to detail.

The Two-Inch Putt: Selecting Stocks for a Concentrated Portfolio

Glenn Greenberg is not an ordinary investor, not even a typical value investor according to the principles of value investing as we have described them in this book. He and John Shapiro, his partner at Chieftain Capital Management since they founded the firm in 1984, have produced extraordinary returns on the money entrusted to them. From 1984 through 2000, their accounts have achieved a compounded annual growth rate of 25 percent per year (before deducting advisory fees), compared with 16 percent for the Standard & Poor's 500. For a value investor to have outperformed the index during the best seventeen-year run in its history, when growth stocks did especially well, is remarkable.

These favorable returns are the result of the iconoclastic approach to investing that he and his associates practice at Chieftain. The Pudd'nhead Wilson quotation regarding the wisdom of putting all your eggs in one basket only hints at the implications of a concentrated investment strategy. For starters, it is far more important to select the proper eggs to put into that basket than to watch them once they have been chosen. No amount of vigilance will make a rotten egg palatable. Greenberg attributes a great deal of his success to the firm's approach to finding the right stocks.

Concentrate

Under the rules they established for themselves, the Chieftain partners will not begin to buy a stock unless they are willing to put at least 5 percent of their assets into it. This is an antidiversification device, and it has a manifold influence on their entire investment process. First, they need to have two types of confidence in the selection: confidence in their ability to understand the company, its industry, and its business prospects; and confidence in the company, that it will continue to perform well and increase the wealth of its shareholders. Their portfolio is not filled with "tracking positions"—that is, miniscule amounts of a large number of stocks that an investor buys on the basis of cursory research as a reminder that additional work needs to be done before a real commitment can be made. Greenberg doesn't even start his purchasing until he has done most of the research that will make him an expert in the company. Obviously, there is always more to learn, and in the time that he holds the stock, which can be years, his knowledge and understanding deepen and broaden.

The Chieftain portfolio has far fewer than the 20 names that a strict 5 percent rule might imply. The partners normally hold 8 to 10 stocks in their accounts, and they are willing to invest heavily in a situation that they are thoroughly convinced will work out for them. To improve their odds, all four professionals in the firm study the same stocks, and they have to agree before they buy a share. If diversification is a substitute for knowledge, then information and understanding should work in reverse.

Buy Good Companies

Second, the companies they are looking for have to fit through a fine mesh screen in order to meet their standards. They want to buy "good" businesses, by which they mean those that are unchallenged by new entrants, have growing earnings, are not vulnerable to being technologically undermined, and can generate enough free cash flow on a regular basis to make the shareholders happy, either through dividends, share repurchase, or intelligent reinvestment. They are not attracted to companies that have hit a rough patch and need to recover. Although they buy shares with the expectation that they will one day sell them, they prefer to hold on to them for a number of years and ride the companies' performance. If they are going to commit at least 5 percent of their assets to a company, they must be sure that it has considerably more than a fair chance of working out. Though they do not want to control the business, Greenberg and his partners see themselves as owners of a business and its surplus cash flow. They expect to get their returns from the company's profitable operations as these become reflected in the price of its shares. This stance is considerably different from that of value investors who buy cheap stocks that have fallen below the reproduction cost of the assets and wait for the market to realize that it has overreacted.

They look for other signs that identify the kind of good businesses they covet. High profit margins are a positive mark; these make the company's earnings less vulnerable to changes in the level of sales. They may also indicate that the company is operating within a franchise and is less susceptible to having its profits eroded by a new entrant. They like duopolies, like Freddie Mac and Fannie Mae, because the two firms generally do not compete intensely with one another, and certainly not on price, so each is left with a high return on capital. Monopolies, by contrast, are always subject to government intervention, either to break them up or regulate their earnings. And even if governments do nothing, they are an invitation to new competitors to try to capture some of their very lucrative business, often by using a newer technology that allows the entrant to leapfrog the incumbent with lower prices or better products.

In making its long-term commitments, Chieftain wants to invest with smart management that has the shareholders' interests in mind. They have had generally bad experiences when they tried to influence managers to change direction, and they are not contentious enough by temperament to enjoy the struggle. It may be true that a company being run by superior executives has nowhere to go but down once those managers leave, and that buying the stock of a poorly run company at a deeply depressed price can position the investor for a profit once management improves. But that is a speculative bet; sometimes bad management stays in place for decades. Greenberg expects to own his stock for four or five years. He doesn't want to wait on the chance that better management will show up, and he doesn't want to lead a shareholder revolt to make that happen. All he needs to know is that the current managers are healthy and young enough to keep the company on course for a few more years.

Buy Them Cheap

Chieftain Capital manages $3 billion for its clients. If it normally holds shares in 10 or even fewer companies, then on average it needs to put hundreds of millions into any one name. Because great situations are so difficult to find, they are prepared to buy 20 percent or more of any one company. While there are around 1,500 or more companies large enough for them to own, their "good business" requirement probably shrinks that list by 80 percent, leaving them with no more than 300 possible candidates. But even within this restricted universe, Greenberg and his partners are brutally selective. They are looking, he says, for "two-inch putts," by which he means investments that will provide them with a high rate of return while subjecting them to a low level of risk. There is only one way they can meet that goal. They have to spot companies that meet all their standards and are still available at a price that will provide them a high rate of return based on future earnings growth.

He is not attracted to turnaround companies or cyclicals, where a successful investment depends on timing. He does not believe in speculating that an underperforming company will be taken over, because most managements resist selling out. Opportunities to make his kind of investment arise irregularly, and then due to unpredictable circumstances. For example, a change in governmental regulations can be the vehicle. In the late 1980s, the entire savings and loan industry was suffering from the bad loans many had made and the illegal activities others had pursued. Congress decided that an inexpensive way—no taxpayer money required—to infuse new capital into the thrifts would be to allow them to sell to the public their shares in the Federal Home Loan Mortgage Corporation (Freddie Mac). Although the shares of the Federal National Mortgage Association (Fannie Mae) had been public for decades, and there was no substantial difference between the business of the two corporations, Greenberg was able to buy Freddie Mac stock at a deep discount on the first day it was offered. The taint of the savings and loan associations, the newness of the issue, and the volume of shares available at one time kept them cheap, at least initially. Within the year they had doubled in price.

Sometimes a cloud settles over whole industries based on little more

than questionable assumptions about the future. In the mid-1990s, the belief that satellite TV receivers would replace cable as the means of plug-
ging couch potatoes into the infotainment universe became prevailing
wisdom. *Business Week* gave the notion its stamp of approval with a cover
story in 1996, and the shares of cable companies fell even further. Greenberg and his partners were not convinced. The satellite medium had a
number of significant drawbacks: it did not carry local stations; it was expensive and complicated to install; all the televisions sets in the house
had to be tuned to the same channel, or else additional and expensive
equipment would be needed; and it wasn't suited to all areas, like dense
urban settings. Instead of satellite replacing cable, Greenberg anticipated
that the two would coexist, often within the same households. Cable
stood to profit from new services and technologies that it was well posi-
tioned to deliver, such as digital TV, telephone service, and a broadband
connection to the Internet. Customers would pay extra for these features,
and although delivering them would require that the cable companies buy
new equipment, they had the heaviest investment—the last mile line
into the home—already in place. Also in the wings was the potential
deregulation of the cable industry, a move that would by itself allow the
companies to raise their prices.

Thanks to the gloom generated by the supposed threat from satellite
receivers, the shares of well-run cable companies were selling in 1996 and
early 1997 at 6 or 7 times current cash flow. All the potential growth—
from new subscribers, new services, and rate increases—was available for
free. Greenberg's firm ignored the two biggest names in the industry, TCI
and Time Warner, because TCI had too much debt and Time Warner was
part of a much larger company not focused on cable. Instead, they bought
two smaller companies, TCA Cable and U.S. West Media Group. In both
cases, they were paid handsomely for their investments; the share prices
rose five or six times, and the companies were ultimately acquired as the industry consolidated. They then found another undervalued cable company, this one in Canada, whose price was depressed by a discount applied
to Canadian investments in general. All told, they had 40 percent of their
assets in cable companies by the end of 1998.

The thrift industry presented Chieftain with a two-inch putt in the late 1980s and early 1990s as savings and loans were converting from a mutual to a stockholder form of organization. When the shares were being offered for sale, a thrift's managers, who had been given options to buy the shares, tried to keep the offering price as low as possible. The supervisory bodies who were responsible for seeing that the conversions went smoothly also had an interest in making sure that all the newly offered shares would sell, so they also opted for a low price. As a result, a savings and loan with a book value of $50 per share could be bought at $25 or $30. With new equity from the sale, the thrift was now overcapitalized. The conservative managers were not interested in making risky loans. As a result, not long after they went public, many thrifts started to buy back their shares. Because they were still selling at below book value, each share the bank retired increased the book value of the shares still outstanding. This was pure financial engineering; the book value rose not because of retained earnings but simply through the repurchase of stock at a discount. With the financial sector in the midst of a substantial consolidation, the thrifts were all acquired within a few years at a premium to book value. Investors who paid $30 per share for a book value of $50 could sell out at $75, a gain of 150 percent. The whole episode may have taken two or three years, giving the investors an annualized return no less than 35 percent for minimal risk.[1] If all putts were this easy, fewer frustrated golfers would consider the game a good walk spoiled.

Valuation of Shares in a Concentrated Portfolio

Valuation is central to all value investors. For someone like Glenn Greenberg, running a portfolio committed to a select few companies, valuation is especially crucial. He has to be very confident that he knows the real worth of the companies he looks to buy. Diversification is not going to bail

---

[1] Other value investors, including Michael Price and Seth Klarman, also participated in the thrift conversion opportunity. Klarman's explanation of the investment arithmetic is somewhat different from Greenberg's, illustrating that even among successful value investors, there are alternate paths to the same goal.

him out. He can't depend on the law of large numbers to turn his rough estimates into good enough guesses; his sample size is too small. Also, given
the kinds of companies he is looking for, he needs a valuation method appropriate to their features. He isn't a vulture investor. Because he doesn't
expect his selections to expire, it isn't relevant to him what their carcasses
will fetch. And he is skeptical about applying an asset-based approach to
the kind of companies he likes. As he points out, many old industrial firms,
such as steel mills and textile plants, had assets on their books that no
longer produced income. Competition from abroad, sometimes subsidized
by governments or able to take advantage of labor costs many times lower
than their domestic counterparts, drained the value out of the bricks, mortar, and equipment of these firms. Unless there are industrial buyers for
their plant and equipment, which isn't likely given the specialized uses for
which they were built, the assets aren't worth much even in liquidation.
Benjamin Graham would not have disagreed. He sought to buy shares in a
company for less than two thirds of its net working capital, ascribing no
value at all to the fixed assets.

Greenberg likes companies that produce a stream of free cash flow, so
it makes sense that he uses an estimate of cash flow to tell him the value of
those firms. Before the arrival of the personal computer and the electronic
spreadsheet, he and his partner would analyze a company by isolating its
business segments and projecting revenue and expenses no more than two
or three years into the future. By assuming that it would grow steadily from
then on, they could calculate its current value by discounting that cash
flow back to the present, using only a hand calculator. Now, with spreadsheets, they can make their projections more detailed and carry them forward further in time. Discounted cash flow analysis, a method about which
we expressed some reservations in the first part of this book, is Greenberg's
valuation technique of choice for all the investments he makes.

Greenberg's discounted cash flow approach is bounded by a set of
restrictions that keep him securely within the value investing camp. He
is only interested in companies with stable earnings and relatively predictable cash flows. He subjects every investment to an "Internet test," trying to anticipate how its business might be affected by this new and disruptive technology. He does not invest in companies that have never

earned any money on the expectation that they will be stars in the future. He doesn't depend on heroic and unsustainable rates of growth to multiply the cash flow four or five years down the road. He invests in companies in which the *terminal value*—what the projections indicate the company will be worth 10 or more years in the future—does not dominate the cash flows of the near and intermediate-term future. And he is careful to make sure that all of the assumptions that are built into a present value analysis are reasonable and conservative: sales growth rates; profit margins; the market prices of assets such as oil, gas, and other fuels; capital expenditure requirements; and discount rates. Common sense serves as the touchstone against which all spreadsheet projections are assessed. He uses the model; he doesn't let it control him.

Would You Buy This Stock?

In November 1999 Greenberg asked students in the value investing course at Columbia Business School whether they would buy a stock that had the features shown in Table 11.1. The back of a small envelope is adequate space to calculate some of the common valuation ratios. The price to earnings ratio (P/E) is almost 28; if we reduce annual earnings by the $7 per year write-offs, it rises to 31. With the dividend yield at 1.5 percent, an investor looking for a 10 percent return would need to get 8.5 percent in capital appreciation. If we take growth at the high end, then the PEG ratio (P/E divided by the growth rate) is 3.35. PEG is not a measure that value investors make much use of, but even devotees of growth must blanch at this high ratio, especially for a diversified and cyclical company. And the presence

Table 11.1   **A Stock to Buy?**

Price	$1,340	
Earnings per share	$50	(before write-offs that averaged $7 per year)
Dividend	$20	
Growth rate	6–8% per year	
Business	diversified and cyclical	
Options	many, but not considered as diluting earnings until they vest	

of a mass of outstanding options can only dampen the returns to investors, diluting earnings as the options are exercised. This stock seems so unpromising that it is hard to imagine anyone buying it.

Now, as many will have recognized, this was no stock at all but a snapshot of the S&P 500 index in November 1999. One year later, not much has changed. The price is down a little, as is P/E. The investment still looks unsound even though the index has beaten the great majority of active money managers for many years. Only the future will tell us with any certainty whether these multiples will be sustained. If they are not, then the index's status as a brilliant investment choice diminishes.

Discounted Cash Flow in Practice: A Diversified Energy Company

To perform better than the S&P 500 index, Greenberg and his partners have had to do a superior job in valuing a company. Though they may test other approaches, they only will invest if a discounted cash flow analysis indicates that the shares are available at an attractive price. They applied it to a diversified energy company operating largely in Canada in order to determine a price at which they would be willing to buy the shares. The process is straightforward but requires a substantial amount of work. The company has proven reserves of oil and natural gas. It owns pipelines, storage facilities, and processing capacity. Though the company has an exploration and development arm that is adding to these reserves, Greenberg ignores the potential from future exploration and assumes that the company merely produces the reserves it already had. The main assumptions that are incorporated into the analysis are a benchmark price for energy in each year, the exchange rate between the United States and Canada, and expenses the company has to pay, including energy royalties and taxes. Greenberg uses West Texas Intermediate as the benchmark for energy pricing. He has it increasing at 2 percent per year over the entire period, starting from a low base of $20 per barrel.

Greenberg's analysis extends for 12 years and then adds a terminal value for the company at that time. He assumes that most of the wells have run dry and that the pipeline, processing, and storage operations increase their income by 2 percent per year in perpetuity. The annual cash flows and

Table 11.2 **Present Value of an Energy Company at Various Discount Rates**

Discount rate	10.0%	12.5%	15.0%	17.5%
Present value per share	$77.31	$64.31	$55.43	$48.85

the terminal values are then discounted to the present using discount rates of 10 percent, 12.5 percent, 15 percent, and 17.5 percent, which produces the valuations on a per share basis shown in Table 11.2.

These present value per share figures are the intrinsic value of the company under four different rate of return requisites. The cash flows in the projection are identical; the only difference is what they are worth today, and that depends on the discount rate. An investor willing to earn 10 percent on his or her money would buy the stock if it were available at $77 per share. Someone insisting on a 17.5 percent return could only purchase it at $49 or less. During the year 1999, the shares of the company actually traded between a low of $32 and a high of $49. Someone looking to earn 15 percent had plenty of opportunity to purchase the stock, and, except at the high end of its price movement, with a substantial margin of safety.

The real value of doing all the work required for a full discounted cash flow analysis is that it forces the investor to think long and hard about all the factors that will affect the future of the business, including the risks it may face that are currently unexpected and unforeseen. If Greenberg ran money with 200 names in his portfolios, he would not have the time—nor would it be worth the effort—to do all this work. But because of his concentrated approach and his determination not to lose his clients' money, he can't afford the luxury of a casual relationship with his companies.

The discounted cash flow approach requires that all crucial assumptions about the future, such as rates of production or the price of energy, be made explicit. It is a guard against untested speculation. As another check, Greenberg asks whether his discounted cash flow results are reasonable. Is it reasonable to assume that energy prices will increase 2 percent per year for a decade? Unless some new and as yet unnoticed source replaces the hydrocarbon realm in a big way, the chances are good that prices will rise at least that much. Will the company be able to maintain the rates it charges for storage and pipeline transmission? That requires a look at the potential competition and whether there may be new capacity on the way. These questions can be answered, provided that one knows where to look and whom to ask. No one said it would be easy.

While the Paint Dries: Keeping Informed

With few stocks in their clients' portfolios, each of them purchased as a long-term investment, the partners of Chieftain do not need to find many new companies to add to their list. In some years, they buy no additional names, in other years three or four. This slow turnover leaves them time to keep thoroughly informed about the firms they do own, a necessity given the large stakes they maintain in each of their companies. All the partners go to the companies' meetings; all of them scrutinize the quarterly filings; and all of them keep current about the industry. They talk with management regularly, and they read the trade journals and other relevant material. In addition to the superior returns we described, their work has earned them the respect of the executives with whom they speak. They have been told by management that they understand the company better than all sell-side analysts covering it.

This praise is gratifying to hear, and it confirms Greenberg's poor experience with outside analysts. On those occasions when Chieftain has hired consultants who are industry specialists to advise them about a particular company, they have been disappointed. Retail experts did a survey for them in the early 1990s and recommended that between Nike and Reebok, Chieftain should purchase Reebok, a cheaper stock with a strong franchise. Reebok shares went nowhere for two years, while Nike increased sixfold. The message Greenberg has taken from these experiences is that he and his partners do better to rely on their own efforts and judgment in making an investment. There is no substitute for homework.

All the intelligence, experience, and hard work that Greenberg and his partners have brought to bear has rewarded them with superior returns; but, as Greenberg readily acknowledges, they make plenty of mistakes and are often quite inexact in their estimates of a company's revenues and earnings. They tend to err on the high side, which puts them in the camp of most analysts. How then have they done so well? For one thing, as value investors, they have not based their investment decisions on expectations of perfection. They do not buy high multiple stocks for whom an earnings disappointment can mean a punishing drop in the share price. The companies in their portfolio are sound enough to recover from short-term problems. As a consequence, the mistakes they have made have not buried them. Their poor investments, Greenberg says, have resulted more in dead money than fatal declines.

Unburdened by the need to offset severe losses, the successful investments have been strong enough to account for the superior performance. Stocks that increase six or eight times in price over a three- or four-year period have provided sufficient energy to lift the entire portfolio by 25 percent per year. So the common precept of value investors about not losing money has worked for Greenberg in two ways: his portfolio hasn't had to recover from disastrous years, and his winners haven't had to balance off large losses just to get back to even. If there are only a few eggs in the basket, they had better be the right ones.

Chapter 12

Robert H. Heilbrunn
Investing in Investors

In 1929, shortly after Robert Heilbrunn had enrolled at the Wharton School, his father died. Heilbrunn left school to take over the management of the family leather trade business. That challenge would have been large enough for anyone his age, but the onset of the Great Depression made things even more difficult. In addition to the business, his father had also left an investment portfolio of stocks and bonds. This too became Heilbrunn's responsibility. It was not one of the joyful moments in investment history. The markets were already down by a sickening amount in that year alone. And Heilbrunn, though he had worked in the leather business in summers and on vacation, had no experience in managing money.

To gain some understanding, he enrolled in courses given by the New York Stock Exchange and by New York University. With none of them providing him with the kind of practical information he needed, he remembered that his father had told him about an investment advisor he knew and trusted, a man named Ben Graham. Heilbrunn looked up Graham in the telephone book and called him. Graham did remember Heilbrunn's father, and the two made an appointment. As Graham later told Heilbrunn, given the circumstances of the time, he thought Robert was coming to ask for a loan. In fact Heilbrunn wanted more; he wanted Graham to become his investment advisor and help run the portfolio. Graham agreed but told Heilbrunn there would be a fee of $25 a month. Heilbrunn, recognizing a bargain when he saw one, accepted.

They started to examine the holdings in the portfolio. Heilbrunn's father had taken a large position in high-grade utility bonds. Though some utility firms had become holding company pyramids and collapsed in the crash, Heilbrunn's bonds held up well; they were paying interest and selling at close to par. Graham's advice took Heilbrunn by surprise. He said they should sell the bonds. "Why?" Heilbrunn asked; "They are good securities." "Exactly," Graham told him; "And they will never be worth more than they are today." Heilbrunn also wanted to know what they would buy with the proceeds from the sale. Graham recommended bonds of Fisk Tire and Rubber. He told Heilbrunn that although the company was in bankruptcy, and the bonds were selling at $.30 on the dollar, Graham was confident that Fisk would reorganize and that holders of the bonds would receive $700 in new securities for each $1,000 bond they held. This was Heilbrunn's introduction to value investing.

Heilbrunn decided to follow his advice—after all, he was paying $25 per month for it—and called his broker with instructions to sell the utility bonds and buy Fisk. An hour or so after he placed the order, the brokerage firm called him back. They would not buy the Fisk bonds, they told him. They were a high-class firm, and they thought their reputation might be tarnished if word got out that they were dealing in bankrupt paper. When Heilbrunn recounted this response to Graham, Graham told him that the brokerage firm was simply wrong, that the bonds would prove a successful investment. Heilbrunn moved his business to another broker, who was Graham's brother, and stayed with him for many years. The Fisk bonds did come through as Graham predicted, and Heilbrunn was convinced that Graham was indeed a brilliant investor. He sent other members of his family to see Graham, and he himself began to advise them using the knowledge and insights he was picking up from Graham.

In 1934 Graham and Dodd published their book *Security Analysis*. Heilbrunn was so taken with it that he enrolled in Graham's course at Columbia, taught then as an extension course at night and thus available to people working during the day. Heilbrunn found him a superb teacher, and the fact that Graham dissected the financial statements of companies that he was buying for Heilbrunn's portfolio did nothing to diminish Heilbrunn's interest. By the time the course was over, Heilbrunn realized that he had had enough of the leather business. He wanted to work for Ben Graham, a desire shared by many students fortunate enough to take the course. But Graham at that time had no need of another employee. Instead, he suggested that Heilbrunn become an independent investigator. He and Graham would discuss certain investment ideas, and Heilbrunn would do the leg work: call the companies, visit them, and find less obvious ways to get more information about them. Though the Securities Act of 1933 and the Securities Exchange Act of 1934 had recently been passed, it took time for companies to make public all the information we now expect. There was no Internet, no EDGAR database, no Free Edgar, or any of the other wonderful tools investors can now summon at the click of a mouse. So much the better for energetic and clever researchers.

Around 1937, Graham bought a large block of stock in a gas pipeline company for Graham-Newman, the investment partnership he had formed with Jerome Newman. To get the information he needed, Graham went to the state public utility commission, where all public utilities were required to file detailed documents describing their operations. Heilbrunn adapted the approach to investigating Government Employees Insurance Company, an insurance company in Texas, and found what he was looking for in the state insurance office. Graham-Newman owned a large position, and Heilbrunn was able to enrich their knowledge and understanding of the company. But Heilbrunn also discovered that it was a violation of the law for an investment company to own a controlling interest in an insurance company. Graham-Newman solved this problem by distributing the shares directly to their limited partners, who then owned it directly. Government Employees Insurance Company, now known as GEICO, has been the object of value investors' interest for decades. Sometime after Graham-Newman distributed the shares, the company attracted the attention of Warren Buffett, who made a well-chronicled trip to Washington to learn what he could about the company and spent a Sunday talking with the chairman. After some ups and downs—the company nearly went bankrupt—it eventually was bought out entirely by Berkshire Hathaway.

Heilbrunn worked on other Graham-Newman depression-era investments that also paid off handsomely. The real estate market in New York was pummeled by the depression, the damage made more severe by overbuilding in the 1920s. When developers and owners defaulted on their mortgages, title companies would take a number of them, package them together, and sell them as bonds. (Securitization of loans has a longer history than many of us realize.) Bonds backed by mortgages in default sold at deep discounts to their face value, and Heilbrunn, along with Graham-Newman, bought a substantial amount. They anticipated that at some point the demand for New York City real estate would return. Another series of bonds had been issued to finance the building of the Waldorf-Astoria Hotel. These bonds came out in 1929, paying 6 percent interest. Even the city's most prestigious hotel could not fill its rooms in the early 1930s, and interest payments were suspended. With the bonds in default, prices dropped to $.30 on the dollar, or $300 for a $1,000 bond. At that price they looked attractive, and since Chase Bank was willing to lend buyers $250 on each bond, the outlay for the investor was only $50. Some years later the bonds were repaid in full, including all the accrued interest. Buying damaged goods paid off handsomely.

Heilbrunn continued to invest with Graham-Newman, to do research that he shared with them, and to do some investing on his own. He sold his leather business to concentrate on investing. His approach was to apply what he had learned from Graham—find the bargains. In that period, when *Barron's* published annually a list of 30 low-priced stocks, Heilbrunn and Graham would examine the companies on the list and buy the 10 best as a basket. Some might disappear, but the ones that worked out more than made up for the losers. And he followed Graham's practice of comparing two companies in the same industry, like Bethlehem and Crucible Steel, to see which was cheaper on an intrinsic value basis. Their focus was the balance sheet, not the income statement. They were able to discuss these ideas and pick up other suggestions from a community of value investors that had formed around Graham.

One lasting interest of Graham and this circle was the search for quantitative trading formulas that could be used to direct market investment strategies in a disciplined way. Heilbrunn contributed to the development of these kinds of rules in an article published in 1958. The method prefigured many of the formulas used by quantitatively oriented value investors today. Heilbrunn examined the price, earnings, and dividend histories of specific companies to establish the ranges of the price to earnings (P/E) multiple and the dividend yield within which the securities had traded. The investment strategy based on this information is to buy stocks when they sell within the lower portion of their historical P/E multiple range, within the higher portion of their dividend yield range, or both. By establishing the ranges with precision, this approach provides a check on the emotions that can distort investment judgment, both the exuberance engendered by a rising market and the despair occasioned by a falling one. It applies a discipline for buying stocks—when they are cheap—and, usually more valuable, a discipline for selling them—when they are dear. In a paragraph as timely today as when he initially wrote it, Heilbrunn warned that

> a feeling of over-optimism in bull markets is one which must be very carefully guarded against by the professional investor as well as by the amateur, since it is generally acknowledged that . . . [both are] . . . influenced by the tremendous quantity of bullish sentiment . . . in newspaper and magazine article, speeches, reports, analyses . . . which emanate from the financial district. This statement is in no way to be construed as a criticism of the security analyst, but being human, and this is probably a disadvantage in this profession, he is subject to the same psychological pressures as everyone else.

Heilbrunn's innovation was to focus on the variability of a single stock as it traded within its historic ranges, identifying its highs and lows as compared with itself. The more customary value approach has been to search for stocks with low P/Es, high dividend yields, or low price to book multiples as measured simultaneously against other stocks in the universe. Modern quantitative techniques developed by major value-oriented institutions like Sanford Bernstein have combined the two approaches. They look at where stocks are trading relative to their historic valuation ranges, and then compare stocks with one another based on these results. They identify those at the lower end of their own ranges, and then test each stock against certain other criteria. If the price of the stock no longer falls when additional bad news is announced, that is a good sign. If insiders and other knowledgeable investors are buying, that is another positive sign. The initial quantitative screen as confirmed by the subsequent stock-by-stock examination produce a disciplined overall evaluation.

In his own practice, Heilbrunn embodied one of the core principles of value investing. The circle of professionals that formed around Ben Graham included two men who actually worked for Graham-Newman: Walter Schloss and, in the mid-1950s, Warren Buffett. Buffett, as all his followers know, had come to Columbia Business School to study with Graham, after having read *The Intelligent Investor*. After a while Heilbrunn began to think that the best investments he could make were in Graham, Schloss, and Buffett. He put money into Buffett's partnership a year or so after it started, and he also entrusted some funds to Schloss after initially deciding against it. In later years he added other prominent value investors to his portfolio of managers. These decisions paid off handsomely, and Heilbrunn was able to retire, more or less, from direct active investing.

By entrusting his assets to other managers, Heilbrunn embodied a version of one of the enduring precepts of value investing: Know what you know and stay within your circle of competence. Investments records are not definitive, but it does seem clear that a small number of professional investors, disproportionately of the value persuasion, have been able to earn above-market returns over the long term. The likelihood of mere good fortune as an explanation is small. When that performance is tied to a carefully designed investment approach and expertise in particular industries, and when the abilities involved are available to others at a reasonable price—Graham charged Heilbrunn $25 per month, but that was in 1929—then investing through these individuals or institutions makes a great deal of sense. Knowing when other full-time investors are likely to outperform your own part-time efforts may be the most fundamental of all value insights.

Several years ago, when Wells Fargo Bank looked like a promising investment to the value firm Tweedy, Browne, the company was about to assign an analyst to study Wells Fargo in detail. Then they discovered that Berkshire Hathaway had acquired a large position in the bank. Tweedy, Browne reassigned the analyst and simply bought the stock. They felt that their own research was unlikely to be superior to Buffett's. Over the years, Heilbrunn has exercised a similar degree of judgment, enriched by his own experiences as a value investor, in evaluating candidates to manage his money. He has made wise choices.

Chapter 13

Seth Klarman
Distressed Sellers, Absent Buyers

Margins of Safety

Like a number of other people who become money managers, Seth Klarman bought his first share of stock before he was old enough to drive, with birthday present money. He served an apprenticeship for a summer and almost two years after college with the legendary value and bankruptcy investor Max Heine and Heine's younger associate Michael Price, at a time when there were few other people in the shop. Klarman then enrolled in the Harvard Business School, from which he graduated in 1982. He then helped to form The Baupost Group, an investment company that today manages over $2 billion of client assets. The staff includes 12 investment professionals and an administrative team of nearly 30 people.

There are good reasons behind the growth of Baupost. The two oldest investment rules, generally honored in the breech, are first, don't lose money, and second, don't forget the first rule. Klarman has always taken this prescription to heart. From the start, his role at Baupost had him handling all the investment assets of a number of wealthy families, so he sees it as essential that he worry about risk before he begins to think about the potential return. The rich are not the only ones who feel this way. Offer a large group of people even odds on winning or losing half their wealth, and few will accept the bet. Psychological studies have demonstrated repeatedly that most people feel more intensely about the losses they may incur than about the gains they may earn. It makes sense, because the incre-

231

mental benefit of a 50 percent improvement in circumstances is valued less than the adversity of a 50 percent decrease. The experience that Klarman had with Heine and Price and his own work taught him that value investing was the only strategy that took care to limit risk while still holding out the prospect for attractive returns over time.

Klarman is the author of *Margin of Safety: Risk-Averse Value Investing Strategies for the Thoughtful Investor,* published in 1991 by HarperCollins. We have discussed repeatedly the margin of safety concept, as set forth by Benjamin Graham and used by many of his intellectual progeny. For Klarman, it would be more accurate to say margins of safety. The securities he likes to buy are cheap on a host of measures: price to book value, price to earnings, price to cash flow, break-up value, dividend yield, and private market value. He also evaluates objective factors such as insider buying, corporate share repurchases, and the like. If one of these factors disappoints, the others are likely to provide some support for the share price. When he invests in other kinds of assets, such as real estate, he requires similar evidence that he is getting a bargain. All these measures divide into two basic categories: assets and earnings. Klarman is most comfortable when the belt of asset value is reinforced by the suspenders of earnings.

As Klarman will be the first to admit, the markets do not always accommodate the value investor in offering securities that meet all, or any, of these requirements. When he started in 1982, the Dow-Jones Industrial Average was no higher than it had been 16 years earlier, even though the economy and corporate profits had tripled in real terms. While no one could have been certain at the time, it has turned out that the summer of 1982 marked the start of the longest bull market in history. So in Klarman's early years as an investment manager, he was able to find many securities that met his stringent criteria for value. But as the stock market continued its long ascent, and was joined for many years by the bond markets that rose as interest rates dropped, identifying undervalued securities became more difficult. Klarman had to extend his search into less populated and less traditional investment areas, such as distressed debt, direct real estate ownership, and foreign equity and property markets. The charter of his fund allowed him to be flexible in his choice of investments, and he took full advantage of this freedom. Consistent in his demand for value, he has been opportunistic in the practice of his craft.

The Klarman Principles

Each value investor operates by a set of principles, or rules that they impose on themselves, that serve to focus their attention and restrict their choices. The one tenet to which all subscribe is that the best investments are made when the intrinsic value of a security is significantly higher than the market price. Klarman is more explicit than most about the other rules that guide his work.

Evaluate Risk First

As we said, Klarman examines the risks—by which he means the likelihood and magnitude of possible losses—of any investment before he starts to think about the returns. A gain of 10 percent with no possibility of loss may be more attractive on a risk-adjusted basis than an expected return of 15 percent with a meaningful possibility of material capital loss. Risk also needs to be considered within the context of return. Many investors claim to attend carefully to risk, but few are as committed or as careful as Klarman. For example, *hedge funds*, a term now applied loosely to just about any investment limited partnership, were originally pools of money whose managers were supposed to succeed in both up and down markets. The strategy was to "hedge" by buying favored securities while selling short those the managers felt would decline. Even if the overall market went nowhere, the fund would profit from its long/short positions. But as many hedgers found out, making two correct calls is more difficult than making one. Even the more contemporary and supposedly scientific version of hedging—the idea that certain positions can be counted upon to converge in price over time and that money can be made by pairing long and short positions as a bet on that convergence—has proved vulnerable to the point of a Federal Reserve intervention. Klarman, recognizing how much rides on those kinds of bets, especially when leverage is employed, steers clear of that kind of hedging. He does not employ naked short selling as a strategy, fearing the skewed risk of unlimited loss on a short position that moves higher. He will commit a portion of his funds to buying put options on a stock index, to hedge against a broad decline in the market. But that strategy is genuinely buying an insurance policy, a cost that will slightly reduce returns if everything works as intended but will offer some protection should the market drop.

Motivated Sellers

In most parts of the investment world, especially the heavily traded and regulated stock and bond markets in the United States and a few other large, rich countries, it is difficult to find an edge, some pocket of inefficiency where knowledge is unevenly distributed and the smart or informed investor has a genuine advantage. Company insiders obviously know what is going on before the fund manager finds out, but they are limited in what they can do to take advantage of their information. The arguments about market efficiency, which continue to fill academic papers four decades after the debate was initiated, merely divide those who think it is extremely difficult for a manager to beat the market averages from those who think it is hard but possible, at least for the talented few.

Klarman tries to improve his chances by finding situations that exist outside the normal buy and sell world of the secondary (stock and bond) markets. The feature on which he places most emphasis is what might be called a *motivated seller*, someone who, as Klarman puts it, is selling for a noneconomic reason. Motivated selling has many sources. Probably the most obvious occurs when a stock is expelled from a major index. Because so much money is invested in funds that seek to mimic the performance of the indexes, everyone knows that a stock selected to join the Standard & Poor's 500 has to be bought by the funds. The shares run up in price in anticipation of the enormous buy orders that will hit the tape a few days after the announcement. But there are only 500 slots in the index, and for every stock that gains admission, one has to be dropped. Some are eliminated through mergers or other corporate activities, but some lose their status because of poor fundamental performance. These stocks are sold into the market by motivated sellers—funds that look not at all at the companies' fundamentals but merely at the fact that they are no longer in the index. Motivated sellers, as Klarman has found repeatedly, create opportunities. When Venator, the name Woolworth chose to make people forget its not-so-illustrious recent history, lost its place in the S&P 500, the share price dropped from $6 to around $3 in a few days. Less than three months later, it was selling at $10.

When assets are sold for noneconomic reasons, the most common explanation is that some type of institutional constraint obligated the owner to move. An index fund's charter is one such constraint—own only the securities in the index. Some of the other constraints that have given Klarman an opening include the following:

- Spin-offs, in which a large company takes a division, creates a new firm, and sends shares in the new company to existing stockholders in some proportion to their holdings. Unlike initial public offerings (IPOs), spin-offs are not supported by investment banks; they do not receive the powerful sales push that these banks use to market their IPOs, and there are few if any analysts covering them. That explains the paucity of buyers. The motivated sellers generally manage large pools of money and don't have the time or desire to own shares in a small, new company. They often take their distribution and hit the sell button, without even looking at the assets they are dumping. Investors who are not subject to this constraint can make up their minds based on the new company's business fundamentals.
- Bankruptcy filings, in which a company petitions the court for legal protection from its creditors, generally with the aim of continuing its operations while it reorganizes its financial obligations. There are many reasons companies file for bankruptcy (some bankruptcies are the result of creditors' actions, not company initiative), only some of which portend the termination of the firm and the liquidation of its assets. Because bankruptcies come in different forms, most of them offer some prospects for gain to the investor who has the skill and experience to read all the fine print and estimate what the outcome will be. Nevertheless, many institutional investors are pre-

vented by their charters from holding the securities—generally the debt—of companies that have filed. So shortly after the announcement, they are actively in the market selling their bonds, even if the prices they receive are substantially lower than a less-constrained seller would demand. For investors unburdened by these limitations, the fire sale creates opportunity.

- Real property in the wrong hands, in which banks or other lenders find themselves in possession of real estate because the previous owners have defaulted on the debt and the lenders have, in their minds, been stuck with the buildings or land. This is not a business they chose to be in, and many of them cannot or do not want to make the effort to figure out what to do. The simplest path is to get rid of the asset, and if they have to take a price for it that seems suspiciously low, it is worth it to them to be rid of the headache, or to be in conformance with their charter. They create another opportunity for the buyer without the restrictions.

Missing Buyers

The other side of the motivated seller advantage is a situation in which there are only a few other buyers considering the same asset for purchase. The ideal number is none. One of Warren Buffett's more notable aphorisms, previously cited, is that if you have been in a poker game for thirty minutes and still don't know who the patsy is, you can be fairly certain it's you. Klarman's variant is that he never wants to show up at an auction to discover that all the other bidders are more knowledgeable and have a lower cost of capital than he does. In those cases, he would have to wonder why it was he who ended up owning the asset.

Fortunately, some of the same characteristics that make for motivated sellers also render the properties being sold unsuitable for many buyers: small size, no coverage (spin-offs), or distressed debt (bankruptcy or the threat of it). Klarman has noticed that over time, as similar assets are disposed of at bargain prices, more buyers begin to turn up. Experience may breed contempt, but it also attracts new players as they become accustomed to the formerly odd-looking asset. Like any good frontiersman, Klarman moves on to new territories when he begins to feel the pressure of the crowds. He was a buyer of Resolution Trust Company portfolios of real properties in the early 1990s when few investors were interested. As the sales continued and more buyers turned up, he moved on.

Catalysts Independent of the Market

Remember dividends? Most stocks used to pay them to shareholders, and they were a large part of the return investors could expect. Between 1929 and 1959, the dividend yield on the stocks making up the S&P 500 index was higher than the yield on long Treasury bonds. In the early 1980s, the yield exceeded 4 percent, and on a rare occasion topped 6 percent. Since then, however, it has fallen steadily, until it dropped below 2 percent in the late 1990s. Many firms, including some of the largest, pay no dividends at all. As dividends have shriveled, shareholders have been left with only one path to realize any return on their investment. They have to wait until the price goes up and sell the shares to someone else. With rare exceptions, they are completely dependent on the market—meaning the sum of all other investors—to pay them for their effort and risk. And, as we have seen, Mr. Market is a fickle fellow. An investor in a company that meets all its performance targets may still find that the market is depressed and unwilling to shell out. Also, though this may be difficult to remember at the end of one of the truly great decades in investment history, the market may go nowhere—or even downwards—for long periods. When returns are entirely dependent on a rise in the share price, this fallow stretch is difficult to take.

There are alternatives, and Klarman is committed to finding investments that have a pay-off route other than the market. Given his focus on absolute returns—that is, his desire to provide positive returns to his investors each year—having investments independent of the market is a requirement. At some level, they are not hard to find. Bonds with fixed interest rates pay out a predetermined amount, generally every six months, and they pay back the principal at a predetermined time. Even though the quoted price of a bond will fluctuate with changes in interest rates and credit ranking, in the absence of a default there are no surprises about repayment, and the market is irrelevant. But the price for this predictability is a lower rate of return, and Klarman is not content to invest in plain vanilla debt instruments simply because they may be secure. The trick for him is to find situations with limited risk that will reward investors with a high return regardless of the level of the market.

Distressed debt, especially the bonds of companies in default, can fit these requirements. The prices of these securities are depressed; the current interest payments are halted although perhaps accruing; and there is uncertainty about when and whether the principal will be repaid. Klarman and other investors in defaulted securities need to be confident that the specific paper they own is covered by sufficient asset value for them to get paid. But once they have made that determination, their returns depend more on the proceedings of the bankruptcy than on the whims of the market.

There are other situations in which the overall market plays little or no role in the timing and amount of return. For example, liquidations—orderly processes through which companies go out of business—march to a schedule set by the company; there may be a stream of payouts over a long period, and the investor has to evaluate both the certainty of payment and the time value of each slice. Takeovers are another investment type that depends on the timing of the deal, not the mood of the market. Once the terms have been set, the investor only has to wait until the deal closes. As with every investment, the more certain the return, the lower the reward. Klarman needs to find deals that are in some way outside the area of investor attention in order to earn more than a riskless rate of return.

Bottom Up—and Side to Side

Just as the investment world may be split into growth and value investors, it may also be divided into those of the top-down and bottom up persuasion. Top-down investors begin by looking at large economic (macro) conditions, and only move on to specific stock selection after they have identified sectors and industries that they think will do well in the coming months or years. They are attuned to the business cycle, and they also make projections about long-term trends in technology and other features of the economy. Like most value investors, Klarman starts his work at the bottom—that is, with a specific security that looks like a value. He thinks it is easier to be correct about a single company than something as large and variegated as the economy. Not only do top down investors have to make the right forecasts, they have to make them better and faster than their competitors do. And then they still need to link the forecast to a particular investment vehicle from which they can profit. Forecasting inflation is the easy part. Finding a stock that will benefit is the tough feat, especially because many other analysts have already predicted inflation and helped to bid up the price of the shares. Also, macro investors are in a bind if their predictions aren't working. If inflation goes down instead of up, do they abandon their investment picks or wait for the economic variable to turn around? Faced with a stock that has fallen in price, the bottom up value investor rechecks the analysis. If he or she believes that the fundamentals are still in place, now is the time to buy even more since the discount has widened. The macro analyst does not have so clean a choice.

But even for the bottom up investor, not every investment decision is unique. Sometimes an entire class of firms can offer a buying opportunity, and the knowledge and skill developed in doing the analysis of the initial company can be easily applied to similar situations. In the early 1990s, in an effort to restructure an industry that needed to raise additional capital, many thrift institutions—savings banks and savings and loan associations—converted from mutual to stockholder organizations. The process was the same from bank to bank. Before selling shares to the public, the thrift was required to get an independent appraisal of the bank's worth. They could then go public and sell shares equivalent to that appraised value. For example, the ABC Savings Bank has assets of $100 million, liabilities (i.e., deposits from its customers) of $90 million, and equity of $10 million. It earns $1 million per year, which is a return on equity of 10 percent and a return on assets of 1 percent. The appraisal (see Table 13.1) indicates that that bank is worth $10 million.

Now comes the conversion. In the IPO, one million shares are sold at $10 per share, raising $10 million in equity. The thrift's managers, realizing this is a wonderful arrangement, buy as many shares as they can, unlike a standard IPO in which management and early investors unload as many

Table 13.1   Thrift Financials before Conversion

Assets	Liabilities and Equity	Earnings
$100 million (loans and cash)	$90 million debt (deposits) $10 million equity	$1 million ROA = 1% ROE = 10%

Note: ROA = return on assets. ROE = return on equity.

shares they can get away with. The converted balance sheet initially looks like Table 13.2.

The first thing to note is that the $10 million investment bought equity worth $20 million, meaning that the shareholders simply purchased their own cash and got the operations of the company for nothing. Second, this is a bank, and the new equity will allow the bank to increase its borrowings and thus its assets. The $10 million of new capital, in Klarman's conservative model, will initially be invested in U.S. Treasury bills and earn only 3.5 percent after tax. Over time, this capital will be deployed and leveraged in the core business. If the debt-to-equity ratio returns to the pre-conversion level, the bank will grow to $200 million in assets, supported by borrowings of $180 million and equity of $20 million. If it continues to earn the same 1 percent on assets, the thrift's income will double to $2 million.

The truly wonderful aspect of this investment is that it became a template for Klarman to apply to many other thrift conversions. Even though each situation was small, as a group they provided a high return on a substantial investment. At first there was little competition to get into these situations. Large value-oriented mutual funds, which might have been lining up with Klarman (and thus reducing his returns), did not want to spend the time analyzing dozens of deals, each of them too small to put much

Table 13.2   Thrift Financials after Conversion

Assets	Liabilities and Equity	Earnings
$110 million (loans and cash)	$90 million debt (deposits) $20 million equity	$1.35 million (approx) ROA = 1.2% ROE = 6.8%

Note: ROA = return on assets. ROE = return on equity.

money to work. In another round of consolidation in the late 1990s, value funds were losing assets after several years of underperformance, so they had to abstain. Finally, thrifts, whether mutual or shareholder owned, are not ordinarily an exciting business. They did not appeal to investors looking for high returns. But the returns were outstanding, both because the price of getting in was so low and because the market quickly realized the extent of the undervaluation.

It is the rare situation in which separate investments are so similar that a simple template can be used repeatedly to analyze each. In many of these cases, some governmental action, because it applies to classes of firms, is the spark. The conversion of the thrifts from mutual to stock corporations was set in motion by regulatory changes that encouraged the thrifts to raise more capital. Klarman has also been a buyer of portfolios of properties sold by the Resolution Trust Corporation (RTC), a federal agency created to dispose of the assets of busted thrifts and banks that had come into government hands as part of a giant bail-out. In these cases, a simple template did not suffice because on some dimensions each piece of real property is an entity unto itself. But as he persevered as a buyer, he learned both the skills necessary to negotiate the bidding process and the special set of valuation techniques that real estate investors employ. When more bidders began to show up at the RTC auctions, he shifted his focus toward buying single pieces of real estate from banks and insurance companies that wanted to get rid of the properties they had ended up with from defaulted borrows. At some level, a rent roll is a rent roll.

New Times, New Competitors, New Markets

Because he looks for situations in which the seller has a noneconomic reason for getting rid of the property and in which there are few other buyers eager to accommodate that desire, Klarman needs to move from market to market as conditions change. Bankrupt debt provided rich opportunities in the late 1980s, until large funds, attracted by the stellar returns, showed up with big pools of money. The thrift conversion experience was a phase, and as it wore on, the obvious values began to surface and attract more investors. The same thing happened to RTC real estate portfolios; what seemed exotic and untouchable in the early years became ordinary and popular as time went on. The stocks of small companies are always off-limits to some managers of large funds, but there are times when so much money has flowed into small cap funds that there are few bargains left. Klarman moved on.

In the mid-1990s, he turned his attention to Western Europe. What he saw there reminded him of the United States a decade or so earlier. Corporate restructuring was just getting started, sparked by changes in tax laws and a realization that businesses were falling behind. Companies were beginning to spin off nonessential divisions, were buying back shares, and were trying to become more flexible. Because major investors in Europe were committed to brand name companies even more than investors in the United States were, values could be found among the stocks of smaller companies. And there was substantial room for the companies to improve their operations, as returns on equity were considerably lower than those in the United States. As a bottom up investor, Klarman did not buy shares simply because the overall environment looked good, but he did discover a new pond in which to fish. As more investors followed, he continued his eastward march. Countries behind the former Iron Curtain, emerging from communism into some type of market systems, had nascent stock markets and shares that were offered at what looked like fire sale prices. Even those that were sitting on fields of oil or natural gas, like Lukoil in Russia, were priced at 1 percent to 5 percent of what they would have fetched in the West. Mindful of the enormous political risks inherent in these countries, Klarman realized that he could lose 100 percent of anything he invested. He limited risk by keeping his exposure at a manageable level. Klarman bought in early—in 1995 and 1996—and rode the shares up. In 1997 he took substantial profits off the table. In 1998, with Russia more or less in default, he rode his remaining shares down. The economics of the companies may have been working out, but the political risks overwhelmed the financial fundamentals. Russia hurt Klarman's results in 1998, but viewed over the five year period from 1995 to 1999, he was still ahead of the game.

Texaco Bonds and Texas Law: How Bankruptcy Pays

During the takeover wave of the 1980s, Pennzoil tried to buy the much larger firm Getty Oil. Before the deal was completed, Texaco topped

Pennzoil's offer and won the bidding. Pennzoil brought a civil suit against Texaco for "tortious interference," and in April 1987 was awarded more than $11 billion by a Texas judge. Under Texas law, in order to appeal Texaco would have to post a bond equal to the judgment issued against it. Even for a firm like Texaco, it was a struggle to raise that mountain of cash. To protect itself from having to come up with that money and to prevent Pennzoil from placing liens on Texaco's assets, Texaco filed for bankruptcy. The company now had some breathing room, but a pale of uncertainty was cast over the size of its liabilities.

Among those obligations were Eurobonds (bonds denominated in dollars but issued outside the United States) that paid 12 percent annually, with only one payment per year. Klarman was attracted to this security. It was a senior obligation of Texaco, and, in his view, it was well covered by the assets of the company, no matter how severe the penalty Texaco might ultimately have to pay to Pennzoil. At any conceivable price for oil, Klarman reasoned, the company would have adequate assets to pay the judgment and still make good on its debts. In addition to the oil, it owned refineries, chemical plants, and a host of other marketable assets. At the end of 1986, the book value of its equity was over $13 billion. Given all this protection, Klarman was convinced that the Eurobonds were a safe investment.

What kind of return did he anticipate? The Eurobonds paid 12 percent interest once a year. When the company filed for bankruptcy protection, it was spared the need to make the interest payments, although the obligations did accrue. In the fall of 1987, the bonds traded at around $90. By that time, they had missed one interest payment of $12, and another six months of interest had accrued, meaning that Texaco would owe an owner of the bond $118 when the bond matured, which was 1989,[1] provided Texaco had emerged from Chapter 11. Klarman did the arithmetic (see Table 13.3), and he saw favorable returns even if it took several years to get paid. The sooner the better, naturally.

Texaco settled with Pennzoil for slightly more than $3 billion some nine months later, and Klarman was rewarded with a return that exceeded his best estimate. Since this was the largest position he has ever taken rel-

---

[1] Klarman's firm owned several issues; its largest position matured in 1989, but it also owned some due in 1987.

Table 13.3   Texaco Bond Returns (Approximate)

	Principal ($)	Interest ($)	Total ($)	Annual Rate of Return (%)
Current	100	18	118	
1 year	100	30	130	44
2 years	100	42	142	26
3 years	100	54	154	20
4 years	100	66	166	17
5 years	100	78	178	15

ative to money under management, the investment turned out exceptionally well.

Why? After all, Texaco was hardly an obscure or small company, and other analysts could reason along with Klarman that the company had adequate assets to pay off the bonds even if it did have to shell out $10 billion to Pennzoil. Here several of the Klarman principles help explain why he was able to take advantage of this opportunity.

Motivated sellers pushed down the price of the bonds. Many of them were prohibited by their charters from holding on to defaulted securities. Once Texaco missed an interest payment, the bonds fell into that category, and it did not matter that the default was going to be temporary. To these investors, distressed debt was forbidden fruit, even if the distressed was only a superficial blemish.

Absent buyers allowed Klarman to fill his needs at the $90 level. Even though there were investment funds whose strategy was to purchase distressed securities, many of them had high rate of return requirements. If the Texaco bonds did not pay off in less than two years, the return would fall below a 30 percent hurdle rate that made them unacceptable by the standards of these investors. So they stayed away. From Klarman's perspective, a rate of return only makes sense when set against the risk involved. Texaco bonds were subject to what he calls process risk and timing risk—how would the case work out in the courts and how long would it take?—both of which were easier to live with than credit risk, the possibility that the investor never gets paid. So Texaco worked out well for Klarman, and it worked out for the right reason—namely, that he had assumed the correct risks.

Chapter 14

Michael Price
Discipline, Patience, Focus, and Power

For a young man, Michael Price has had a long and prominent career as a value investor. In his twenties and thirties, he worked for, and then with, Max Heine, one of the most highly regarded men in the field, managing the Mutual Shares mutual fund. Price started his career there in 1975, directly out of college. When Heine died in an automobile accident in 1988, Price assumed direction and control of Mutual and its smaller fund siblings. In 1996 Price sold his fund business to Franklin Resources for a great deal of money. Franklin was prompted by corporate imperatives: They were strong in fixed income funds and wanted to expand their offerings of equity products. Price had both institutional and personal reasons for selling: His funds had grown so large that they required enormous physical and human overhead to manage, and a lot of that human overhead was coming from him. These complementary goals brought Franklin and Heine Securities (the corporate name for the Mutual series of funds) to an agreement between professionals. Price consented to stay on for a few years and keep a large part of his proceeds invested in the funds. That was not a problem for him, since in his mind there was no better place for his money. In 1998, when he did leave, it took him two days to get back into the business, albeit on a smaller scale with far fewer shareholders to worry about. Why not? He is good at it, and he enjoys it. Everyone should be so fortunate.

What actually brought Franklin Resources and Michael Price together was success. When Price started at Heine Securities, Mutual Shares had about $5 million under management. In 1973 and 1974, two disastrous years for the overall market, the fund had held up well. It continued to post strong returns for the rest of the decade and beyond. The late 1970s were not characterized by unrestrained enthusiasm for stocks. *Business Week's* infamous cover story "The Death of Equities" ran in 1979. The magazine listed a host of reasons why even the most experienced investors were abandoning stocks for real estate, gold, diamonds, and anything else but an ownership share of a business. In an environment like this, even a successful fund like Mutual Shares was not inundated with new money. But Heine and Price persisted, adhering to their value strategy, and when investment sentiment changed in the 1980s, they had a record of success that investors found appealing. *Found* is the perfect word here, because without spending money on advertising, promotion, or sales commissions, the fund still grew over time until it and its siblings passed $15 billion in assets. That is a compounded growth rate of around 50 percent a year, a combination of returns of around 20 percent and the new money that sought out Mutual Shares and Michael Price.

It is a mark of Price's craft as a value investor that he was able to maintain his performance even as the money under his care swelled. We have the sworn testimony of other value investors in this book that they prefer to work away from the crowd, that opportunities are more attractive when there are fewer players, and that small size is an advantage both regarding the companies they look at and the assets they have to manage. While it may be difficult to provide superior returns with a mass of money to invest, it is not impossible. Michael Price met the challenge by combining a strict adherence to the principles by which he was raised with a pragmatic exploitation of the power that size can convey. Too big to fly under the proverbial radar screen or to move unnoticed into diminutive niches, Price realized that owning a large block of securities could give him a voice in company decisions. He did not have to sit patiently and wait or pray for the executives to turn the company around; he could encourage them to take the steps that actually would, in what must be managements' most clichéd phrase, "enhance shareholder value."

Even in those instances in which he could use his size to become his own catalyst, Price has operated consistently within the framework of a set of value investment principles that guide his practice. He has followed these principles when Mutual Shares was small, when it was huge, and again today, when the portfolio he runs is small again, by his choice.

Lower the Risk First, and Higher Returns Will Follow

Before Price joined Mutual Shares, the fund was already known for its ability to weather down markets. Max Heine was a pioneer in bankruptcy investing, and the securities he owned in companies undergoing reorganization were more or less immune from market fluctuations. The cheap stocks that made up the value portion of the portfolio also proved less vulnerable to bear markets. This stability served the fund well in 1973 and 1974, when the Dow-Jones Industrial Average declined by 40 percent over the two-year period. The Standard & Poor's 500 posted similar losses, and two years later neither index had climbed back to its level at the end of 1972. Mutual Shares, by contrast, fell 8.1 percent in 1973, then gained 8.2 percent in 1974, 34.1 percent in 1975, and 55.2 percent in 1976. Over the four-year period, the fund had produced a compounded return of more than 100 percent. The message to Price was clear: if you don't do too badly during the down years, you only have to perform decently during the up years to beat the averages over time. His goal has been clear since then: to earn compounded returns of 15 percent per year. At that rate, assets double in less than five years. Because the strategy has less volatility than the market as a whole, shareholders are spared the sickening feeling of seeing their holdings cut in half. They are much less likely to take their money and run. The business grows in part because it doesn't have to pay out massive redemptions.

Structuring the Portfolio to Match the Strategy

There are few professional money managers who will admit that their approach to investing subjects their clients to stomach-turning levels of risk. Even the most audacious momentum players like to think that their skills, their stop-loss systems, or other tested techniques will keep their portfolios protected from market crashes. Thus, a goal frequently invoked is to match the market when it is going up but to decline less when it is going down. This is unquestionably a respectable ambition, but it takes more than wishes to bring it about. Price and his colleagues at Mutual, reflecting on their performance in the turbulent years of the mid 1970s, concluded that they owed a large part of their success to the structure of their portfolio. They kept about two thirds of the investments in (to use Price's technical language) cheap stocks. The other third was divided as opportunity dictated among bankruptcy plays, arbitrage positions, and cash, with the cash never falling below 5 percent of the portfolio.

The bankruptcy investments moved to the timing of the legal procedures, not to the stock market or the economy. The arbitrage positions were all in publicly announced deals, largely takeovers for which financing was available. Price saw these investments as a more profitable use of cash than money market alternatives such as Treasury bills or bankers' acceptances. The returns available were generally in the range of 15 percent to 20 percent, on an annualized basis, and they existed because there was always some risk that the deal might collapse or take longer to close than was initially anticipated. By putting together a group of 5 to 10 out of the 300 or so deals generally available and liquid enough to be traded in quantity, Price had managed to protect another portion of the portfolio from the turbulence of the market while earning more than a decent return. Over the years, the volatility of his portfolios has averaged around 40 percent less than that of the market itself. The system has worked so well that when Price sold Heine Securities and began to manage money for family and friends, he naturally adopted the same approach to portfolio structure.

Streetwise and Wise to the Street

When the market raced to new highs in 1998 and 1999, driven in part by the demand for stocks of companies with new, promising, and as yet unprofitable technology, Price did not participate. Like all value investors, he was not convinced that many of these companies would ever earn a dollar, and he believed strongly that the price the market was willing to pay for nothing more than hope was ludicrous. As a private money manager, Price did not have to worry about being punished for poor relative performance. Given his long-term record and history of adhering to his discipline, there is no doubt that even if he were answerable to shareholders, he would still have stayed away from what has proved to have been a bubble.

Price's refusal to be swept up in the Internet and associated enthusiasms stems both from his valuation principles and from his understanding of the ways of Wall Street. We may regard the rise and subsequent decline of the new technology stocks as just another in the long list of manias that periodically sweep through investment markets, but in recent years at least, these manias have had a motivator more corporeal than the madness of crowds. Though there are a number of ways in which investment banks can earn money, traditional stock brokerage is not among the more lucrative ones. Commission rates are too low. Investment banking fees, by contrast, are generous. So these banks make much more money financing deals or taking companies public than they do in handling trades. When the public is hungry for initial public offerings (IPOs), the investment banks are only too happy to oblige. They can make 7 percent on the money they raise in new equity offerings, versus a few cents per share on an ordinary brokerage transaction. (With enough volume, even a few cents can add up to real money.) While this compensation arrangement ought to be a warning sign to investors, it gets ignored amid all the promotion and other hype that accompany the offering.

The message is that IPOs have extremely motivated sellers. But unlike the insurance company that is motivated to sell a nonperforming real estate loan because of regulatory requirements, the motivation of investment banks, the venture capitalists, and the proprietors of the company coming public is to paint this generally young and untried firm as a sure winner in an enormous marketplace now in its infancy. Though Securities and Exchange Commission regulations require that all sorts of disclaimers about the company's potential be included in the prospectus, the interests behind the offering trump that cautionary tale with their own versions of future riches. Inflated expectations drive the share price of hot issues straight up, especially because there will be relatively few shares available for purchase.

For those fortunate or important enough to get a bloc of the stock at the opening price, holding for a few hours and then selling the shares has been an extremely rewarding tactic. For anyone getting in at the end of the first day, overall results have been poor. The earnings of the investment banks, by contrast, have been superb, which is one of the most important reasons why the markets as a whole and the IPO and technology sectors within them rose to heights that were unprecedented when measured by any valuation yardstick.

Wall Street has other games to play. IPOs represent only a small portion of the money it raises for public firms. Seasoned firms may be reluctant to tap the equity market for fear of signaling to the world that they need an infusion of equity capital, but they issue debt continually, spin off and sell divisions, and find other ways to raise money from the public. The bigger the company, the more likely it is to be client of an investment bank. At the top of the ladder, companies in the Dow-Jones index or at the head of the Fortune 500 list deal with a stable of investment banks, each of them ready to take more of the company's banking business. There is nothing wrong with that; it is how capital is raised in a market economy. But then, as Michael Price knows and we should remember, these are the same investment firms writing research reports on their clients, and making buy or hold (sell recommendations have disappeared) recommendations regarding their shares. With all the talk about Chinese walls separating the various functions of the large investment/brokerage firms, investment professionals take as a given that no sell-side analyst is going to prejudice his or her firm's ability to win banking business from the company under examination. This fact of business life encourages a positive bias in analysts' reports and helps explain why many value investors claim they never rely on sell-side research.

Michael Price certainly does not rely on sell-side research, but he is willing to use it for a convenient summary of a complicated firm's business segments and as a check on his own valuation approach. For example, in October, 2000, General Electric snatched Honeywell away from another suitor by offering to pay $45 billion in GE stock. Since GE has probably the lowest cost of debt capital of any American industrial firm, Price wondered whether its decision to make the acquisition by issuing equity might be an acknowledgment that its shares were overpriced. Should he short GE? Here was probably the most highly respected company on the globe, with a CEO who had been elevated to near deity status by the media—hardly a candidate for the underappreciated stock award. To speed his work, Price started with a recent report from an analyst at one of the largest investment and brokerage houses.

At the time of the report, just before the announcement of the Honeywell purchase, GE shares were priced at $56.63. The 10 billion shares outstanding gave GE a market capitalization of $570 billion. The analyst estimated that GE would earn $1.27 per share in 2000, and, given the precision with which the company had continually met expectations, that number was a pretty safe bet. It did mean, however, that GE was selling at almost 45 times estimated earnings and 36 times estimated cash flows. These are high multiples for a mature giant, a company that was already first or second in virtually every market in which it operated. The analyst was not deterred; she argued that putting a 48 multiple on next year's estimated earnings could justify a target price for GE of $70.

What caught Price's attention was neither the *buy* recommendation of the report nor this optimistic forecast of what lofty multiple the market would reward GE's estimated earnings. Both were to be expected. He turned instead to the breakdown by business segment and did his own informal valuation by putting a realistic multiple on each of the segments' operating earnings, leaving aside only GE Capital, the company's financial businesses.

By his calculations (shown in Table 14.1), the nonfinancial segments of GE deserved on average a pretax operating multiple of 10.8, the equivalent of around 17 times the fully taxed operating earnings. These were primarily manufacturing businesses, some as unglamorous as home appliances, some with a little high-tech cachet, but none of them capable of explosive growth with little additional capital investment. In November, 2000, Maytag had a price to earnings ratio of 9, and Whirlpool's was less than 7; these are after-tax ratios. The power generation business was so unattractive that Westinghouse abandoned it. Though one might argue with Price's multiples, it is hard to increase them substantially and still keep a straight face. To err on the side of liberality, let us say that the nonfinancial

Table 14.1   **GE Segment Analysis**

	Estimated Operating Earnings, 2000	EBIT Multiple	Value
Aircraft engines	$2,415	12	$28,980
Appliances	$595	10	$5,950
Broadcasting	$1,780	15	$26,700
Power generating	$2,640	10	$26,400
Lighting	$770	9	$6,930
Transportation	$560	9	$5,040
Industrial systems	$875	9	$7,875
GE supply	$120	6	$720
Materials	$1,910	10	$19,100
Medical systems	$1,600	10	$16,000
GE info systems	$125	8	$1,000
Total	$13,390	10.8	$144,695
GE Capital	$5,200		
Shares outstanding	10,068		
Price per share	$56.63		
Market cap	$570,151		

Note: All dollar figures are in millions except for price per share.

segments of GE were worth, at the time of the report, 15 times operating earnings, or $200 billion. With a market value of $570 billion, that left a $370 billion hole to be filled by GE Capital, a company with operating earnings of $5.2 billion. What kind of legerdemain does it take to transform a financial services company's pretax earnings of $5.2 billion into a market value of $370 billion, giving it a multiple in excess of 70? We know the answer: Wall Street magic, energized by the potential of investment banking business.

The moral is clear and adds to the lesson of the IPO phenomenon: Trust the Street at your own peril. Wall Street needs to generate excitement. That is how investment firms get paid. When the game is working and the public is motivated more by greed than by fear, value investors will be left out and left behind. Their performance will look puny when compared to their growth-oriented peers. The pressure to abandon the discipline and dive into the pool will be intense, especially for those managers who do not have the institutional support to stay the course. But for those who can wait out the eruption of enthusiasm—those with patience and job security—opportunities will abound when the excitement wanes and fear reappears.

Valuation: How Much Is That Business Really Worth?

To estimate the intrinsic value of a firm, Price asks one question: How much is a knowledgeable buyer willing to pay for the whole company? He finds his answer by studying the mergers and acquisitions transactions in which companies are bought and sold. Every transaction produces voluminous documents in which the parties to the transaction spell out in detail the basis for the price that is agreed upon: How much is being paid for each revenue stream that makes up the company being acquired? The investment bankers who turn out these documents provide a range of multiples. Price and his associates accumulate that information into a knowledge base that tells them the current prices actually being paid in the mergers and acquisition markets, which is the market for control of the company. New transactions allow them to update the knowledge base while still sticking to the principle that the deal price determines the multiple, not the other way around. Because each large company operates in more than one line of business, the knowledge has to be organized on a business-segment basis. No two companies will be exactly alike, but each is made up of divisions for which Price may have sufficiently current information about the prices at which these are changing hands.

Price does not rule out more traditional approaches to valuation: reproduction costs of the assets, how much they are insured for, multiples of cash flow, and even book value. But he uses these as checks on the transactions-based valuations that he assembles from studying the market for control. His preference for the deal-based valuation is that it is current, that it incorporates the informed buyer's valuation of the business, and that it includes a premium for control that may be worth a lot to the share owner who finds that his or her investment is now in play.

The Search for Cheap Stocks

The newspaper is a steady and fertile source of information for Price. He pays little attention to anything about the economy at large, where he feels that his ignorance is no greater than that of the experts, but a great deal of attention to specific items about real companies. He looks at all the deals, of course, but also at news about companies missing earnings expectations, companies in trouble, and companies hitting new lows. His definition of a cheap stock is one that is selling at 40 percent below his estimate of its intrinsic value. Many of the companies he spots aren't there yet, so he waits until the price drops to meet his standards.

In the interim, he does his homework on these potential investments. He wants to know about the business on a segment-by-segment basis, so that he can be confident about his valuation. He is also interested in the management. Are they owners themselves, and have they acted in the interests of shareholders? Have they engaged in self-dealing—that is, paying themselves for consultations or renting real estate for the company in buildings they own? Who is on the Board of Directors? Should Price expect them to act in the interests of the shareholders, or are they functionaries of current management? Are there other reasons why this company is not a candidate for a takeover? Nobody is going to buy GE or Cisco; they are simply too big. There are additional impediments that Price pays attention to, such as too much debt on the balance sheet to allow a purchaser to finance an acquisition, or a control class of stock that doesn't trade in the public market. GM may be put in play, but Ford seems invulnerable because the family owns the control stock. He does not expect that all of his cheap stocks will be taken out by control buyers, but he wants to have that as a prospect for as many as possible. The premium for control can transform a mediocre investment into an extraordinary one.

The search strategy also identifies industries undergoing consolidation. Changes in the economic environment, in governmental laws and regulations, and in technology all can be spurs to consolidation. When real estate investment trusts (REITs) became a fashionable investment, they grew in number from 30 to around 350. Wall Street will supply what the market demands. But as there are no sound business reasons for there to be that many, the chances for consolidation are good if only because a lot of overhead can be eliminated. When the prices for many of their shares dropped, REITs caught Price's attention both as cheap stocks and candidates for acquisition. These features are obviously linked; even control buyers like bargains.

Bankruptcy Investing Is Value Investing, Only Better

The same newspapers and trade journals that point Price to cheap stocks lead him to potential bankruptcy situations. And he is looking for basically the same thing: assets selling for less than their intrinsic value as determined by the market for control. The difference is that the companies that have filed for bankruptcy have more severe problems, generally from one of two sources. Either they have taken on too much debt and cannot meet their interest obligations, or they are being sued for a mammoth sum and have filed for bankruptcy to protect them from the claimants. In either case, a bankruptcy is an opportunity, provided the investor knows what he or she is doing. That means being able to analyze the liability side of the balance sheet as well as the asset side, and understanding the legal pathways through which bankrupt companies move as they either reorganize or liquidate.

Price wants to spot companies that are headed for bankruptcy before they file, not to buy securities immediately but to build up his store of information. On the liability side, it is crucial to identify the hierarchy of claims and whether any of them have specific assets pledged as security. In the event of liquidation, the assets will probably not be sufficient to pay off all the debt, so it may help to be standing in front of the line. If the company is reorganized and does emerge from bankruptcy, the creditors will be paid in cash or new securities depending on the kind of debt they hold. Early in the bankruptcy process, before anyone can predict the outcome with certainty, it is much safer to hold senior debt. Price's rule is to buy it only after the price has fallen to 30 percent or 40 percent of what the enterprise is worth. As events unfold and the outlines of the reorganization begin to take shape, the knowledgeable investor may decide to move down the seniority ladder and assume higher risk for the promise of a much higher return.

There are four main stages to most bankruptcies:

1. Before the filing, when the company may be trying to get creditors to agree on a solution (meaning that creditors will accept less than the face value of the debt they own in exchange for a speedier and more certain outcome) or to attract new capital
2. The filing itself, either with this solution in hand (known in the trade as a *prepack*) or not
3. The reorganization plan as offered first by the firm in bankruptcy and then negotiated with and among the various creditors until an agreement is reached
4. Emergence of the firm from bankruptcy, with a new capital structure and new securities issued to claimants

An investor can make a profit in each of these stages. Before the filing, while the company is scrambling to avoid bankruptcy, someone with cash can negotiate with the company, which is now under considerable duress, to buy a large chunk of equity or debt on extremely favorable terms. If the new infusion of cash helps the company right itself and return to profitability, the investment will have been a triumph. This is one of the areas in which managing a large fund helps; if the company needed only a small infusion, it would not find itself in such dire straits to begin with.

After the filing, some holders of the debt will be obligated by their investment policy to sell it, and bonds that have traded at 85 cents on the dollar can now fall to 70 cents or less. Some banks will be anxious or compelled to sell their loans, and though this paper may be higher on the claims ladder than the most senior bonds, it may fall in price below them. This is another place in which size is an advantage, because banks will want to sell off their loans wholesale to a ready buyer. At the same time, all the levels of bonded debt are being repriced in the market. In this tumultuous period, the prepared investor may be willing to trade down in seniority level because the junior debt has gotten so cheap. During this period, the company is filing monthly papers with the bankruptcy court spelling out in great detail what the company is doing. Investors who take the trouble to read these filings can learn more about the company in bankruptcy than they can about any healthy company that files a Form 10Q only quarterly.

The company itself has the first shot at filing a reorganization plan. Owners of the various classes of securities have been trying to anticipate what the plan will look like, especially the proposals for satisfying the creditors' claims. There is money to be made by figuring all this out in advance and holding that class of security in which the gap between price and payout is largest. Under bankruptcy law, owners of two-thirds of each class of debt have to approve the plan of reorganization. Here again size can be an advantage, since an investor has to own only one third of any class to be able to block an agreement. The negotiations among the creditors can be spirited; they are carving up a finite pie, and each wants to secure a decent return on the money invested. Price tries to own a large enough block to have a voice in the negotiations, even veto power, without becoming a member of an official creditor committee, which would prevent him from trading the bonds while the settlement was in progress.

The last stage is either liquidation or emergence from bankruptcy. If the company liquidates, that is the end of the story, and the holders of debt will be paid with the proceeds from the sale of assets according to their place in the claims line. The situation is more interesting if it emerges as a new company. During the bankruptcy, the firm has not had to pay interest or taxes, so its cash position has generally improved. It may have sold off assets such as land or buildings, also increasing its liquidity. The divisions that were a drain on profitability may have been closed or otherwise disposed of, leaving the new company with the better businesses. And it has restructured its liabilities, reducing its debt load to something the new company's cash flows can handle. For all these reasons, the new company is likely to be stronger than its predecessor.

It has also disappeared from view, as far as Wall Street is concerned. No analysts cover it, and the owners of shares in the old company have probably received little if anything and have nothing but enmity for the successor company. Bond holders may have received new equity as part of their settlement, and a number of them want to dispose of the shares. Thus, conditions are ripe for the informed value investor to acquire a mass of cheap stock. They may have received some for their bond holdings, one of the reasons they bought the bonds in the first place, and now they will be able to buy more from the motivated sellers. The connecting thread through all the stages of bankruptcy and the various ways of profiting from an investment is knowledge: knowledge about the company and the intrinsic value of its assets, knowledge about the classes of debt and the assets backing them, knowledge about the bankruptcy process and the ways in which creditors can influence decisions, and knowledge about the condition of the new company and its underlying value. The more knowledge the better, and the earlier an investor can figure out what is likely to happen, the greater the payoff. This isn't particle physics; the field has gotten more crowded in recent years, and Price has started to look elsewhere for ways of acquiring cheap stock. But anyone wanting to profit from bankruptcy investing ought to be certain that they do understand all of the elements that are involved in a bankruptcy episode. With corporate debt at historically high levels, there will be no shortage of opportunities to put that expertise to work.

Encouraging Companies to Do the Right Thing

In 1995 stories about Michael Price moved from the financial pages to the front pages thanks to his investment in Chase bank and the steps he took to raise the price of its shares. Chase stock was selling for around $34. The bank had earnings in 1994 of $5.87 per share, with the book value of its common equity at $38. Price also calculated that among the bank's credit card, mortgage servicing, and several other businesses, there was the equivalent of another $30 of hidden assets per share that simply were not recorded on the balance sheet because of accounting rules. By this estimate, Chase's stock was deeply underpriced. The bank must have agreed; they had bought 8.5 million of their own shares in 1994. Now Chase was about to issue 11 million shares to purchase a business with $300 million of revenues from U.S. Trust. That is, as Price saw it, it was going to use stock to buy a business that was not worth the $380 million in market value that

Chase was paying, much less the $700 million in the intrinsic value of the stock.

For passive investors, a group that historically has included most of the large pools of capital like pension, insurance, and mutual funds, the way to deal with poor management decisions is to sell the stock if you own it or to avoid it if you do not. Life is too short and the outcome too uncertain to get into a contest with management when there are hundreds and even thousands of other companies to buy. Price took a different approach. Because Chase stock was cheap, he bought a lot of it: 11 million shares, or more than 6 percent of the stock outstanding. When investors buy more than 5 percent of the shares of a company, they have to file a Form 13D with the SEC. Many investors never get to that 5 percent, not wanting to let the world know what they are doing. Price was not reticent. He announced in the 13D filing that he thought the shares were undervalued by the market. He was trying to get the attention of Chase's management; more than that, he wanted them to abandon that intended acquisition.

To buttress his case, he started to visit the other larger shareholders of the bank, explaining to them what he thought its shares were worth and why management's proposed acquisition was a mistake. Chase executives made the same rounds, arguing that the investors should be patient and that their own plans for Chase would produce even more value. But Price was not deterred. He made the legal arrangements necessary to buy additional shares and to get seats on the board of directors. In the interim, all this activity made its mark on the analysts at the brokerage houses, who began to write about the merits of Chase merging with another money center bank. The price of the bank's shares began to rise, and after a few months, Chase and Chemical Bank sent out their wedding announcement, which was a euphemism for Chemical's purchase of Chase. Shareholders of Chase received around $54 worth of Chemical stock in the deal. Those who held on saw the price more than double over the next two years.

This is a story with several messages. One certainly is that size can be made to pay, provided that the manager knows how to apply the leverage. In Chase's case, it took more than a phone call to the CEO to get the bank to change course. Price had to consult with other large holders and threaten to move for seats on the board of directors to force management's hand. He sees a general trend having developed over the last decade or so in which managements have become more attentive to the views of their institutional shareholders, and he no doubt played his part in that change. Second, his valuation of Chase may not have been perfect, but it was substantially better than management's. That valuation was confirmed when Chemical bought them out for $20 more than the pre-deal price, and the success of the bank after the merger added additional support. Third, catalysts are important in realizing the value of an investment. In the end, he succeeded in the Chase episode by becoming his own catalyst. Most of the time, however, it is business buyers who perform that role, at least for the cheap stock portion of his portfolio. The reason that deals add so much to his overall performance is that his analysis is done with the prospects of a deal always in mind. Companies that no one can buy do not end up in his portfolio. The Chase investment was made during a period of bank consolidation, which is another reason he found it appealing.

Do Your Homework, and Do It Early

There are three or four attributes that define Price's approach to investing. One is discipline: Don't deviate from the valuation standards, especially as the sirens of momentum are enticing the unwary. Also, don't alter the policy you have established for the composition of the portfolio just because other approaches are currently more favored. Price's own structure was carefully designed to control risk and still provide excellent returns. A second quality is patience: After the analysis has been completed and the intrinsic value is determined, don't chase the stock. It is important to wait for the market to offer a price with a discount large enough to allow for a margin of safety. The third virtue is focus: Don't be distracted by global predictions or macro forecasts, either by listening to them or making them yourself. It is much easier to understand a security than an economy, and the way to profit is by using that understanding.

Finally, do your homework. Each investment is a wager against the party on the other side of the trade. Only one of you will be right, and the prize usually goes to the person who knows more about the security and knows it sooner. The best strategy for the investor is to broaden and deepen the store of relevant knowledge. Each of the areas Price focuses on—cheap stocks, arbitrage, and bankruptcies—leads him to examine the businesses as a control buyer would look at them. The arbitrage positions are generally takeovers; they offer useful information about how much acquirers are paying for what kinds of businesses. The bankruptcies add additional information; as assets are sold off by the restructuring company, Price records the prices at which they change hands. Cheap stocks, such as Chase bank in 1995, and expensive stocks, such as GE in 2000, all have business segments that can be valued by reference to what buyers are paying for similar operations. The store of knowledge expands with each deal, each stock purchase, and each arbitrage position. With a large and current base of knowledge, the value investor can move quickly to take advantage of a fleeting opportunity. Patience is certainly a virtue for investors, but so is alacrity when the situation demands.

Chapter 15

Walter and Edwin Schloss
Keep It Simple, and Cheap

Walter Schloss started his limited partnership in the middle of 1955. He tracks his performance from January 1, 1956, a date sufficiently historic to give him one of the longest uninterrupted records—same manager, same organization—in investment history. He also has one of the best. Over the entire 45-year period from 1956 through 2000, Schloss and his son Edwin, who joined him in 1973, have provided their investors a compounded return of 15.3 percent per year. During the same period, the Standard and Poor's Industrial Index[1] had comparable total returns of 11.5 percent. Every dollar a fortunate investor entrusted with Schloss at the start of 1956 had grown to $662 by the end of 2000, including all charges for management (see Figure 15.1). A dollar invested in the S&P Index would have been worth $118. The Schlosses' accomplishment is even better than this initial comparison suggests. Over that entire 45-year period, their portfolio had seven years in which it lost money; the S&P Index had 11. The average loss in the Schloss partnership was 7.6 percent; in the S&P, 10.6 per-

[1] Walter Schloss began using the S&P Industrial Index in 1955 because without utilities or transportation companies, it more accurately matched the investments in his portfolio. He has kept that index as his benchmark comparison even as the S&P 500 has become the proxy of choice. Comparing the two over the last two decades, we found that they tracked each other very closely and that the Industrial had a slightly higher return than the 500.

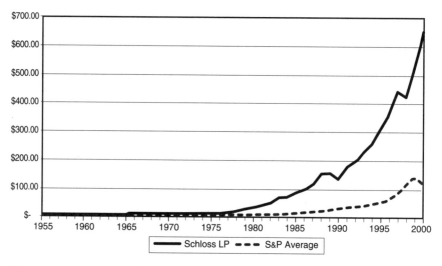

Figure 15.1   Value of $1.00 Invested in the Schloss partnership versus the S&P Industrial Index, 1956–2000

cent. Modern investment theory argues that return is compensation for risk, that higher returns are achieved only by increasing the volatility of the portfolio. The investment success of the Schlosses does not confirm the theory.

Walter and Edwin Schloss are minimalists. Their office—Castle Schloss has one room—is spare; they don't visit companies; they rarely speak to management; they don't speak to analysts; and they don't use the Internet. Not wanting to be swayed to do something they shouldn't, they limit their conversations. There is an abundance of articulate and intelligent people in the investment world, most of whom can cite persuasive reasons for buying this stock or that bond. The Schlosses would rather trust their own analysis and their long-standing commitment to buying cheap stocks. This approach leads them to focus almost exclusively on the published financial statements that public firms must produce each quarter. They start by looking at the balance sheet. Can they buy the company for less than the value of the assets, net of all debt? If so, the stock is a candidate for purchase.

This may sound familiar. If Walter Schloss was not present at the creation of value investing, he showed up shortly thereafter. He started on Wall Street in 1934, at age 18, in the midst of the Depression. During the late 1930s, Schloss took courses from Benjamin Graham at the New York Stock Exchange Institute. He was in good company; his fellow students included Gus Levy, head of the arbitrage department at Goldman Sachs; Cy Winters of Abraham, at one time president of the New York Society of Security Analysts; and other Wall Street heavyweights. At the time Schloss was working at Carl M. Loeb and Company, Graham's brother Leon was a customer's man at the firm, and Graham kept his account there, allowing Schloss to confirm that Graham did indeed practice what he preached in class. And he preached value—the advantage of paying less for stocks than for the value of the current assets after deducting all liabilities. Graham hired Schloss in 1946, as soon as Walter was discharged from the service.

One of Graham's favorite teaching strategies was to analyze two companies side by side, even if they were in different industries, and compare the balance sheets. He would take Coca-Cola and Colgate, related to one another only by alphabetical proximity, and ask which stock was more of a bargain relative to the net asset values. Graham's primary concern was the margin of safety, a focus which prevented him from recognizing the great growth potential in Coke. Not all of Graham's tactics worked out. He would buy a leading company in an industry, such as the Illinois Central Railroad, and sell short a secondary one, like Missouri Kansas Texas, as a hedge. As it turned out, the two securities were not correlated, and the hedge did not work. Another type of hedge that Graham used repeatedly was to buy a convertible preferred stock and short the common. If the common rose, he was protected by the convertible feature. If it fell, he made money on the short. In either case, he collected the dividend. This approach has become a standard practice in the industry even though it no longer has the tax advantages it once did. Schloss sees Graham as a legitimate genius, someone whose thinking was original and often contrary to established wisdom. Graham's motivation, Schloss thinks, was primarily intellectual. He was more interested in the ideas than in the money, although that too had its rewards.

Looking for Cheap Stocks

Ask either Schloss about his investment strategy and you will get the same succinct response: We buy cheap stocks. Identifying "cheap" means comparing price with value. What generally brings a stock to the Schlosses' attention is that the price has fallen. They scrutinize the new lows list to find stocks that have come down in price. If they find that the stock is at a two- or three-year low, so much the better. Some brokers with whom they have done business over the years call them with suggestions. These securities tend to be at the opposite end of the spectrum from the momentum stocks that most brokers are peddling. The Schlosses are especially attracted to stocks that have gapped down in price—stocks where the price decline has been precipitous.

This taste for fiasco is very contrarian. Stock prices sink when investors have been disappointed, either by a recent event such as an earnings announcement below expectations, or by continued unsatisfactory performance that ultimately induces even patient investors to throw in the towel. Over the many years that the Schlosses have managed money, they have found themselves investing in different industries, in large, medium, and small companies; in companies with shares that have plummeted in price, and in those that have slid downward gradually but persistently. The unifying theme is that the stuff they buy is on sale.

The other term in their strategy is equally important. They buy stocks. They don't buy derivatives, indexes, or commodities. They don't short stocks; they have in the past, and have made some money, but the experience was uncomfortable for them. They don't try to time the market, although they do let the market tell them which stocks are cheap. At some points in their careers, the Schlosses did invest in bankrupt bonds, and if the situation presented itself to them, they might again. But that field has become more crowded over the years, and like most value investors, they don't want too much company. As for ordinary fixed income investments, they steer clear. The potential returns are limited, and they can be negative if interest rates rise. Their business is making money for their partners by investing in cheap stocks.

When they find a cheap stock, they may start to buy even before they have completed their research. They have at least a rudimentary knowledge of thousands of companies, and they can consult Value Line or the S&P stock guide for a quick check into the company's financial position. Both Schlosses believe that the only way really to know a security is to own it, so they sometimes stake out their initial position and then send for the financial statements. The market today moves so fast that they are almost forced to act quickly.

What Is It Worth? Valuing Assets, Earnings, and Companies

For the nine-and-a-half years that Walter Schloss worked for Ben Graham and for some years after he left to run his own partnership, he was able to find stocks selling for less than two thirds of working capital. But sometime after 1960, as the Depression became a distant memory, those opportunities generally disappeared. Today, companies that meet that requirement are either so burdened by liabilities or are losing so much money that their future is in jeopardy. Instead of a margin of safety, there is an aura of doubt.

Nevertheless, Walter has retained his preference for valuation based on assets. A company's assets are more stable than its earnings. If a company has a tangible book value of $15 per share, then even if it is not earning money at the moment, the chances are good that the value of the assets will not drop precipitously. An investor paying $10 or even $12 per share has some comfort in knowing that the assets are there to back up the shares. And in Schloss's long experience, company's whose shares can be bought for less than the value of the assets will, more often than not, either return to profitability or be taken over by another firm. All of this may take time; their average holding period for a stock is around four years. Walter has the patience to hold on. The underlying bet he is making is that overreaction by the market has offered him a bargain, and that given enough time, he will be rewarded. "Something good will happen," he likes to say. And in the interim, the asset value provides some protection against another steep drop in the price of the shares. Though he tends to make his initial purchase before the stock has bottomed, and likes the opportunity to add to his position at lower prices, he also sleeps better at night knowing that if there is a cliff out there, his shares have already fallen over it.

Edwin Schloss pays attention to asset values, but he is more willing to look at a company's earnings power. He does want some asset protection. If he finds a cheap stock based on normalized earnings power, he generally will not consider it if he has to pay more than three times book value. There are some durable companies in industries such as food, defense, and even plain old manufacturing, that sell for more than book value even when their share prices are depressed. Depending on his estimate of what the companies can earn, Edwin may still find the stock cheap enough to buy.

When they begin to take a hard look at a new company, the Schlosses make sure to read the annual reports thoroughly. The financial statements are important, no doubt, but so are the footnotes. They want to be certain that there are no significant off–balance sheet liabilities. They look at the history of capital spending to see what condition the fixed assets are in. A company that has a fully depreciated plant may be reporting higher earnings than a rival that has just completed a new factory, but if the rival has spent its money carefully, it is likely to have a more modern and more efficient operation. Ten years of advertising expenses don't show up on the balance sheet, but they do create some value for a brand, provided that the company knows how to exploit it. The Schlosses are looking for recovery potential. The stocks they buy have become cheap for a reason, and their success lies in their ability to form a sufficiently accurate estimate of whether or not the market has overreacted. They do not try to get inside the business, to know the details of the operations better than management itself. They don't claim or want that expertise. Instead, they limit their exposure to any single company and use their broad and deep investment experience to guide their judgment.

Because the Schlosses have been in the business so long, they have been forced to adjust their criteria as market conditions have changed. When markets are very expensive, their definition of cheap has to be somewhat more flexible and relative. As certain strategies, such as investing in bankrupt bonds, became popular, they moved to other areas. Like many great athletes and some other value investors, they let the game come to them. They have core principles that do not change. They buy cheap stocks, and they like to hold them until they have recovered. Otherwise, they are willing to take what the market offers them on the grounds that if they have bought correctly (i.e., if the stock was sufficiently cheap), the chances are that something good will happen.

Keeping Track

The Schlosses joke that they will go to corporate annual meetings that are held within a 20-block radius of their office. Since they work in mid-Manhattan (New York, not Kansas), that is a less severe restriction than it might initially appear. When they do show up, they like to be lonely, not surrounded by analysts and investment managers. Once, they owned shares of Asarco, a copper mining and smelting company; they went to the meeting and found the room full. On closer inspection, the other attendees turned out to be wives of directors, employees, and people working for the company's investment relations firm. Needless to say, the cheap stock had not yet been discovered. In this case, the company did recover from its price decline and was ultimately bought out by Grupo Mexico.

Because the Schlosses hold their positions on average for four or five years, they have time to become more familiar with the company. They continue to look at each quarterly report, but they do not obsess about day-to-day price swings or two-cents-per-share earnings disappointments or positive surprises. Their approach, as we said, is minimalist. If a company announces an acquisition that they regard as foolish, that would be cause for concern, and they might decide to sell. Since everything about their approach orients them toward companies that are not in rapidly changing industries in which technological innovation may undermine value in weeks if not days, they can afford to sit back and wait.

They are not entirely passive. Having started with a bottom up approach to finding a cheap stock, now that they own it they look laterally to analyze other firms in the industry. Are these also cheap, and for the same reasons? They may decide that one of these other companies is a better investment than their initial purchase. Perhaps it is a higher quality company, with better profit margins or lower debt levels. If so, they may trade up in quality, provided that they can still take advantage of the depressed status of the industry.

When to Buy, When to Sell

The notion that an investor can buy a stock that has reached the bottom of its fall is a fantasy. No one can accurately predict tops, bottoms, or anything in between. More often than not, value investors will start to buy a stock on the way down. The disappointments or reduced expectations that have made it cheap are not going away anytime soon, and there will still be owners of the stock who haven't yet given up when the value investor makes an initial purchase. If it is toward the end of the year, then selling to take advantage of tax losses can drive the price down even more. Because they are aware that they are—to use an industry cliché—catching a falling knife, value investors are likely to try to scale into a position, buying it in stages. For some, such as Warren Buffett, that may not be so easy. Once the word is out that Berkshire Hathaway is a buyer, the stock shoots up in price. Graham himself, Walter Schloss recounts, confronted this problem. He divulged a name to a fellow investor over lunch; by the time he was back in the office, the price had risen so much that he could not buy more and still maintain his value discipline. This is one of the reasons why the Schlosses limit their conversations.

Still, when asked to name the mistake he makes most frequently, Edwin Schloss confesses to buying too much of the stock on the initial purchase and not leaving himself enough room to buy more when the price goes down. If it doesn't drop after his first purchase, then he has made the right decision. But the chances are against him. He often does get the opportunity to average down—that is, to buy additional shares at a lower price. The Schlosses have been in the business too long to think that the stock will now oblige them and only rise in price. Investing is a humbling profession, but when decades of positive results confirm the wisdom of the strategy, humility is tempered by confidence.

Value investors buy too soon and sell too soon, and the Schlosses are no exceptions. The cheap stocks generally get cheaper. When they recover and start to improve, they reach a point at which they are no longer bargains. The Schlosses start to sell them to investors who are delighted that the prices have gone up. In many instances, they will continue to rise, sometimes dramatically, while the value investor is searching for new bargains. The Schlosses bought the investment bank Lehman Brothers a few years ago at $15 a share, below book value. When it reached $35, they sold out. A few years later it had passed $130. Obviously that last $100 did not end up in the pockets of value investors. Over the years, they have had similar experiences with Longines-Wittnauer, Clark Oil, and other stocks that moved from undervalued through fairly valued to overvalued without blinking. The money left on the table, to cite yet another investment cliché, makes for a good night's sleep.

The decision to sell a stock that has not recovered requires more judgment than does selling a winner. At some point, everyone throws in the towel. For value investors like the Schlosses, the trigger will generally be a deterioration in the assets or the earnings power beyond what they had initially anticipated. The stock may still be cheap, but the prospects of recovery have now started to fade. Even the most tolerant investor's patience can ultimately be exhausted. There are always other places to invest the money. Also, a realized loss has at least some tax benefits for the partners, whereas the depressed stock is just a reminder of a mistake.

The Portfolio: Diversification with Leeway

In the minds of some money managers, diversification is a defense against ignorance. The thoroughly informed investor, knowledgeable about the industry, the company, and even the economy, can take fewer and larger positions in situations in which he or she is fully informed. Value investors come down on both sides of the question of diversification, although all of them think there is an important role for active stock selection. The Schlosses run a diversified portfolio, but they do it without prescribed limits on the size of a position they will take. Though they may own 100 names, it is typical for the largest 20 positions to account for around 60 percent of the portfolio. They have occasionally had up to 20 percent of their fund in a single security, but that degree of concentration is a rarity. They are buying cheap stocks, we must remember, not great companies with golden futures. Though history has shown that most of their investments work out, there are always some that don't. The difficult task is to tell which will be which ahead of time. Diversification is a safeguard against uncertainty and an essential feature of the Schlosses's successful strategy.

Here as with other aspects of their approach, they rely on judgment rather than fixed rules. Although they are not going to end up with the portfolio invested in one or two industries, they will overweight their holdings when they find cheap stocks clustered together in out-of-favor sectors. At times like these, they can pick the better companies within these discarded securities. If the price of a commodity such as copper has plummeted, then copper-related stocks will be on sale. Unless copper disappears permanently from use as an industrial and communications material, the supply and demand cycles have a way of righting themselves. Companies with low costs that are not overburdened by debt are safe bets at these times, primarily because nobody wants to own them. A cheap price can make up for a multitude of cyclical, operational, and even managerial shortcomings.

Take Care of the Clients

When Walter Schloss had been in business for 20 years, including several with Edwin, Warren Buffett sent a letter to some friends describing the Schloss partnership. Schloss left Graham-Newman, Buffett told his readers,

> in 1955. And Graham-Newman closed up in 1956. I would prefer not to dwell on the implications of this sequence.
>
> In any event, armed only with a monthly stock guide, a sophisticated style acquired largely from association with me, a sublease on a portion of a closet at Tweedy, Browne, and a group of

partners whose names were straight from a roll call at Ellis Island, Walter strode forth to do battle with the S&P.

We have seen the results of that contest.

Other than an additional 25 years of superior performance, little else has changed. The Schlosses still sublet from Tweedy, Browne, although they have moved into a full-sized room. They supplement the monthly stock guide with Value Line and a quotation machine. And the nature of their clients has persisted—something that does distinguish the Schlosses' partnership from most similarly structured funds. There are partners in the fund whose parents were partners; some are even third-generation clients. As a group, they are not wealthy by the standards of limited partnerships. The money invested with the Schlosses is important to them, which is one reason why the Schlosses are determined not to lose it. It may also explain why the Schlosses do not disclose to their partners the names of the companies whose shares they own. In the main, they invest in unpresentable securities, stocks no one wants to brag about at cocktail parties or anywhere else. Through painful experience—agony both for the limited partners and themselves—they have found that letting the dogs out of the bag does not add to their clients' comfort level. Quite the reverse; some people have left the fund out of fear that the beaten-down shares in the portfolio were too risky. Despite all their experience with value investing and how the Schlosses practice it, these former clients were unable to incorporate the idea that at the right price—very low—the shares of a troubled company make a good investment.

The Schlosses are very attentive to the taxes their partners will have to pay. They do not like to sell shares in which they have a profit whenever the sale would constitute a short-term capital gain. This occasionally may put an investment at some risk; tax laws currently in place make it difficult, if not impossible, to protect the gain by a hedge until it goes long-term. Given the different tax rates between short- and long-term gains, that is a risk the Schlosses are willing to take.

There are two policies that the Schlosses follow in their partnership that set them apart from most money managers running similarly structured investment funds. First, they assume that they will distribute all the realized gains to their partners each year. If a partner asks that the money be kept in the fund, they will oblige, naturally. Most partnerships require an affirmative request, made many weeks in advance, for the withdrawal of any money, whether realized gains or not. The Schlosses do not regard the money entrusted to them as captive, requiring a rescue by the partner to pry it free. This policy also helps them keep a rough cap on the size of the fund. They don't want to manage billions of dollars; returning a large portion of the gains each year is like pruning back a shrub to the desired height. Second, the Schlosses get paid for their work by taking a portion of the investment returns. This is the typical practice for limited investment partnerships. Where they depart from the standard is that they also assume the same portion of the losses. If the fund has dropped in value over the year, the accounts of the limited partners decline less than the fund itself. The Schlosses are charged their proportional share of the loss. Also, they do not take a management fee from the fund; most of their peers do. They only get paid for performance. As their long history shows, in 7 years out of 45 they ended up worse off than they began. This arrangement is another incentive for them not to lose money.

Example 1: Asarco—Cheap Assets Find a Buyer

In 1999 Asarco was a copper company with a past more glorious than its current situation might suggest. Once a member of the Dow-Jones Industrial Average, it lost $1.70 per share in 1998, down from a gain of $5.65 in 1995. When the stock dropped below $15 per share, its market cap fell to under $600 million, less than the $885 million in long-term debt on its books. Despite all these troubles, however, Asarco had a book value of around $40 per share. Its assets included its 50 percent ownership of the Southern Peru Copper Company, the equivalent of one share per each share of Asarco. Southern Peru traded between $10 and $14 for most of the year. A purchase of Asarco at anywhere from $15 to $20 would leave the investor with a margin of safety of at least 50 percent based on book value; he or she would be paying between $5 and $10 for the potential earnings of the company, after deducting the value of the Southern Peru share.

Walter and Edwin had actually been buying and then selling Asarco since 1993. They picked up some at around $20 and sold it out above $30 the following year. When the stock fell in 1999, they moved back in. This turned out well. The company agreed to a merger of equals with Cyprus Amax Minerals. The larger copper firm Phelps Dodge then bid for both companies, trying to buy them before the merger. They turned Phelps down, even though its bid for Asarco was worth around $22. Now that Asarco was in play, it was just a matter of time before a higher offer appeared. The Schlosses finally sold their shares to Grupo Mexico for almost $30 in cash. If the assets are there, as Walter likes to say, something good will happen.

Example 2: J. M. Smucker Co.—Selling Sugar to Americans

Warren Buffett didn't say it, to our knowledge, but some of his investments—Coca-Cola, See's Candies, Dairy Queen—suggest a faith in the notion that no one ever went broke selling sugar to Americans. That is the business the Smucker family has been in for years, packaging the sugar in the form of jams, jellies, and other sweet treats. Although the company has earned money consistently, their outside shareholders have not fared so well. The shares hit a high of $39 in 1992, but from then through 1999 they seldom sold for as much as $30. Earnings varied little over this period, from $1.27 in 1993 to $1.26 in 1999; the book value increased from $7.55 to $11. The price-to-book ratio never fell below 1.5 to 1, and the price-to-earnings ratio only dropped below 15 on a bad day in 1999. On neither an assets nor earnings based valuation did Smucker qualify as a value investment.

Then, in 2000, the price dropped below $15 per share. Food stocks in general were a depressed group, and Smucker fell along with the others. The Schlosses bought some. At that price, the company was selling for 10 times earnings, well below its historic range. Though it was not a company with a franchise, it did have an established brand and a share of supermarket shelves. On an earnings power basis, it was cheap enough to take a position.

Two events made this a sweet investment. First, when Best Foods was bought out by Unilever, the prices of other food stocks rose in sympathy. Then, the Smucker family, which was the controlling shareholder of the firm, decided to simplify the share structure and do away with a class of super voting stock. This reorganization made the stock more liquid and also introduced the possibility that the company could be taken over, now that the super voting shares were eliminated. Thanks to Unilever and the family, the stock rose from $15 to $25 within seven or eight months. The Schlosses now had to chose between taking a short-term capital gain, not something they like, or continuing to hold a stock after it had ceased to be cheap and may have become overvalued. They took the rational course and decided that paying the tax would be less painful than seeing the shares decline to $15. Naturally, the stock rose to $27 before the end of the year, but now, at this higher price level, it is someone else's worry.

Chapter 16

Paul D. Sonkin

Small Is Beautiful, Especially When It's Ugly

The Old Time Religion

Paul Sonkin's career is shorter than the other investors profiled here, but only because he is the youngest. Like many of them, he bought his first shares before he started to shave. Today, he saves time by ignoring the sports pages, and he isn't the person to ask about the hottest restaurant or the latest novel. But if you want to learn about a small company whose shares have recently plummeted in price, Sonkin is the person to talk with. The chances are good that the stock will have turned up in one of his searches for cheap companies. If it has attracted his attention, he will have investigated sufficiently either to pass, which happens most of the time, or to be interested, in which case he will settle in to learn a lot more. Either way, he has added the stock to the list of firms he knows something about. Given his interest and his youth, he retains this information, and his list gets longer.

Sonkin is a graduate of the business school at Columbia, where he teaches courses on security analysis and advanced value investing. Before entering Columbia, he worked at the Securities and Exchange Commission and Goldman Sachs. Upon finishing school, he joined Royce & Associates, a money management firm specializing in small and microcap value securities, and served as an analyst and portfolio manager. From Royce he moved to First Manhattan Company, another value house, this one concentrating on larger company shares. Since November 1999 he has been the chief investment officer of the Hummingbird Value Fund, a limited partnership in which he has been able to return to the small and microcap world he loves.

The old testament of value investors is undoubtedly *Security Analysis*, the book that Benjamin Graham and David Dodd wrote in 1934. The book is currently in its fifth edition, but Sonkin and many value buffs prefer earlier versions. For Sonkin, the third edition, published in 1954, stands out. It is the last one actually written by Graham, and thus it benefits from the enriching of his own experience between the depths of the Depression and the post-war recovery. Sonkin also appreciates the letters that Graham wrote to the investors in the Graham-Newman partnership, as he does Warren Buffett's letters from the days before Berkshire Hathaway, when he was running the Buffett partnerships that made so many of his investors into genuinely wealthy people. Sonkin has less interest in, if no less regard for, the Berkshire annual letters. They date from a period in which Buffett had so much money to invest that he was forced to concentrate on large cap stocks that he could hold forever. Though the value discipline can still be applied in these circumstances, it is considerably more difficult. The investor is now betting against some of the most informed and intelligent players in the game, and the margin of error, if not the margin of safety, has been squeezed. Like other value investors, Sonkin prefers games with few if any other participants.

Following Graham, Sonkin's favorite place to locate value is on the balance sheet. And here, the higher up the asset list—cash and accounts receivable—the better. Though Graham's net-nets are much harder to find today than in 1934, the only place where one has a chance to locate any of them is in the small and especially the microcap area. No decent-sized company is going to escape the searches that investors perform every day looking for value. The small ones may not escape either, but people managing big pools of money will still stay away, and occasionally a net-net may fall through the cracks.

There is a better chance of finding a company that is still cash rich, though it doesn't meet the net-net standard. Sonkin loves to spot situations like the following. Say the firm has a market capitalization of $20 million with earnings of $1 million. Ordinarily this looks like a price per earnings (P/E) ratio of 20, and in most cases the stock is no bargain. But if the company has $15 million of net cash (cash after all the loans have been subtracted), then the whole company can be bought for an outlay of $5 million. The real P/E is closer to 5 (the interest earned on the $15 million has to be subtracted from net income), and the stock becomes a screaming buy. As a measuring device to spot these companies, Sonkin uses the *cap rate*, short for capitalization rate. The denominator in a cap rate equation is the market value of the debt plus the market value of the equity minus the cash or cash equivalents. The numerator is the operating earnings (EBIT) times (1 – tax rate). The purpose is to expose what an investor would have to pay to own all the after-tax operating earnings of the company. The cap rate analysis is a starting point for Sonkin, a kind of screening test to see if the company merits further work. Unlike more commonly used screens such as price to earnings or price to book, the cap rate differentiates among the assets and looks at operating earnings rather than net income, which can be misleading.

If It Ain't Broke, Don't Buy It

It is a truism that though all value investors are contrarians, not all contrarians are value investors. The difference is simple. While both are looking for beaten-down securities, the contrarians are content with measures like low P/E or low price to book, and they like to see a graph that shows the current price substantially off from the high. But for contrarians, that may be the end of the research effort. Value investors want to compare the current price of the securities not simply to its former high—all that means is that some investors are deeply disappointed—but to the intrinsic value of the firm, which means examining the assets and the earnings power. The fact that the security has tumbled in price may be a necessary condition for a value investment, but it is hardly sufficient.

In this vein, Sonkin likes to examine what he and others call *broken IPOs* (initial public offerings). During periods when the stock market has risen, there are powerful incentives to take new companies public. One inducement motivates the early investors in the company, whether family and friends or a venture capital firm. At last they are on track to cash out. Another applies to the people running the firm, who almost invariably own a large portion of it; the IPO allows them to raise cash for expansion at a relatively inexpensive rate. A third incentive drives the investment bankers who do the underwriting. The fees they receive from a successful IPO, around 7 percent, dwarf their payouts on other transactions. The brokers who get to distribute (sell) the offering to their clients are pushing for IPOs, as are those large investors who are given first crack at hot issues and can often buy and sell them during the first day for exorbitant returns.

To accommodate all these interests, the firm being taken public makes a strenuous effort to put its best face forward. It can freeze hiring in the year before the offering to show a decline in expenses. Other discretionary spending will be deferred, and revenue will be accelerated wherever possible. It may be that the need for these practices abated in the late 1990s, since the public appetite for IPOs in sexy industries was so intense that companies that had never come close to profitability were able to sell shares. Still, anyone buying shares in a new offering should be aware of how much hype and fluff has been built into the story, and into the price.

Take the case of SCC Communications (SCCX), a firm that provides specialized software to telephone companies. It came public in June 1998, underwritten by Robertson Stephens and Hambrecht and Quist, first-tier bankers in high-tech offerings. For the year ending December 1997, SCCX had net income from continuing operations of $2.45 million, although it had lost money on discontinued operations. Sales had virtually doubled from 1995 to 1996 and again from 1996 to 1997. The prospectus indicated that the company intended to sell 2.1 million shares at around $12 per share, to raise around $24 million. The company planned to employ some of the proceeds from the offering to pay off $4 million in bank debt; the rest would be used for general corporate purposes, including R&D. In addition to the 2.1 million shares being sold by the company, early investors were selling 1.2 million; none of the money for these shares would go to the company. Though each of these sellers would be selling only a small portion of their holdings, the fact that insiders were cashing in even some of their chips is never a great sign.

After the offering, there would be roughly 10 million shares outstanding, with a book value of around $3.50. In other words, for an investment of $12, the purchaser of a share of SCCX received $3.50 worth of assets that the company used to generate income, after paying off the debt. For

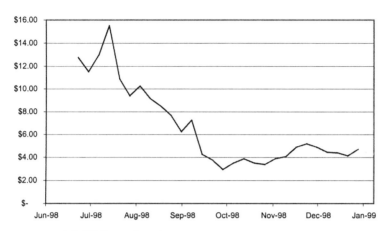

Figure 16.1   SCCX Price Graph, 1998

the year ending December 1998 (see Figure 16.1), that income turned out to be around $.50 per share not counting extraordinary items or dilution, and $.29 per share counting both—hardly figures that quicken the heart of a value investor.

Like most IPOs, the shares of SCCX moved upward from the initial price. A month later they traded at close to $16. But then reality and the outside world started to impinge. When the company announced its results for the second quarter of 1998, investors could see that the rate of growth both of revenue and earnings was starting to flatten out. While this damp-ening might not have had a major impact on a stock with a less inflated share price, for SCCX it was the start of a severe downward correction. By the end of August 1998, the shares were selling at around $7. They con-tinued a ragged decline until they fell below $3 in September 1998, a time in which the whole market was tumbling thanks to Russian debt default, the Long Term Capital Management fiasco, and general malaise. SCCX re-covered somewhat, to the point where it closed the year at around $4.70. This IPO was definitely broken.

The worst was not over, however, and in the first months of 1999 the stock fell even more (see Figure 16.2). Sonkin spotted it on his daily scan of the new lows list, and after he did some research on the company, he came to believe that the bad news had been overblown. One reason that

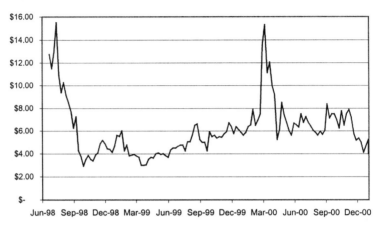

Figure 16.2   SCCX Price Graph, 1998–2000

the company's revenues and earnings growth had slowed was a delay by Congress in passing legislation mandating that phone companies install the services provided by SCCX. Convinced that this was a temporary set-back, Sonkin began buying the stock when it fell below $4 in March. He held it as it moved up in the spring and then down in the summer. The company's results were mediocre, but the legislation did pass Congress in the fall, and SCCX developed new services to sell to the telephone oper-ating companies. Then, in the first three months of 2000, during the gen-eral euphoria that lifted the shares of virtually any company in the tele-communications business, SCCX stocks spiked up from $8 to above $16. For a value investor, this was nose-bleed territory, and Sonkin was happy to let Mr. Market have his shares, some at $13, some at $15, and some, on the way down, at $8.

The investment worked only because Sonkin waited until the great expectations with which the underwriters had promoted the stock had been sufficiently deflated for the shares to sink to a more than reasonable valuation. And it also worked because he did not buy into—instead he sold into—the overblown optimism that inflated the price of telecommu-nications shares in early 2000. As a good value investor, he has learned to accommodate Mr. Market.

The Value of Incremental Information

The standard arguments in favor of small companies are that they have better growth prospects than those that are already large, that they can be more nimble to take advantage of new opportunities or changes in markets, that their shares may be a bargain because many funds are prohibited from owning them, and, finally, that because there are fewer if any analysts following the company, information or insight about the company is less likely to have already been incorporated in the share price. If there are 500 analysts following General Electric (not an extreme estimate, based on the number of institutional accounts that own the stock added to the sell-side analysts who cover it for the brokerage firms and all the other experts), the 501st is not likely to add much to the store of information or understanding about the firm. But if there has been only one analyst covering the company, a second one certainly has a chance of discovering something important. And if the analyst is not publishing the findings but is using them to make investment decisions, then the value of that research and analysis should be found in the portfolio's performance.

Sonkin agrees with all these reasons and adds another: Small companies are much easier to understand. Both their financial statements and their business models tend to be simple. Usually they operate in one line of business, not the 5 or 15 of a Standard & Poor's 500 firm. They probably have a few competitors and a few major customers. It takes almost no time to make the phone calls that analysts rely on to feel comfortable about the business. Put in economic terms, the marginal value of time spent studying a small company far exceeds that spent on a large one.

Small Stocks, Big Portfolio

A number of value investors have made the case for a concentrated portfolio. The argument for a portfolio holding a large number of names comes out of modern investment theory, which differentiates between systematic and nonsystematic risk. Nonsystematic risk is the risk (uncertainty) inherent in owning any single security. This risk can be reduced or even eliminated by diversification—owning enough securities that do not move in tandem with one another. Systematic risk is the risk that cannot be diversified away—the uncertain return of the market itself or, more universally, of all markets together. According to the theory, since there is no payoff for assuming a risk that can be eliminated, it is better to be diversified. That usually means owning securities in 20 or more companies, or, more globally, in many more markets. A number of value investors, having questioned many of the tenets of modern investment theory, don't buy the diversification argument. They argue, first, that security price volatility is not the only nor even the most appropriate measure of risk, and that they can reduce risk by having more information and better analysis, which leads to purchasing securities with a large margin of safety. Second, they feel that they have few enough great ideas and do not want to dilute the performance from these potential stars by filling the rest of the portfolio with more mediocre opportunities.

Sonkin is not a member of the "focused" value investor school. In fact, he embraces diversification with a passion. The portfolio he runs is divided into two major parts, each with three subsections (see Table 16.1). Following Benjamin Graham, he calls one part *General Portfolio Operations*. Here he invests in the traditional value stocks: small and microcap companies that have lost favor with Wall Street or never found favor in the first place. He locates these stocks on the new lows list, which he looks at daily, and by using various screens to identify stocks that are cheap relative to cash in the bank, other tangible assets, or normalized earnings. He also buys hybrid securities, which are usually preferred shares or convertible bonds, that are also depressed in price.

The other half of the portfolio is devoted to various types of arbitrage situations. Sonkin uses the term *arbitrage* broadly, but the unifying element is that some event will change the price of the shares. Announced takeovers, spin-offs, company liquidations, corporate restructuring, and similar kinds of events can be golden opportunities: high return on investment and low level of risk. These exceptional possibilities are available because Sonkin is operating in a niche that is too small for the bigger arbitrage

Table 16.1 The Diversified Portfolio

	ARBITRAGE OPERATIONS			GENERAL PORTFOLIO OPERATIONS		
	Microcap Arbitrage	*Liquidations*	*Spin-offs and Reorganizations*	*Moderate Neglect*	*Deep Neglect*	*Hybrid*
Time horizon	1 to 3 months	1 to 18 months	1 to 18 months	1 to 3 years	3 years or more	3 years or more
Intrinsic value	set	set to growing	set to growing	growing	growing	set to growing
Discount to intrinsic value	small	varies	varies	large	extreme	large
Time table	predictable	predictable	predictable	unpredictable	totally unpredictable	unpredictable
Market cap	micro to small	micro to small	micro to mid	micro to small	micro to small	micro to small
Market correlation	low	low	low	moderate	low	low
Liquidity	poor to good	poor to good	low to excellent	fair to excellent	poor to low	poor to low

funds. In addition to the high-return and low-risk qualities of each position in the Arbitrage section, the differences between the Arbitrage and General Portfolio portions is what makes combining them in one portfolio so valuable.

All of the positions in the Arbitrage section, by definition, have a catalyst through which value will be realized. They are only there because some event has or will occur that will spark a change in price. The stocks in the General Portfolio section, by contrast, may take a long time before market price catches up with intrinsic value. If they were not out of favor, they would not be in the portfolio in the first place, and it may take several years before either their operations or their assets get enough attention to drive up the price. On the other hand, it may happen overnight. Sonkin owned one stock in his Deep Neglect subsection, a company with no coverage and no attention. In the course of one week, the price moved from around $1 to almost $4 on the basis of a news story that saw the company as a potential beneficiary of a potential relaxation of the U.S. embargo on trade with Cuba. The stock was in the portfolio because it represented value, and Sonkin expected that it might double or triple over the next two years. When all of that change was compressed into a week, he sold a large part of his position to gratify Mr. Market's appetite. A few weeks later, after the rumors subsided, the new owners began to wonder why they bought the shares in the first place, and prices drifted back to below $2 per share, where Sonkin bought some back.

Under normal circumstances, however, it is the Arbitrage positions that will turn over more quickly, providing a steady flow of cash back into the portfolio. Because they were chosen through different selection processes and for different reasons, the two halves of the portfolio are not highly correlated with one another, and the Arbitrage section is not correlated with the market as a whole. Thus, the principle purpose of diversification, which is to dampen the price swings in the portfolio, is accommodated much more fully than if diversification simply meant owning 30 stocks and making sure they all aren't in the same industry.

Centennial Technologies: Unloved, Uncovered, Undervalued

In November 1999, the shares of Centennial Technology hit the new lows list and caught Sonkin's attention. He knew of the company because it had been in the headlines a few years earlier when a large accounting scandal was disclosed. The shares plummeted, class action lawsuits were filed, and the stock was delisted. Like many other investors, Sonkin thought that the firm had gone out of business. He was surprised when it showed up on the list. He decided to do a little work to see if Centennial warranted more attention.

He found that the company had settled its legal troubles in May 1999 by distributing almost 5 million shares to claimants in the law suits. Many of these shareholders, due to their unhappy experience with the company, sold their stocks over the next few months. By the end of September, the shares had fallen from $7 to $4 without any change in the underlying business, a clear case of sellers motivated by something other than the firm's economic condition. That condition was excellent. Centennial manufactured a range of PC cards and other computer-related products using flash memory chips. They were earning high returns on invested capital and had strong and growing free cash flows. To confirm his initial impressions that Centennial was a genuine value, Sonkin did a back-of-the-envelope calculation, shown in Table 16.2.

He found that the whole company could be purchased for around $900,000, using the company's own cash and its shares in another firm. For that money, the owner would acquire a firm with $1.3 million of operating earnings for the last 12 months. These were increasing to a current annual rate of around $2.4 million per year. Thanks to a $50 million net operating loss carry forward, the company would have to pay no taxes on these earnings for many years into the future.

To confirm that the company had returned from the dead and was being well managed, he checked the background of the new CEO and discovered that he had successfully run another public company for many

Table 16.2   Centennial Technologies Capitalization Rate

Price	$4.313
Shares outstanding	3.250
Market value of equity	14.016
Total debt	0.000
Cash	6.400
Interest in Century Electronics	6.700
Enterprise value	0.916
Operating income last 12 months	1.300
Cap rate	142%

years. Still not convinced that a company could look this good and sell for so little, Sonkin spoke with the chief financial officer (CFO) and was assured that business was strong and improving. Then he did one more calculation: a rough estimate of intrinsic value. He took the earnings for the trailing 12 months of $.40 per share and gave them a P/E multiple of 10; the value came to $4.00 per share. To this he added the net cash and securities of $4.03, for a total intrinsic value of around $8. With the stock selling at slightly more than $4.00, the margin of safety was also $4.00, or 50 percent of the intrinsic value. Shortly after he bought his first lot, the stock dropped to as low as $3, on no news. This prompted him to place another call to the CFO, who again assured him that business was on track. As a good value investor, Sonkin added to his position.

Enter the catalyst. On Thursday, December 30, Centennial announced that they had purchased a unit of Intel for 600,000 shares and $6 million in cash and notes (see Table 16.3). Another phone call to Centennial, at 8:30 A.M., assured Sonkin that the purchase would add to earnings immediately and that very little in the way of fixed assets was included. Centennial was buying inventory and customers; it had enough manufacturing capacity to support the growth in volume. Sonkin redid his intrinsic value calculation, factoring in the business bought from Intel and the cash and shares paid.

Expecting the stock to rise in price once the news was digested, Sonkin bought some at the open at $4.63. By noon it was up to $5.00. He left the office for an appointment, and when he returned around 1:30 P.M. the stock had climbed to $9. At first he thought it was a Y2K bug arriving a day

Table 16.3   Centennial Technologies Intrinsic Value with Intel Acquisition

Enterprise Value Calculation	
Price	$4.625
Shares outstanding	3.850
Market value of equity	17.806
Total debt	0
Cash	0.400
Interest in Century Elect	6.700
Enterprise value	10.706
Earnings Power Value Calculation	
Projected EBIT from existing business assuming $600,000 run rate	2.400
$20 million of Intel revenue at 8% operating margins	1.600
Projected operating income	4.000
Taxes (NOL carry forward)	0%
Net income	4.000
Shares outstanding	3.850
Earnings per share	1.04
P/E multiple	10
Earnings power value per share	$10.39
Cash and securities	7.100
Share outstanding	3.85
Cash and securities per share	$1.84
Total intrinsic value per share	$12.23

or two early, but a call to the trader disabused him of that thought. The $9 was real. Mr. Market was hungry again, and he had eaten up most of the margin of safety. So in the last two days of the year, Sonkin sold 60 percent of his position, at an average price of around $9.00.

This story has several more legs. Value investors, as one might expect, often sell too soon. Their valuations are based on assets and current earnings power, and they are skeptical about the potential for profitable growth. When the price of the shares rises to the point where it approaches the full asset or EPV, value investors say farewell. The margin of safety is a requirement not only at the time the shares are purchased, but also every day they are held. When it disappears, so do value investors. In the case of Centennial, Sonkin felt that the increase in EPV might be legitimate, so he held on to 40 percent of his shares. He sold the rest largely because with the rapid run-up in price, the stock had become too large a part of his portfolio, and he used his position limits rule to force him to sell.

A benefit of continuing to own some shares of the stock is that it forces the portfolio manager to pay attention. Sonkin examined carefully Centennial's Form 10Q for the quarter ending June 24, 2000. Earnings had come in stronger than anyone had expected. Sales were up and margins up even more. The company was on track to earn at least $8 million for the year, or $1.60 per share. Given the problems in their history, the CFO assured Sonkin that they were going to be careful and conservative in their estimates. Though they had spent most of their cash in the purchase of the Intel business, the intrinsic value had moved up thanks to the growth in earnings. Also, the inventory they carried on their books at cost had risen substantially in value, providing a margin of safety not reflected on the balance sheet. Sonkin revised his intrinsic value estimate, as shown in Table 16.4.

Table 16.4   Centennial Technologies Intrinsic Value in July 2000

Enterprise Value Calculation	
Price	$11.250
Shares outstanding	4.800
Market value of equity	54.000
Total debt	0
Cash	0
Interest in Century Elect	0
Enterprise value	54.000
Earnings Power Value Calculation	
Projected EBIT	8.000
Taxes (NOL carry forward)	0
Net income	8.000
Shares outstanding	4.800
Earnings per share	1.67
P/E multiple	10
Earnings power value	$16.67

During July and the first half of August, shares prices fluctuated around $10. With an intrinsic value above $16, the investment now had a margin of safety of around 40 percent. Sonkin became a buyer, paying $8 and $9 for the shares. New information requires new valuations, and a company that looks fully valued in January can become a bargain by June.

The revaluation proved a worthwhile effort. On January 23, 2001, Solectron, a large contract manufacturer in the electronics business, offered to buy Centennial for the equivalent of $21 per share. In little more than a year, the price had risen fivefold, from $4 to more than $20; in the same period, the Nasdaq index fell by 15 percent. As Sonkin likes to say, value investors aren't supposed to have this much fun.

References

Preface

By and on Benjamin Graham:

Benjamin Graham and David L. Dodd, *Security Analysis* (New York: Mc-Graw-Hill, 1934). This is the first edition.

Benjamin Graham, *The Intelligent Investor: A Book of Practical Counsel*, 4th Revised Edition (New York: Harper & Row, 1973).

Benjamin Graham: The Memoirs of the Dean of Wall Street (New York: McGraw-Hill, 1996) edited and with an introduction by Seymour Chatman.

Janet C. Lowe, *Benjamin Graham on Value Investing: Lessons from the Dean of Wall Street* (Chicago: Dearborn Financial, 1994).

Chapter One

Two major papers by Eugene Fama and Kenneth French:

Eugene F. Fama and Kenneth R. French, "The Cross-Section of Expected Stock Returns," *Journal of Finance*, XLVII:2, June 1992, 427–465, and Fama and French, "Size and Book-to-Market Factors in Earnings and Returns," *Journal of Finance*, March 1995, 131–155.

Other studies confirming and expanding the Fama-French findings are summarized and described in a pamphlet produced by Tweedy, Browne Company, L.P., 52 Vanderbilt Avenue, New York, NY 10017: "What

Has Worked in Investing: Studies of Investment Approaches and Characteristics Associated with Exceptional Returns."

On risk as (un)related to return:

Joseph Lakonishok, Andrei Shleifer, Robert Vishny, "Contrarian Investment, Extrapolation and Risk," *Journal of Finance* (1994).

Warren E. Buffett, "The Superinvestors of Graham-and-Doddsville," can be found as an appendix in Benjamin Graham, *The Intelligent Investor*, 4th revised edition.

Chapter Two

On the various tests that have been run to compare value stocks with growth, glamour, or otherwise popular securities:

Michelle Clayman, "In Search of Excellence: The Investor's Viewpoint," *Financial Analysts Journal*, May/June 1987.

James P. O'Shaughnessy, *What Works on Wall Street: A Guide to the Best-Performing Investment Strategies of All Time* (New York: McGraw-Hill, 1994), p. 193.

and the Fama and Lakonishok articles referred to in Chapter One.

On cognitive biases, the starting point is the collection of papers:

Daniel Kahneman, Paul Slovic, and Amos Tversky, editors, *Judgment under Uncertainty* (New York: Cambridge University Press, 1982).

The consequences for investments form the relatively new field of behavioral finance. Books and articles to consult:

Andrei Shleifer, *Inefficient Markets: An Introduction to Behavioral Finance* (Oxford: Oxford University Press, 2000).

Richard H. Thaler, editor, *Advances in Behavioral Finance* (New York: Russell Sage Foundation, 1993).

David Dreman, *Contrarian Investment Strategies: The Next Generation* (New York: Simon & Schuster, 1998), makes use and has references to many of the articles in this field.

Chapter Four

We owe the analysis of Hudson General to Mario J. Gabelli, whose investment company was a major shareholder of the firm, and who presented this material in Bruce Greenwald's course on value investing at the Graduate School of Business, Columbia University.

Chapter Eight

Jeremy J. Siegel, *Stocks for the Long Run: A Guide to Selecting Markets for Long-term Growth* (Burr Ridge, Il: Irwin Professional Publishing, 1994), p. 31.

Warren Buffett

The Loomis passage is from Carol Loomis, "The Inside Story of Warren Buffett," *Fortune*, April 11, 1988, p. 28.

The Web site for Berkshire Hathaway is *www.berkshirehathaway.com*, where the letters and much else can be found.

There is no shortage of books on Warren Buffett. To list them all would take up too much space; to select a few would be an unintended slight to those omitted.

Mario Gabelli

The Web site for Gabelli Asset Management, *www.gabelli.com*, is the source of the quotation and of a wealth of information on the Gabelli approach to investing.

Seth Klarman

Seth Klarman, *Margin of Safety: Risk-Averse Value Investing Strategies for the Thoughtful Investor* (New York: 1991, HarperCollins).

Acknowledgments

We want to thank all the people who have contributed over the years to the value investing program at Columbia University Graduate School of Business or directly to the writing of this book. That includes all the investors we have profiled in this book and a host of other individuals:

Bill Ackman, Barbara Dodd Anderson, David Berkowitz, Chris Browne, Bob Bruce, Chuck Brunie, Hirsch Cohen, Pat Duff, the late Tom Ebright, Geraldine Fabrikant, Bill Falloon, Meyer Feldberg, Bob Gottesman, David Greenspan, Larry Hilibrand, Irving Kahn, Thomas Graham Kahn, Marilyn Kohn, Helene and Sid Lerner, Carol Loomis, Ronald Mayer, Catherine Murray, Joe Reich, Chuck Royce, Mina Samuels, Lew Sanders, Jace Schinderman, Andy Weiss, and Marty Whitman.

As value investors know, families are invaluable. We thank ours: Diana Greenwald, Gabriel Kahn, Lavinia Lorch, Anne, Katie, Frank and Sally Rogin, Ava Seave, Stacy and Zev Sonkin, Fiamma and Tristan van Biema.

Index